CONTEMPORARY HISTORY SERIES

General Editor: JAMES F. MCMILLAN
Professor of History, University of Strathclyde

AFRICAN DECOLONIZATION

D0826623

African Decolonization

HENRY S. WILSON
Senior Lecturer in History, University of York

Edward Arnold
A member of the Hodder Headline Group
LONDON NEW YORK MELBOURNE AUCKLAND

First published in Great Britain 1994 by
Edward Arnold, a division of Hodder Headline PLC,
338 Euston Road, London NW1 3BH

British Library Cataloguing in Publication Data
Wilson, Henry S.
African Decolonization. - (Contemporary
History Series)
I. Title II. Series
960.32

Library of Congress Cataloging-in-Publication Data
A catalog record for this book is available from the Library of Congress

ISBN 0 340 55929 2

1 2 3 4 5 98 97 96 95 94

Typeset in 10/12.5 Ehrhardt by York House Typographic
Printed and bound in Finland by Werner Söderström Osakeyhtiö

Contents

Preface

Since 1945 the great European empires in Africa have come to an end. This book analyses the processes of decolonization which produced that major change in the world order.

Like every author I have many debts to acknowledge. Professor Jim Macmillan suggested the topic. Christopher Wheeler and his staff at Edward Arnold provided constructive and patient support and advice throughout the project. I have learned much in discussion with colleagues and students in the Department of History and Centre for Southern African Studies at the University of York. Finally, thanks to my wife, Ellen, who has helped me in more ways than I can say.

A Note on some Key Terms

Certain concepts such as 'self-determination' were part of the public cant of the age of decolonization. But the fact that all parties felt able to pay lip-service to them reflected their inherent ambiguity. Their specific interpretation in any given historical situation was contested politically – sometimes even by force of arms – so can only be elucidated in context. The meaning of 'decolonization' itself has been debated, especially by Africans, throughout its implementation and aftermath, as the Introduction makes obvious. But it seemed helpful to provide the reader with a short preliminary glossary of certain specialized terms which retained a relatively stable meaning throughout the period covered by this book.

Cultural Functionalism: A theory of culture which analyses the interrelation and interdependence of patterns and institutions within a cultural complex or social system, and which emphasizes their interaction in the maintenance of socio-cultural unity or in meeting biosocial requirements. In Africa it was particularly associated with the efforts of anthropologists, such as Malinowski and his followers, to understand the workings of traditional societies. It was regarded as supplying the intellectual justification for Indirect Rule. Not to be confused with 'international functionalism' (see below) though the context should usually make this clear.

International Functionalism: The theory or practice of achieving cooperation between governmental units by gradual integration of economic and other functions rather than by immediate political union or federation. It was particularly associated with the political scientist David Mitrany. Mitrany in fact believed that this approach need not be confined to interstate and international relations. It could, for example, replace conventional political decolonization as a way of defusing conflict between ethnic groups, as well as rulers and ruled, within a colony. (See his account of his encounter with the Indian nationalist Tilak and members of the Labour Party in his *The Functional Theory of Politics*, p. 32.) However, the term 'international functionalism' seems appropriate as it was in the context of the League of Nations, the United Nations, such bodies as the International Labour Organization, and the general development of international aid, that it came into general currency. Not to be confused with 'cultural functionalism' (see above) though the context should usually make this clear.

Lusotropicalism: The ideology used to explain and justify the Portuguese presence in Africa. Its exponents claimed that because the Portuguese were exceptional among European imperialists in being non-racist, their colonization of tropical territories was characterized by racial egalitarianism in both legislation and informal human interaction. The term was coined by Gilberto Freyre, the celebrated Brazilian sociologist, who argued that miscegenation had been a positive force in Brazilian history, creating a unique fusion of races and cultures. The ideologists of Salazar's New State adopted the ideology of lusotropicalism as a vindication of their unique 'civilizing mission'.

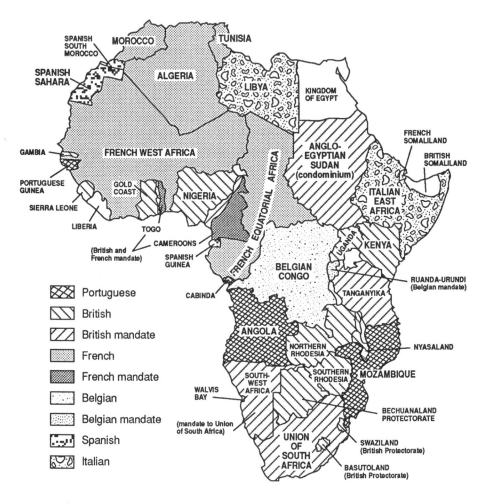

Map 1 Africa in 1939, indicating areas controlled by European powers

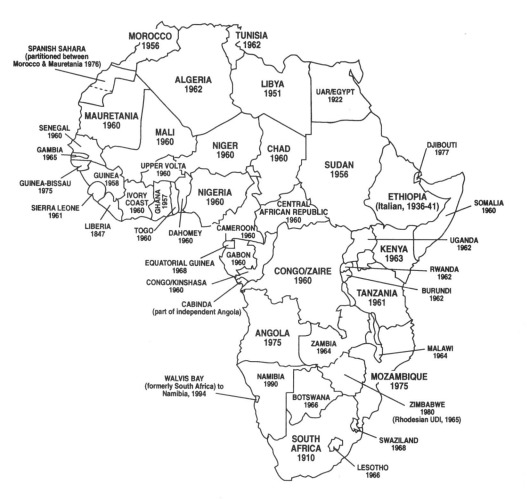

Map 2 The chronology of independence

I

Introduction

Since the end of the Second World War the political map of Africa has been transformed by decolonization. Before the mid-1950s almost all of Africa was controlled by European empires or white-settler states. Since then the empires and settler states have gone, and have been replaced by more than 50 sovereign African states, the largest addition to the comity of nations since the consolidation of the nation-state. A precise date can be attached to each new country signifying exactly when the preceding imperial power or settler regime renounced sovereignty. Independence Day pageantry dramatized these constitutional and diplomatic formalities for a mass audience at home and abroad.

Yet even on this basic political and diplomatic level African decolonization can be read two ways. From the metropolitan standpoint decolonization, with its strong prefix denoting decisive action, implied a planned ending to Europe's African empires. The ceremonial lowering of the imperial flags signified the successful culmination of policies initiated and to some degree controlled from London and Paris. (The agency of Brussels and Lisbon was more problematic.) Thus, Arthur Creech Jones, Colonial Secretary in Britain's postwar Labour government, reflected comfortably in 1959 on a 'remarkable record of liberation and nation-building' by enlightened rulers.[1]

From the local standpoint, though, the term 'African' implied collective action, African agency, even African ownership, as well as geographical location. On 6 March 1957, Ghana gained its independence from Britain, becoming the first Sub-Saharan African colony to do so. More than 100,000 people crowded into the Polo Ground in Accra, the capital city, to watch the midnight ceremony. The Union Jack was lowered, the new Ghanaian flag hoisted in its place, and Kwame Nkrumah proclaimed to the jubilant crowd: 'At long last the battle has ended! And thus Ghana, your beloved country, is free for ever.'[2]

A very similar scene would be played out in Africa in the next few years as state after state attained political independence. The Kenyan writer, James Ngugi, in his novel *A Grain Of Wheat* (1967), describes independence night:

Kenya regained her Uhuru from the British on 12 December 1963. A minute before midnight, lights were put out at the Nairobi stadium so that the people from all over the country and the world who had gathered there for the midnight ceremony were swallowed by the darkness. In the dark the Union Jack was quickly lowered. When next the lights came on the new Kenya flag was flying and fluttering, and waving in the air. The police band played the new National Anthem and the crowd cheered continuously when they saw the flag was black, and red and green. The cheering sounded like one intense cracking of many trees, falling on the thick mud of the stadium.[3]

The new flags unfurled in place of the imperial banners gave focus to the patriotic euphoria of the Independence Day crowds. In 1957 at Ghana's independence Nkrumah proclaimed his Pan-Africanism by superimposing the lodestar of African freedom on the red, green and gold of Ethiopia. Several other new states followed his example in honouring Ethiopia's role as a beacon of African independence during the colonial period by adopting the same colours. In 1960 Somalia simultaneously celebrated and questioned the new international order with a flag of light blue with a white star, the United Nations' colours, to honour that body's sponsorship. But the star had five points: two for Italian and British Somaliland, which had united to form the new state, and one each for the Somalis of Djibouti, Kenya and Ethiopia, as yet condemned to live outside the national homeland. The Kenyan flag which Ngugi's crowd cheered had a black stripe for the African majority over a red stripe for the independence struggle and a dark green stripe for agriculture. Narrow white stripes represent the non-African minorities and in the centre is a traditional shield with weapons, based on the shields of the Masai people, many of whom had been opposed to Mau Mau and Jomo Kenyatta, the leader of the new state. It was a flag expressly designed to symbolize reconciliation in a fully multiracial state.

For Europeans, like Creech Jones, decolonization constituted an ending, a more or less successful finale, but for Africans it was a beginning and their view of it was liable to be revised in the light of the subsequent history of the postcolonial states it ushered in. Again Ngugi captures the mood of expectation that underlay the excitement: 'Everybody waited for something to happen. This "waiting" and the uncertainty that went with it . . . was a taut cord beneath the screams and the shouts and the laughter.'[4] The uniquely thrilling moment of decolonization, when achievement and expectation were blended in the joy of liberation, gave way to the protracted political and economic crises of the postcolonial regimes. Disenchantment over the failure to fulfil the promises of independence has led many Africans to agree with Frantz Fanon's celebrated characterization of the transfer of sovereignty as 'false decolonization'.

Some mocked the formalities of independence by dubbing it mere 'flag decolonization'. Like the concept 'false consciousness' to which it is akin, 'flag decolonization' has a fine dismissive ring. The powerful rhetoric of nationalism, like that of socialism (and in Africa the two were frequently combined) had given individuals the sense of simultaneously shaping history and being swept along by its irresistible tide. With the approach of independence Africans reimagined their history; all the defeats they had endured in the past were now seen as links in a chain of resistance culminating in liberation. Samora Machel, first president of independent Mozambique, in his Independence Day address, 25 June 1975, commemorated 'our heroes – those who fell in the struggle against the foreign invaders, those who perished in the slaughter-house of Portuguese colonialism, through deportation, the slave trade and forced labour, those who were condemned by colonial fascism to slow death, family disintegration and depersonalisation . . . .Their blood laid the foundations for the new Mozambican nation.'[5]

'False decolonization' and 'flag independence' were cries of protest, intended to call the successor regimes to account for betraying the promise of liberation and the struggles of all those who suffered to bring it about, but they have tended to close off historical analysis with an easy ideological sarcasm. (They contain their own beguiling rhetorics either of Africans as hapless victims of the decolonization process or of liberation by 'cleansing violence', with frequently an intoxicating blend of the two.)

The flags enshrined ideals which patriots have taken too seriously to be dismissed from the historical record. In 1964 Nkrumah replaced the gold stripe which he had chosen for the Ghanaian flag with a white one to bring it into line with the colours of his own Convention People's Party. The move was widely resented as a gross manipulation of sacred national insignia for party-political purposes. When he was deposed in 1964 the original gold was restored and has been retained. Somalis have been willing to kill and be killed for the irridentism symbolized by the five-pointed star. Vexillology, the study of flags, is a necessary if certainly not a sufficient discipline for the historical analysis of African as for any other modern nationalism.[6]

The analysis of decolonization from an African, as against a metropolitan, standpoint has shifted through three stages which more or less correspond to equivalent stages in Africa's own historical development. The first approach was essentially concerned with the specific process of ridding Africa of alien rule. The second searched for the precise origins of the successor regimes in the colonial state and decolonization, especially if they had developed into one-party states or governments by the military, as so often happened. Lastly attention has returned to the development of African civil society outside the control of the colonial and postcolonial bureaucratic state with a view to locating the springs of political freedom and competition.

The earliest stage, dating from the 1950s, focused on nationalist efforts to forge an effective anticolonial coalition. These first students of African liberation were virtually all drawn to it by intense sympathy for its aims, working in Crawford Young's happy phrase in 'intimate symbiosis' with the nationalist struggle on the ground.[7] They assumed that European colonialism would resist tenaciously in line with the 1944 Brazzaville Conference declaration of French colonial officials that self-government was ruled out 'now or in the future' and British official expectations that independence for Kenya or Tanganyika lay some 15 or 30 years ahead. They assumed therefore that nationalist leaders would have to mobilize the broadest possible coalition to make a convincing case before the bar of world opinion and unsettle such determined rulers. Thomas Hodgkin's *Nationalism in Colonial Africa*, dating from 1956, provided the classic synthesis, adopting an inclusive definition of nationalism as all forms of anticolonial protest and any organizational or group assertion of 'the rights, claims, and aspirations of a given African society (from the level of the language group to that of "pan-Africa") in opposition to European authority, whatever its institutional form and objectives'.[8]

Harmonizing anti-colonial rhetoric from the nationalist leadership matched this inclusive conceptualization by students of nationalism. Nkrumah continued his Independence Day oration by thanking 'the chiefs and people of this country, the youth, the farmers, the women, who have so nobly fought and won this battle. Also I want to thank the valiant ex-servicemen who have so co-operated with me in this mighty task of freeing our country from foreign rule and imperialism.'[9] The nationalist rhetoric was reductive. It proclaimed that there was only one struggle to be waged and that it was negative: directed against colonial rule rather than for anything specific. It was taken for granted by both the nationalist leaders and academic experts that foreign rule was bad. Argument focused on tactics and timing – 'Self-Government Now!' as against 'Self-Government in the shortest possible time!' – deflecting attention from critical questions concerning what the precise nature of this 'Self-Government' should be.

The next stage in elucidating decolonization from a local perspective was to direct attention to the regimes which emerged as the Europeans withdrew. This developed naturally as scholars followed the careers of nationalist leaders into government. Already in March 1957 there was a large amount of ceremonial reconciliation involved in Nkrumah's embracive oratory. He had won three hard-fought elections – in 1951, 1954 and 1956 – disciplining his own party malcontents as well as defeating his opponents to earn a statesman's right to address his fellow countrymen from the independence podium. Political realism prompted analysis of the party politician as well as the founding father. Western political scientists, especially American ones, who had learned from their own domestic history to regard party machines as pivotal to the democratic process, focused on African parties as necessary mechanisms for organizing an acceptable division of the spoils and so essential to the process of nation-building.

The emergent postcolonial situation tended to dissolve, however, even while under investigation as party competition was replaced by single-party regimes. By 1960 some of the most prominent African nationalist leaders – including Nkrumah himself, Sekou Toure of Guinea, Julius Nyerere of Tanganyika and Habib Bourguiba of Tunisia – had argued that the mass single party was the most effective machinery for nation-building. Leading political scientists continued to display solidarity with the nationalist leadership. (Influential sections of the Western media were so sour about the whole independence process, especially over the Africans' failure to express thanks fervently enough, that some academic reaction redressing the balance is understandable.) In 1961 Immanuel Wallerstein reported that African nationalists regarded the mass single party 'as a peculiarly African contribution to the theory of *democratic* society', while in 1964 Ruth Morgenthau's, *Political Parties in French-Speaking West Africa* synthesized the arguments for the mass single party as a potentially democratic form.[10]

The claims made for the single party were soon challenged. As early as 1963 Martin Kilson had pointed to the authoritarian impulses increasingly apparent beneath the single party's democratic façade, while in 1966 Aristide Zolberg argued convincingly that its mass character was also exaggerated. These judgements were confirmed by the general trends of the postcolonial period. In 1982 the Nigerian historian Jacob Ajayi, looking back over more than two decades of independence considered that 'The most fundamental aspect . . . has been the elusiveness of development . . . in many ways the quality of life . . . is even worse than on the eve of independence.' He listed the failure of many states to provide 'sufficient food and energy resources for the bare necessities of life' and the failure of most of the new states to evolve stable political structures.[11]

Conceptual tools were introduced which would analyse these disappointing postcolonial regimes more effectively. Ethnicity crept back into consideration in the mid-1960s to account for some of the new states' salient characteristics, while since the 1970s class has dominated Africanist discussion of the formation of the new regimes. Both concepts enriched understanding of the complex interplay of collusion and conflict that marked the relationship between metropolitan decolonizers and the emergent political class in the lead-up to independence and the consolidation of the new states.

Recently the Africanist approach to decolonization has directed attention away from preoccupation with government and towards greater concern for civil society. This corresponds to a general tendency which developed in the 1980s to look sceptically at all governmental pretensions and performance, not just that of the postcolonial African state. (The collapse of the Soviet Empire and the decolonization of Eastern Europe which contributed to this reconsideration thus brings fresh perspectives to bear on the previous round of imperial dissolution and state-making in Africa three decades earlier – and doubtless will encourage revisionism in other ways as well.) The 1992 collection edited by Goran Hyden and Michael Bratton, *Governance and Politics in Africa* is a good example of the new approach. As the title illustrates it does not ignore government but focuses closely on its relationship with civil society.

In some ways this comes full circle by corresponding to the strategy adopted by metropolitan liberals when they first began to take African decolonization seriously in the 1940s and 1950s. They promoted a series of new institutions –

local government organizations, co-operatives, trade unions, universities and their extramural extensions – through which civil society could find expression at varying levels of the colonial structure. Creech Jones's reflections on the colonial policy of the postwar British Labour government stressed these activities, such as the development of special training facilities for colonial students at the Co-operative College at Loughborough as well as the dispatch of well-known Co-operators to tour the colonies to raise the profile of the movement.[12] And of course throughout the colonial period and beyond there were the missions which were involved with African society in many more ways than straightforward evangelization. Margery Perham, who did so much to develop the new tutelary approach in the British colonial service through the colonial cadet training courses she organized at postwar Oxford, was already looking beyond govern-ment when she decided in the worst period of the war for the British Empire – after the fall of Singapore – that 'the civilising effects of Christian culture, represented by both missionary work and the establishment African universities might help to check the forces of disintegration'.[13] In line with these convictions she became President of the Universities Mission to Central Africa (UMCA) and a stalwart of the Inter-University Council, the key agency in the development of universities in the British Empire during decolonization and the consolidation of independence.

These stages in the styles of interpretation have hardly been smoothly cumulative. Each new vision of the meaning of independence was prompted by a combination of the switchback progress of postwar African history and a consequent heightened awareness of elements that its predecessor failed to take properly into account. Yet all three elements – the ending of European rule, the construction of the postcolonial regimes and the simultaneous transformations in African civil society – should constitute a single field of analysis, comprising the relationship between metropole and colonies in the process of becoming postcolonial states. The trick is to bring one into focus without losing sight of the other two.

The prospect of decolonization frequently bristled with controversy in the metropolitan countries, at the same time as African nationalist leaders sought to maintain a united anticolonial front. France, facing much the most difficult task of extricating itself, because of Algeria's special status, was so riven and its political fabric so damaged that the Fourth Republic voted for de Gaulle in June 1958, effectively signalling its own demise. Portugal's African wars finally prompted the Armed Forces Movement to overthrow Caetano's dictatorship in April 1974. The Belgians, hitherto most efficient of colonialists, badly botched the decolonization of the Congo amid general recrimination. The British were prone to say that they, by contrast with the rest, had managed things fairly adroitly, with a good deal less damaging controversy, largely because they had been first to come to terms with the principle of African independence. (British officials, though, were often as divided over the means of decolonization as their

European counterparts; they simply found it easier to screen their controversies from the public view.) Certainly despite the Mau Mau emergency, the British continued their tradition of keeping their colonial wars small, avoiding anything so damaging as the French surrender at Dien Bien Phu or the prolonged guerilla wars in Algeria and the Portuguese territories.[14] On the other hand, shortly after Belgium and France were free from colonial crises, protracted impotence in the face of the white Rhodesian unilateral declaration of independence (UDI) in November 1965 damaged Britain's international reputation. Yet once the independence of their colonies was achieved public controversy within the metropoles subsided rather quickly, whereas in Africa the specific structure of the new regimes was fraught with such significance that the character of decolonization remained controversial. So fraught indeed that the new regimes often resorted to draconian powers inherited from their colonial predecessors to curtail public discussion.

Speculation about the relative importance of deliberate imperial policy in ending empire in Africa, as against the pressures of African nationalism and of an international environment transformed by the superpower rivalries of the United States and the Soviet Union, did ultimately confront Europeans with fundamental questions about their changing role in world politics. Ultimately rather than immediately because the slack in the system, the margin of error of a still relatively prosperous Western state with a superpower ally, appeared to give scope for manœuvre. This could seem like procrastination, however, even to basically sympathetic observers; as a former Secretary of State of the superpower in question, the United States, Dean Acheson, commented rather tactlessly in December 1962 when British decolonization was still in mid-career, 'Great Britain has lost an empire and has not yet found a role'.[15] Two fine academic studies that deal with these issues are *Britain, Europe and the World, 1850–1986: Delusions of Grandeur* (second edition, 1987; originally published in 1983) by Bernard Porter, and Robert Holland's *The Pursuit of Greatness: Britain and the World Role, 1900–1970* (1991). Both were drawn to this broad theme by way of imperial history. As well as UDI, Britain's relatively long period of postcolonial supplication before signing the Treaty of Rome in January 1972, and frequently tense relations with fellow-members of the European Community thereafter, were especially conducive to such self-examination. By contrast France and Belgium, with a more traumatic experience of decolonization, were founder members. Although Portugal did not join till 1986, it had enjoyed relatively congenial relations from the 1974 revolution onwards; since joining its relations with the rest of the members have been less troubled than Britain's.

The metropolitan perspective has changed as increasing awareness of such large-scale, long-term transformations in the relationship of the colonial powers with the rest of the world provides the context within which specific events in the process of decolonization are understood. In that sense revisionism about decolonization, both African and European, has prompted fresh consideration about the scope for individuals, local communities and states to shape their own history in an increasingly complex world.

NOTES

1 Arthur Creech Jones, ed., *New Fabian Colonial Essays* (London, Hogarth, 1959), p. 37.
2 Kwame Nkrumah, *I Speak of Freedom* (London, Nelson, 1962), pp. 106–7.
3 James Ngugi, *A Grain of Wheat* (London, Heinemann, 1967), p. 177.
4 *Op. cit.*, p. 177.
5 Samora Machel, 'The People's Republic of Mozambique', *Review of African Political Economy* 4 (1975), pp. 14–16.
6 Michael Faul, *The Story of Africa and her Flags to Colour* (Santa Barbara, Bellerophon Books, 1991) is the best introduction to African vexillology.
7 C. Young, 'Nationalism, Ethnicity and Class in Africa', *Cahiers d'Etudes Africaines* XXXVI (1986), p. 423.
8 *Op. cit.*, p. 425.
9 Nkrumah, *Freedom*, pp. 106–7.
10 Young, 'Nationalism', p. 430.
11 J. F. A. Ajayi, 'Expectations of Independence', *Daedalus* CXI (1982), p. 6.
12 A. Creech Jones, 'The Labour Party and Colonial Policy' in Creech Jones, ed., *New Fabian Colonial Essays*, pp. 19–37, especially p. 33.
13 A. Smith and M. Bull, 'Margery Perham', *Journal of Imperial and Commonwealth History* XIX (1991), p. 10.
14 The standard British manual by C. E. Callwell was entitled *Small Wars* (London, Her Majesty's Stationery Office, 1899, enlarged edition 1906).
15 Speech to fourteenth annual conference on United States affairs at the United States Military Academy, West Point, 5 December 1962.

I

PRELIMINARIES

2

Paradoxes of Imperial Power

Generalizations about European imperial regimes in Africa between the two World Wars tend to adopt two conflicting approaches. Some stress the 'steel frame' of imperial control which brought tranquillity to Africa in contrast to the strife of the immediate precolonial period and the brutalities of pacification. Others emphasize the tenuous character of the regimes and find the steel-frame image seriously misleading. To some extent the differences derive from writers drawing general inferences from that part of Africa they know best. But there is more to it than that. In fact the two views complement rather than contradict each other. Paradoxically the imperial regimes were simultaneously both weak and strong.

They were strong because the local apparatus of control was backed by the coercive force of the metropole. Awareness of this deterrent of last resort stiffened the morale of the rulers and encouraged their subjects to be deferential. Contemporary maps dramatized the imperial order. Mercator's projection reflected Europe's history of putting itself at the centre of a world of which it was only a small part, assigning marginality to other races and cultures. The maps were colour-coded to represent the size and spread of imperial possessions while reassuring those consigned to the peripheries that they were not totally cut off from metropolitan centres of civilization. The self-assurance of imperial agents also derived from their belief in progress or, failing that, their confidence in their special suitability to mediate and ameliorate its impact upon Africa. Such contrary attitudes, progressive and reactionary, deriving from differing interpretations of European experience, were alike in believing that Africa's best hope of coming to terms with the modern world lay in the rational control and disinterested service the European imperial bureaucracies claimed to provide.

The most obvious weakness of the imperial regimes was that the actual number of European rulers in Africa – 'the thin white line' in Anthony Kirk-Greene's evocative phrase – was miniscule.[1] Nor was there easy access to metropolitan reinforcements. Every European colonial power, but most especially Britain, was aware of the danger of imperial 'overstretch'. The vaunted self-reliance of the imperial 'man on the spot' was to a large extent a virtue born of necessity. The Europeans, moreover, knew very little of the societies they ruled and their means of finding out depended on the very people they were trying to control. When, perforce, they delegated authority and decided, sensibly enough, that this should be done in line with local custom the question of who was manipulating whom became highly problematic.

Paradoxically these elements of weakness also contributed to the regimes' strengths. The basis of imperial authority was racial. In African colonies whites commanded and Africans obeyed. Everyone wore a 'uniform of colour' so everyone knew his or her place. The ruling élite was small, exclusive and tightly-knit. Its lack of knowledge of those it ruled was a very effective way of preserving the assumption of white superiority on which the whole edifice of racial control depended.

Stereotypes though were no substitute for objective knowledge when it came down to the detail of field administration. Imperialism needed both a rationale (the 'inferiority of the natives') and working knowledge of some objectivity to serve its purpose of conquering and ruling. Such were the ambiguities in which rulers and ruled were involved and of which they were generally vaguely, sometimes blindingly, aware. The phrase 'working misunderstanding' neatly captures the terms on which Europeans and Africans collaborated.[2]

With good reason, then, both Africans and Europeans usually approached problems of governance circumspectly. Such mutual caution was in large measure responsible for the political tranquillity of Africa between the two World Wars. Nor were these contradictions to be fully unmasked and resolved in the process of decolonization. But that is to anticipate. Now we must turn to a fuller anatomy of the sinews of colonial power between the two World Wars, examining military and police organization, money-raising and administration.

SINEWS OF POWER

The Europeans maintained control during these interwar years with very slender resources. A handful of European administrators was backed by small African garrisons or paramilitary police, led by a few European officers and frequently equipped from the cast-offs of metropolitan armies. Nigeria had only one British administrative officer for every 100,000 Africans or a ratio of 1 : 54,000 if the secretariat is counted in. They were backed by 4,000 soldiers and 4,000 police of whom all but 75 in each force were African. In the Belgian Congo the ratio of European administrators to Africans was 1 : 34,000 and in French West Africa 1 : 27,000. (The ratios for the Portuguese are complicated because parts of Mozambique were not even administered by the government but by concessionary companies.)[3]

The British were notoriously parsimonious, the sheer size of their empire forcing them to husband personnel. Many Africans never saw a white man. Nigeria's northern emirates, with bureaucracies and tax systems sanctified by Islam, offered scope to cut European administration to the bone. In Uganda, where the kingdom of Buganda presented similar possibilities, the ratio was one administrative officer to 49,000 Africans. Yet in Kenya, where much of the best land was given over to white settlers, the ratio was 1 : 22,000, making it the most closely administered British colony in Africa with roughly four times as many British administrators in proportion to the African population as Nigeria. And here settler magistracies, gun clubs and generally relevant military experience reinforced the not-so-thin white line. Clearly the ratio of rulers to ruled was not purely a matter of security; much depended on what the colonial state was expected to do.

As a general rule European empires were committed by considerations of expense to light government. The colonial state had to be financially self-sufficient; this was the basic condition of its legitimacy in the eyes of the metropolitan publics. It was fundamental to the French 1900 colonial reform law and the Colonial Charter for the Belgian Congo of 1908, while the British Treasury had always insisted that all but the most penurious colonies pay their way (if this was impossible, as in the case of British Somaliland, then they could be doled out a tiny annual subvention). The Europeans controlled the upper echelons of government to levy revenue and safeguard their economic and strategic interests without trying to reshape indigenous societies. The classic model, especially of course for the British, was India. There powerful structures of control and fiscal extraction, sanctioned by elaborate and resilient religious systems, were incorporated into the colonial state. In 1939 just 760 British officers in the élite Indian Civil Service ruled nearly 389,000,000 Indians supported by only 15,000 British (and over 250,000 Indian) soldiers. But no indigenous African society could match the effectiveness of India's hierarchies in extracting land revenues or, on the French side, Vietnam's long-established bureaucratic machinery for appropriating rice surpluses.[4]

In the Kenyan case, moreover, unlike India, there were European settlers desperate for labour; hence the state's relatively elaborate mechanisms for recruiting African workers and coping with the consequent crises in the rural areas from which they were drawn. The Kenyan system, which was probably more harshly bureaucratic than that of any other British colony in West or East Africa, pivoted on a 'Native Registration Ordinance' forcing all African men between 15 and 40 to register and carry an identity card with space for employers to record duration of employment, along with the type of work and the wages paid.[5] The difficulties of interwar Kenya ominously suggested that forcing the pace of economic and social change in Africa might mean the end of empire on the cheap.

One imperial institution, the colonial army, turned the belligerence of the frontiersmen to its advantage by select incorporation. The French provided employment for fighting men who would otherwise be troublesome from 1830 in Algeria and from 1857 in West Africa. Prudent posting of soldiers outside their home areas to avoid divided loyalties could easily be finessed into tactics of divide and rule. Berbers were enlisted to counterbalance Arabs and in West Africa they gave preference to certain districts and ethnic groups which could be played off against the rest.

The British, having created the supreme model colonial army from sepoys and Gurkhas in India, believed they were especially adept at selecting good native soldiers. There was much talk of discriminating between martial and effeminate peoples but basically they favoured Africans 'pure and simple' whose ethnic stereotypes were unblemished by too much culture contact. In the Gambia, for example, they chose to recruit up-river rather than 'trouser boys' from nearer the coast who had already been influenced by missionary example.[6] Such partiality paralleled that of the District Commissioners for the 'unspoiled' African and matched that of the British army as a whole which was officered in the main by country gentry who preferred similarly bucolic recruits to the urban working class. Officers assumed that the patterns of deference in rural England and rural Africa were basically equivalent, believing that the African soldier simply switched allegiance from his chief to his European officer and regiment for the duration of his service.[7] Scottish officers must have found the analogue with highland clans even more compelling.

The partition of southern Africa had presented the British, and the English-speaking South Africans of Natal, with the continent's most feared warrior people, the Zulus. Here was a superb, ready-made fighting machine, splendidly organized and disciplined through the regimental system. At first the British army considered incorporating them as a counterpoise to the predominance of Muslims elsewhere in the colonial forces, but the fearful opposition of European settlers ruled that out. Nevertheless the martial presence of the Zulus was too impressive to be ignored; they became the quintessential black policemen and 'boss boys' of the colonial enterprise. (Indeed Anglo-Zulu mutual admiration was central to the imperial mystique, especially in Natal: two consciously martial peoples, each flattering the other's self-image by regarding them as really rather superior to other representatives of their race.)

Elsewhere the colonial armies transformed freelance warriors into formidable combatant units, undeniably effective in Europe and Asia as well as Africa. Imperial propaganda, directed at the metropolitan publics, usually stressed the disciplined ferocity of these African armies. This rallied domestic support for the empire from Europeans very conscious of their country's relative military strength in a war-torn age. It appealed particularly to the French, aware of their long-term demographic decline and general weakness when set against the statistics of German military power. It was also meant to frighten the metropole's enemies – and did so, hence the international outcry when French African troops occupied German territory in the aftermath of the First World War. And it promoted the basic imperial message: savage Africa needed European discipline to function effectively.

African soldiers, including conscripts, were freely deployed in both World Wars, not only to conquer Germany's African colonies in the First World War, but in such distant theatres as Europe, the Middle East and Burma. One million overseas subjects of France served in the First World War and 250,000, most of them African, died. Regimental names indicated African soldiers' availability for peacetime service outside their home colony, for example, the West African Frontier Force and the King's African Rifles, its equivalent in British East and Central Africa, while the Force Publique was responsible for both the Belgian Congo and Ruanda-Urundi. France and Portugal, as more centralized imperial regimes, simply took for granted that colonial soldiers could be deployed as units of the metropolitan army.

Army life was tough but at least it functioned by comprehensible rules. (Whereas for other Africans caught in the mesh of colonialism the invisible line between a proper display of initiative and insubordination was often problematic. Joyce Cary's ebullient tragi-comedy *Mister Johnson* (1939) is the classic fictional account of civilian misunderstanding.) The army offered regular pay and rations at a higher standard than most peasants enjoyed, as well as the prospect of pensions and gratuities.

In colonial armies loyalty to the empire was based on the solid foundation of *esprit de corps*. The depot and the regiment were complementary total institutions based on draconian punishment, possible promotion and routine dramatized by ceremonial. African soldiers displayed the authentic imperialist arrogance. The King's African Rifles were 'filled with unshakeable knowledge that . . . the British had never been beaten in a war . . . their only thought was "pilente patsogolu" (to go forward).'[8] A Senegalese sub-lieutenant harangued his battalion in the First World War, 'You are the first among the Blacks, for the French, first among the Whites, have conferred distinction on you.'[9]

Identification with empire operated against certain African groups inside the colonies as well as the enemies of Britain and France abroad. Economic aspects of the uneven development of colonial Africa have tended to attract most attention, understandably given the importance of the development of the migrant labour system – especially as it operated from relatively remote rural areas to the South African gold mines. But throughout colonial Africa uneven development has had vital security aspects as well. Clayton and Killingray, the chroniclers of Britain's African armies, suggest that although their officers warmly praised the men's loyalty to the Crown, 'It is more likely that the soldier's perception of the Crown was rather different; although British and remote, the monarch was nevertheless a powerful being endorsing and protecting the remote rural peasant ways of life from which the vast majority of soldiers came, especially if those remote rural societies felt themselves disadvantaged in relationship to other more influential ethnicities.'[10] Any system of selective recruitment was liable to be a form of divide and rule but ethnic stereotyping in a colonial situation of uneven development was all the more insidious, and therefore effective, for not being one-way; in Sierra Leone, for example, Freetown Krios despised the soldiers of the Royal West African Frontier Force, and shunned enlistment themselves, because the troops went barefoot.[11]

In policing Africa, insofar as it can be distinguished from garrisoning it, colonial rule generally provided relative peace and greater individual security than had existed before. Harold Blair, District Officer at Tamale in the Northern Territories of the Gold Coast in the 1930s recalled, 'I never once had occasion to call on the military in the tribal battles I dealt with. Generally I rode out with a walking stick and perhaps one policeman. At the most, on one or two occasions, I went out with the mounted [police] patrol. I never had to fire a shot.'[12] But the enforcement of law and order varied enormously. Settler colonies were more rigorously policed than others, employing substantial numbers of European officers. In the depression years of the 1930s the trend was to leave the policing of remote areas as far as possible to some form of Indirect Rule.

The prime justification for the European partition of Africa had been to maintain 'pax' – peace and stability – where the precolonial rulers of Africa were deemed to have failed. Indeed the Berlin West Africa Conference which laid down ground rules for partition, in order that Africa might be carved up without European conflict, charged the would-be rulers to provide evidence of 'effective occupation' by way of legal title. But the peoples on the geopolitical margins of the new European colonies proved remarkably recalcitrant. Difficulties of terrain – swamplands, mountains, dense forests, deserts – combined with guerilla prowess and disdain for many of the consumer goods of contemporary capitalism, enabled them to evade the clutches of the colonial state to live in outlaw, semi-nomadic freedom on the periphery. The initial conquerors left such turbulent peoples as far as possible to their own devices, with some kind of loose treaty arrangement with their 'big men', for if the colonial state had scant attraction for them, they too had normally little to offer in the way of revenue and commerce. Huge tracts of territory were therefore still semi-autonomous, while their nominal European rulers concentrated on the rich pickings nearer to hand, like Lyautey in 1914 who having opened the route from Fez to Algeria was content to have secured what he termed '*le Maroc Utile*' ('the useful part of Morocco'), a fraction of the whole. Paradoxically, that comment was memorable because he was discriminating between parts of one of the few colonies with a strong territorial identity, deriving from its precolonial existence.

District Officers on lonely patrol, like Blair, knew that even hitherto inaccessible areas were becoming a good deal less so due to the development of imperial technology. Europe's latest weaponry, military aircraft, threatened to end the geographical isolation that favoured African defiance. Even before 1914 aircraft had been used in Morocco, as well as by the Italians in the conquest of Libya. In the First World War they were deployed in several theatres. Flying was vital to the futuristic mystique of fascism from the start – Mussolini himself learned to fly in 1919. Bombs and gas were used against civilians as well as soldiers in the annexation of Ethiopia in 1935–6.[13]

Newsreels showing Mussolini's pilots dropping poison gas on defenceless villagers for the fun of it created indelible images of the fascist years.[14] But the confrontation between aviation and the African became a central motif of imperial ideology. During the First World War East African campaign a German officer reported that some Africans were terrified by a British plane believing it was *Muungu*, a supernatural being.[15] Here was the archetypal myth of Western omnipotence in its starkest essentials: superstitious savages panicked by the wonders of science which they confused with the supernatural. Air-power enthusiasts speculated that hitherto stiff-necked tribesmen might be stunned into submission by this novel, cheap and bloodless celestial warfare. This was contested by those who were committed to ground forces rather than aircraft. General Milne, Chief of the Imperial General Staff, opposed the use of air power in the Anglo-Egyptian Sudan in 1928 on the grounds that the 'oriental mind' when aroused to fanaticism by 'religious or racial propaganda' was immune to the terror of aerial attack experienced by more sensitive Europeans.[16] A further twist in the complex interplay of race, religion and ethnicity in colonial stereotyping brought the argument full circle with a vengeance. If tribesmen lacked the finer sensitivities of Europeans then the same humanitarian considerations need not apply. During the complicated negotiations of the 1932 Disarmament Conference the British government agreed that bombing cities ought to be banned but refused to sacrifice 'the use of such machines as are necessary for police purposes in out of the way places'. Ex-Prime Minister Lloyd George commented with brutal contempt, 'we insisted on the right to bomb niggers'.[17]

The Anglo-Egyptian Sudan constituted a critical case study for the arguments over the value of aircraft in colonial control. First, its sheer size, some 1,300 miles north to south and 1,000 miles east to west at its widest, roughly the same extent as Western Europe, represented the geopolitical problems of the British Empire's vast spread writ large. Poor land communications made the southern Sudan virtually impassable except for four months of the year. The Sudan, moreover, lay close to the intersection of several networks of imperial air communications – eastward to the Middle East, India, Singapore and Australia; south to East and Central Africa and the Cape – so that it would be relatively easy to integrate into overall imperial planning. But the aerial policing of British Africa became enmeshed in inter-service rivalries involving, at first, the survival of the RAF as an independent force and thereafter, once this had been assured because of its colonial role, competition for scarce resources doled out by a reluctant treasury. As General Milne's derogatory comments illustrate imperial regimes were never monolithic either in instrumentalities or ideology. The Governor-General, Sir John Maffey, initially quite sceptical, was eventually 'most impressed' by an RAF squadron as a 'swift agent of government' reprisal against a group of Nuer who had killed a DC and 17 others in 1928.[18] In such circumstances aircraft vastly increased the reach and speed of strike of the colonial state.

They had their routine uses, too, providing rapid transport for DCs and, flying at relatively low altitudes, giving them a much better overall sense of the country than could be gained from a slow trek over difficult terrain. Aerial cartography, which was much cheaper than traditional methods of ground surveying, greatly increased the state's capacity for informed action in such remote areas; large air surveys of the Sudd country of the Sudan, as well as Northern Rhodesia, were carried out.

Aircraft were never omnipotent. Rainforests could not be policed as effectively as deserts, for example. They were rarely armoured and therefore were vulnerable to rifle fire. Yet air power irrevocably altered the balance of power between the centralized state and the societies on its periphery. In that sense its contribution, in rendering that state effective and therefore increasing its legitimacy, was significant.

The airplane was only the latest and most spectacular instrument of imperial power. Mobility, in all its forms, was crucial to the maintenance of colonial authority between the wars. The railway, the motor car, the telegraph and telephone, became essential to day-by-day control. Ironically this meant that the man on the spot, the DC or *Commandant du Cercle*, was also under closer bureaucratic control. He spent less time on trek and more at his desk or in court, so that his relations with Africans, as well as with central colonial authority, became more formalized.

LEGITIMACY

The colonial soldiery and police were unique. Their unswerving loyalty was essential to the functioning of the imperial regimes. Here certainly was the indispensable steel in the imperial frame. The British Colonial Office stated crisply in 1936 that the military was 'the power in reserve behind the civil authority to check any subversive movement or incipient disorder among people still to a great extent in a primitive stage of society'.[19] Given unquestioning loyalty from such key personnel the colonial state could manage with reasonable diligence on the part of its civil servants and passive compliance from the great mass of Africans whose taxes kept the machinery running.

Until quite late in the day sustained efforts to justify imperial policy were almost invariably directed to the domestic metropolitan public rather than Africans. (The mandates of the League of Nations were special cases where international public concern was institutionalized.) Recently Anthony Kirk-Greene pointed out that Americans still find it difficult to understand that no attempt was made to inculcate a deliberate ideology of imperialism in the training of Britain's overseas administrators.[20] Imperial propaganda within the colonies, such as it was, therefore, tended to be sporadic and unsystematic, largely confined to certain annual celebrations and parades. (The military and police could then impress the civilian populace with their spectacular drill and disciplined *esprit de corps*.) Nevertheless, if the ideology of imperialism was unsystematic it became increasingly systemic. Both rulers and ruled became progressively enmeshed in its unexamined assumptions. (One implication of Kirk-Greene's remark is that the ideology of imperialism was so deeply held by the British that it did not need conscious indoctrination. With both a monarch and an aristocracy the British had less occasion to think through what was involved in grounding authority on descent – possessing a white skin or, if African, being of chiefly lineage – than republican and more formally egalitarian societies.)

Within barely half a century of the European partition the colonial states had achieved a certain legitimacy, especially with the educated élites. They planned their careers and arranged their children's education around the perceived opportunities provided by the apparatus of administration, along with the missions and expatriate firms. Day by day, year by year, even to the next generation, they shaped their lives to fit the patterns of colonialism. And in the process the colonial state also adapted somewhat to the rhythms of their own routines. But what had they committed themselves to? As they probed the career possibilities, especially in the second generation, it became increasingly clear that it was the modernized generic state, rather than any specific regime, that gave them scope to pursue their chosen lifestyles.

A further point needs to be made about the nature of the educated élite's commitment to the centralized colonial state: it did not involve surrendering their ethnic identity (which was generally assumed at the time to be their precolonial 'tribal' identity). Quite the reverse. With the expansion of literacy and myriad transliterations of African vernaculars, the period between the wars was one of massive proliferation and enrichment of ethnic ideologies. Only the educated élites, literate and bilingual, fluent in English, French or Portuguese, as well as their own vernaculars, could supply and promote the essential primers in language, history and folklore. Only with such consciously crafted ideologies could ethnicities survive and flourish in the highly competitive arena of colonial print capitalism.[21]

At a lower level the colonial administrations worked through the politics of collaboration with local 'big men'. They wanted, in the words of Lord Lugard, the leading British theorist of colonial rule, 'a class who in a crisis can be relied on to stand by us and whose interests are wholly identified with ours.'[22] Where possible they co-opted Africans already in authority who were able to call on existing routines of obedience. The British, through Lugard, developed the theory that Indirect Rule, via the chiefs, was the best form of imperial government, embodying the ideals of trusteeship by 'developing' native African institutions instead of importing alien ones. But even in Northern Nigeria, the model for Indirect Rule elsewhere, this ideal was likely to be modified by pragmatic imperial practice. Lugard himself 'made the point as strongly as he could that all chiefs, even the Sultan of Sokoto, were henceforth agents of the government . . . and that the authority of the local residents was above theirs.'[23]

The crux of all the European imperialists' self-justification was their insistence that they were qualified above all competitors to rule Africans; hence they made much of their patent philosophies of rule deriving from their unique national experience. In practice although the French used direct administration, through a cadre of administrative chiefs, as they theorized about their new doctrine of 'Association' they increasingly recruited from traditional chiefly families so that British and French practice converged. As the French colonial reformer, Robert Delavignette, noted, 'We are well aware that it is essential to preserve the native character of the canton chief and to make use of the traditional feudal spirit which still survives in him; on the other hand, the very fact of colonization forces us to shape him to our administrative outlook.'[24] Similar practical considerations affected Belgian field administration even while their theorists proclaimed their own rhetoric of centralized paternalism. In 1933 they rationalized their system of local administration into approximately 1,000 units of roughly the same size explaining, 'While respecting traditional administration, the legislator wanted to establish a single administrative system: he made the chieftaincy (or sector) the lowest echelon of the administrative organization, and the chief a functionary integrated into the system without prejudice to his traditional role.'[25]

Roland Oliver, doyen of general historians of Africa, has remarked that the so-called 'partition' of Africa was in reality 'a ruthless act of political amalgamation, whereby something of the order of 10,000 units was reduced to a mere 40 [colonial territories]'.[26] Most of the original units were quite small, numbering between 5,000 and 10,000 people. But they tended to form clusters of 20 – 30 statelets, 'each cluster representing a common language or culture', and it was to these that Europeans attached the term 'tribe.'[27] The Europeans then based their local administrative units on these 'tribes' because administrators believed Africans were naturally 'tribal'. Meanwhile missionaries – both black and white – often merged all the dialects into a single written language.

Colonial policy sought the consolidation of these ethnic units thus preventing the emergence of 'detribalized' Africans and the consequent development of a potentially dangerous colony-wide political consciousness. The remarks of Colonel French, a British War Office official in 1917, illustrate this divide-and-rule strategy perfectly:

> [The] spirit of nationality, or perhaps it would be more correct to say, of tribe, should be cultivated and nowhere can this be done with better chance of success than in British East Africa and Uganda, where there are numerous tribes ethnographically quite distinct from one another. It is suggested that in each ethnographically distinct district the schools should . . . form integral parts of the

tribe and centres of folk-lore and tradition . . . [A] method might also be found whereby the efforts of the missionaries may also assist in the cultivation of national spirit. This it seems might be done by allowing only one denomination to work in each demographic area and by not allowing the same denomination to work in two adjacent areas.[28]

The strength of French's military *realpolitik* was that it could be implemented in good conscience. All the imperial powers promoted the study of African societies so as to understand their point of departure. Anthropologists, amateur and professional, regarded African societies as more or less self-contained tribal units. By focusing on the local situation, holding it steady in their minds, they came up with plausible analyses of the ways in which such societies functioned. On this model African politics were local micropolitics to be conducted at the tribal level. That was regarded as authentic, an authenticity underwritten by the considerable advances in knowledge made by functionalist anthropology. Above that level lay the domain of administration, imperial administration, not politics.

Indirect Rule though would have been built upon shifting sand if it had not converged with similar trends among Africans. Buffeted by social change they too constructed a new political geography oriented to kinship and bolstered by imaginative history such as the mythical Nkhamanga Empire of northern Nyasaland.[29] African ideology, Indirect Rule and contemporary social science all combined in the creation of tribes. But Lugard had devised Indirect Rule partly to negate the political claims of the 'Europeanized Africans' of Lagos, whose counterparts all over colonial Africa were fashioning the tribal histories which supplied its ideological justification.

Sir Donald Cameron, as much as Lugard, believed Indirect Rule was a way to stop Africans following the Indian model of anticolonial nationalism. But he did try to think ahead. He was clear that Indirect Rule should be 'a means and not an end' with the native administrations becoming foundations for wider African political organization, possibly in the Legislative Council, should Africans want that. He preferred though a pyramid of councils culminating in 'a council for the whole of Tanganyika' in 'probably not more or less than three or four generations'.[30] Cameron's rather sketchy scenario in 1930 was one imagined future. He was succeeded in 1932 by Sir Stewart Symes, who ordered the native administrations to confine themselves strictly to local issues, blocking off the possibilities of any such imaginative evolution.

The educated élite meanwhile formed a series of organizations designed to cope with their members' professional and social problems and express their broader aspirations. They ran the gamut from welfare organizations to political pressure groups and have led to the period between the wars being characterized as both 'the age of improvement' – with strong overtones of moralistic self-help – and that of 'secondary resistance' to imperialism. ('Secondary resistance' – as against 'primary', the original patriotic resistance to European occupation and 'tertiary', full-scale nationalism aiming at political independence – worked within the framework of colonial rule to improve African conditions.)[31] The Livingstone Native Welfare Association, for example, was formed in 1929–30 by African clerks, in both government and private employment in Northern Rhodesia, aiming to 'help the government to improve the country and to deal with matters and grievances affecting the native people.' In West Africa these bodies often specifically designated themselves 'improvement associations' or 'progress unions'. Some, especially those with an ethnic base, such as the Ashanti Youth Club and the Akwapim Improvement Society both founded in the Gold Coast in 1930, although led by the élite, reached out to the illiterate and semi-literate. Indeed the structures ranged from local and tribal to colony-wide and beyond. In Tanganyika the African Association, formed in 1929, succeeded in being both a clerks' trade union and a vehicle to express African opinion on a country-wide and sometimes even Pan-African basis.[32]

African associations displayed striking organizational diversity and adaptability as they adjusted to the changing dimensions of townships and tribes and increased their scale to encompass whole colonies, and indeed thrust across imperialism's formal boundaries to follow the lines of trade and labour migration. Many were short-lived and, as in all organizations, there was a tendency for imaginative reach to exceed effective bureaucratic grasp. Certainly such exuberant experimentalism contrasts with the rigid conservatism of imperial officials like Symes.

Africans had never lacked political imagination and their ideas on modernization and schemes for incorporation in the concert of nations predate partition, as James Africanus Horton's *West African Countries and Peoples* (1868) and the constitution adopted by the Fante Confederacy (1873) illustrate.[33] Indeed with a rich variety of religious concepts of community and nationality (again prepartition in origin), as well as the specifically secular versions, Africans could call on a multiplicity of models to give concrete shape to their inchoate hopes. Some of these models, such as those developed by Henry Venn of the Anglican Church Missionary Society (CMS), in partnership with West Africans on 'the euthanasia of missions' and national chuches, were highly suggestive.[34] Others were conservative in orientation, like the *Volkskirche* (ethnic church), which reinforced a somewhat rigid interpretation of tribe.[35] Nevertheless, all contributed to a plurality of possibilities which could not be cramped into the imperial bureaucratic mode where 'indirect rule became an end and not a means'.[36]

By far the largest European empires in Africa belonged to Britain and France who also boasted Europe's best established liberal parliamentary regimes. There were ironies here which Africans and their European champions could exploit. The 'civilizing mission' had not always been tied to notions of race, tribe and Indirect Rule as the instruments of trusteeship. Older ideas of the 'civilizing mission' as 'assimilation', the French notion that indigenous peoples be assimilated to Western – that is French civilization – or its British equivalent, grounded in the evangelical revival, that men and women could be made anew by Christian conversion, survived in segments of the colonial system.

Such ideas might be dismissed as unnatural attempts to transform Africans into 'Black Frenchmen' or 'Black Englishmen' by administrative officialdom but they were powerfully held elsewhere. They were especially vigorous in parts of the mission field. By 1910 there were already nearly 11,000 missionaries and by 1939 this had doubled to 22,000.[37] All figures are relative and these missionary totals are the more significant in view of the scant administrative presence. Given mission responsibility for most colonial education these ideas were especially powerful in that crucial sector. Whatever notions of 'adapted education' colonial theorists might develop to suit the era of Indirect Rule, at Fourah Bay College in Sierra Leone West Africans studied, under the guidance of the CMS, the same Durham University syllabus as their student contemporaries in England. (And they and their parents insisted that this was precisely what they wanted for they had no intention of being fobbed off with an 'adapted' degree.)

With the colonial state generally strapped for cash, its functions were minimal and its main concern was security rather than welfare and social engineering. Missions, therefore, were by far the largest 'aid' donors in the interwar period, providing health and educational services partly through the contributions of their converts and partly through their home congregations in Europe and America. Colonialism was thus never monolithic and the significance of this voluntary conversionist colonialism in the development of African civil society being out of phase with the structures of official colonialism has to be taken into account.

Such 'assimilationism' or 'conversionism' could foster powerful residual loyalties towards the imperial regime. The *Quatre communes* (Four Communes) of Senegal were the showpiece of French assimilationism, where the former customs officer Blaise Diagne was elected to the French parliament by carefully organizing the votes of urban Africans in 1914. When Marcus Garvey, the charismatic Jamaican-born leader of a mass 'Back to Africa' movement in the USA, called on him for support in 1920 on the basis of racial solidarity, Diagne spurned him: 'We French natives wish to remain French, since France has given us every liberty and since she has unreservedly accepted us on the same basis as her European children. None of us desires to see French Africa delivered exclusively to the natives.'[38]

Europe's empires tended to measure their achievements against the great classical exemplar, Rome. So also did some of their educated subjects. Before and during the scramble, Edward Blyden, the great Pan-Negro patriot and educator, recommended a curriculum based on the classics as an antidote to contemporary racism. Certainly Fourah Bay and the denominational grammar schools, which differed from Blyden on many other issues, agreed on the importance of the classics. Insofar as the latter-day Romans fell short of good classical norms through practising racial discrimination or other forms of injustice then their self-proclaimed civilizing mission was discredited.

An American political scientist, Michael Doyle, has recently used the Roman model to analyse the consolidation and disintegration of empires through the ages. Doyle's arguments are complex and deserve careful consideration from all students of empires but for our immediate purpose of comparison it serves to note that he identifies two critical thresholds through which the Roman Empire passed to explain its remarkable persistence over four centuries of Mediterranean domination. The first threshold was the first-century AD Augustan revolution which rescued the Empire from imminent dissolution by bureaucratic centralization, removing its administration from the arena of Roman politics. The second threshold was passed in AD 212 when the Emperor Caracalla declared that all free men were citizens of Rome. Such was the degree of political integration already achieved by piecemeal administrative measures and the spread of a common culture throughout the empire that the actual edict caused scant comment when enacted. Active political participation in Rome, moreover, had declined more rapidly than it rose in the provinces. The year AD 212 thus records the date when the people of the Empire were absorbed into a common tyranny. Survival depended then on administrative centralization and egalitarian subjection. Doyle does not develop the question of survival through the extension of freedom by upgrading provincial citizenship because, first, the reverse happened in the Roman case and, second, because such equality would transform empire into something else – a species of decolonization in fact.[39]

The closest approximation to Doyle's Augustan and Caracallan revolutions was the Portuguese dictator Salazar's '*Estado Novo*' ('New State') with its legal centralization and ideology of a global multiracial lusotropical national community, based on miscegenation. Here the case could be made that the peoples of the Empire were assimilated in a common tyranny and here Empire lasted longest.

Among democratic imperialists the French doctrine of assimilation was closest to Roman universalism, as the organizing officials of the 1900 Paris Universal Exposition boasted 'forty-five million men of all races, who have achieved the most diverse degree of civilization, have entered the French community.'[40] Although the French parliament had the right to legislate for the colonies, in practice colonial law tended to be invoked by presidential decree or governors' ordinances. This duality was translated at the personal level into the division between those enjoying the status of citizens and those subordinated as subjects. The contrast between Muslim and French civil status was to be especially significant in Algeria. Blaise Diagne's proud political achievement, grounded on his citizenship status, bore solid political fruit for France. He was instrumental in recruiting 134,000 'subjects' to fight in Europe. As a successful collaborator he was able to win in return the consolidation of his fellow citizens' privileges and rights to pensions, citizenship and some job opportunities for those soldiers who survived.[41]

The decentralization of Britain's African Empire removes it furthest from Doyle's Roman model. Yet even here British subjects of the Crown colonies (but not British 'protected persons' from the African protectorates) rejoiced in the fact that they were also citizens of the United Kingdom. In March 1920 the National Congress of British West Africa was inaugurated professing loyalty to the British King Emperor and wishing to keep 'inviolate' the connection with the British Empire while calling for half-elected, half-nominated legislative councils, a house of assembly with an elected majority to control finance and a West African University. In its political and economic outlook, as in its social composition, the Congress had 'all the virtues and political limitations of mid-Victorian liberalism', comments Jabez Langley, its historian.[42] The same observation could be made about the politics of the new élite in South Africa which rallied, alongside other liberals, in a rearguard defence of the Cape Colony's non-racial franchise against the attack of the majority white electorate in an increasingly segregationist Union of South Africa.

European racism had sprung a cruel ideological trap on the new élite. They claimed full citizenship, equal civil and political rights, as civilized men and women. They had the certificates, diplomas and degrees, as well as the lifestyles and general cultural achievements, to prove their case. When the imperial regimes' civilizing mission was assimilationist and conversionist professional and political status was coordinated, more or less, with cultural attainment. The switch from achieved to ascribed status – European and chiefly birthright – changed that. As racial ranking consolidated and racist ideology became more strident so the new élite's insistence on its cultural achievement grew increasingly desperate. But this very cultural attainment allowed their white rulers to argue that they had thereby differentiated themselves from the mass of the population in their respective colonies and so disqualified themselves from speaking on its behalf. In December 1920 Nigerian Governor Hugh Clifford sneered at the 'loose and gaseous talk on the subject of popular election . . . from a self-selected and self-appointed congregation of educated African gentlemen [the National Congress]', wondering 'what these gentlemen's experience would be if, instead of travelling peacefully to Liverpool on a British ship they could be deposited . . . among . . . naked warriors of the Ibo country, and there left to explain their claims to be recognised as the accredited representatives of their "fellow nationals".'[43]

Many educated Africans did not fit into such rigid colonial pigeonholing. Sol Plaatje, for example, was the archetypal South African liberal – in local parlance 'Cape liberal'. (So much so that he even supported the 1930 enfranchisement of white women, even though, on one level, this amounted to cynical racist gerrymandering to devalue his own Cape franchise!) But he was also an African nationalist, committed Christian and, as a Tswana patriot, a dedicated researcher into ethnic history and folklore with chiefly patronage. On a personal plane he needed no less than this multiplicity of roles to locate his own and his people's place in history and the wider world; on a public plane his various interests sometimes conflicted, as in the case of the white women's vote, but then conflict and compromise are the stuff of politics.[44] Similarly the career of Stefano Kaoze, the first Congolese to become an ordained Roman Catholic priest, and his seminal role in developing Tabwa ethnicity in what is now south-eastern Zaire in the first half of the century, shatters the colonial stereotype of the 'detribalized African'.[45]

European imperialism's tidy administrative solutions, turning on race and Indirect Rule, were remarkably effective in the short run, but in the long term they were counter-productive. Rejecting the assimilationist and conversionist option of common citizenship through cultural convergence, they forced the educated élite to direct its intellectual and organizational energies into the creation of newly imagined communities outside official channels. Sir Donald Cameron, the reformer of Indirect Rule, clearly understood that it marked a crucial advance in the struggle by the colonial state to capture control of African society: 'Paradoxical as it may seem', he noted on return from trek in Tanganyika in 1928, 'although indirect administration has replaced direct administration there is a great deal more administration than there was before', tracing the linkage, via headman, sub-chief, chief and district office, between the remote peasant 'on the shores of Lake Eyassi' and the Provincial Commissioner.[46] As the colonial state penetrated deeper into local society so it standardized centre–periphery relations towards the point when even the remote peasant and his headman could be caught up in colony-wide politics. It was a two-way process. The state extended its grasp and the peasants of the periphery had, perforce, to enlarge their horizons to engage with it. From the 1930s the efforts of officials to lock African aspirations into local institutions increasingly failed.

THE MANDATE SYSTEM

The peace settlement at the end of the First World War was in part a colonial settlement whereby the victorious powers disposed of the colonies of the vanquished. By Article 22 of the League of Nations Covenant the victorious imperial powers agreed to be held accountable to the League for their administration of ex-colonies of the German and Ottoman Empires. The crux of the mandates system was international accountability; the administering author-ities submitted annual reports to the Permanent Mandates Commission to prove they were fulfilling their obligation to hold the mandates as 'a sacred trust of civilization' for the welfare of the 'natives' rather than for purposes of exploitation.

The colonial settlement of 1919 in effect defined four categories of mankind. First, the victorious imperial powers considered fit to discharge 'the sacred trust of civilization'. These consisted of European colonial powers: Britain, France and Belgium; white dominions of the British diaspora: Australia, New Zealand

and South Africa; and finally, that unique Asian exponent of maritime imperialism, Japan.

The peoples they were to rule were also classified hierarchically. In the top category were the 'A' peoples of the Middle East – the ex-Ottoman territories of Iraq, Palestine and Syria – deemed to have 'reached a stage of development where their existence as independent nations can be provisionally recognized subject to the rendering of administrative advice and assistance by a Mandatory power until such time as they are able to stand alone.' Outside of Category 'A' there was no such recognition of the existence of potential nations which would be able 'to stand alone' in a relatively short period of time. Ranked next were the 'B' peoples of tropical Africa, where the mandatory power was to guarantee freedom of conscience and free trade, prohibit the slave trade and arms traffic and generally behave just as the colonial powers had promised at the Berlin Conference on the eve of the scramble for Africa in 1885. Plainly an indefinite period of economic and political advancement under European tutelage was envisaged for such 'tribal' peoples. In this 'B' category the territories of Togo and the Cameroons were divided between Britain and France (although in the latter case nine-tenths went to France), Tanganyika was administered by Britain and Ruanda-Urundi by Belgium.

The people of one African colony, though, ex-German South-West Africa, were relegated to category 'C', along with the peoples of the Pacific islands considered to be still in the 'stone age' therefore likely to remain colonial subjects for centuries, possibly forever. South-West Africa was to be administered by South Africa. (Indeed the white dominions dominated this category with Australia administering New Guinea and New Zealand responsible for Samoa, the two largest Pacific islands, while the smaller Marshalls, Carolines and Marianas fell to Japan.)

The mandates system exemplifies both the ideological strength and weakness of early twentieth-century imperialism. As in the internal administration of the colonies it embodied racial hierarchy with the colonial mandates themselves ranked 'A', 'B' and 'C' – roughly, Arab, Negro African, Khoisan and South Sea Islanders.[47] One ranking reinforced another in a self-sealing ideological system which endorsed racial division as the basis for social and political organization.

From one viewpoint the mandate system appeared a cynical and hypocritical land-grab by the victorious colonial powers. The behaviour of General Smuts, the South African architect of the League of Nations, might seem to provide strong endorsement for that judgement. Wishing to match South Africa's economic expansion with territorial enlargement, he hoped to incorporate Southern Rhodesia, the High Commission territories of Basutoland, Bechuanaland and Swaziland, and southern Mozambique. His expansionism was disappointed in each of those cases. He did get South-West Africa, even if not quite on the terms he wanted, failing to secure its annexation at the Peace Conference in 1919. Nevertheless, as a 'C' mandate, he was allowed to treat it as an integral part of the Union. Some of the African peoples had expected that the replacement of German rule by the Union Mandate would mean the restoration of their lost lands but were brusquely disenchanted. A dog-tax imposed to stop the Nama people hunting was particularly hated. One group of Nama, the Afrikaans-speaking Bondelswarts, were refused the return of leaders exiled by the Germans. The Bondelswarts rebelled in May 1922 and were machine-gunned and bombed into submission, killing over a hundred. Although the Permanent Mandates Commission asked questions, South Africa escaped formal condemnation.

Through the mandates system, however, the imperial powers had created a special type of colony for whose administration they were held accountable by the international community, even if there was no provision for enforcement against a recalcitrant mandatory power as the Bondelswarts killing demon-strated. Yet the 'Bondelswarts massacre' entered the lexicon of international atrocities, not least because of the blistering criticism of Smuts from fellow South Africans. 'Bondelswarts' became part of the process whereby the South African government gradually took on the role of chief colonial scapegoat, representing what was unacceptable by the norms of international behaviour. If the mandate system was condemned as hypocritical, as it often was by ex-colonial states in the League Assembly, then the old adage about hypocrisy being vice's tribute to virtue is still worth remembering. It definitely marked the end of the kind of imperialism that was so taken for granted by its practitioners that they had no need for self-justification. Henceforth guilt and self-doubt as well as Western notions of superiority were inscribed on the international agenda.

Further, the imperial powers had subdivided this category according to the prospects of particular colonies for self-government, while designating even the most backward as a 'sacred trust for civilization'. The imperial powers publicly, in international concert, thus hedged the very idea of empire with radical qualifications. Their critics – domestic, international and colonial – could hold them to account when their performance fell below their own professed standards. In liberal imperial theory such criticism, if sensitively handled, could strengthen empire as wrongs were righted in ways that confirmed imperial ideals of 'good government'. In practice discrepancies between theory and perform-ance were not always resolved so positively. At the very core of the mandates system, moreover, was the notion of tutelage, asserting that the ultimate ideological justification for empire was provided by presiding over its own liquidation.

Decolonization was now an international issue. In September 1931 the Mandates Commission suggested to the League Council the basic conditions to be fulfilled before autonomy be granted to 'A' and 'B' mandates: the territory should have a government and an administration capable of running public services; it should be able to safeguard its independence and territorial integrity; it should have sufficient and reliable financial resources and a banking system;

and it should possess a legal system capable of dispensing justice for all on an equitable and regular basis.

Nor could the implications of this be confined to the mandates. It was impossible to argue convincingly that the Togolese or Tanganyikans should ultimately be able to exercise their right of national self-determination, because they were inhabitants of mandated territories, while those who lived in the Gold and Ivory Coasts, or Kenya and Uganda, should not. In any case the imperial powers were keen to assert their right to deal with their mandates, for the purposes of administration, like the rest of their colonial domain. They proudly asserted that the League of Nations proclamation of a 'sacred trust for civilization' was already embodied in their practice of trusteeship. Paradoxically, therefore, they assisted in creating an international scenario in which imperial tutelage, culminating in eventual decolonization, was expected to be the norm for all colonies not just mandates. There was still scope, of course, for colonial paternalism. So long as racial theorizing was a plausible mode of discourse colonial peoples, especially if they fell into category 'C', were liable to be accorded a semi-permanent status of immaturity. And even for liberal imperialists the period of tutelage prescribed in quite promising cases tended to stretch far into the future.

CONCLUSION

What do these combinations of strength and weakness in the imperial regimes portend? First, the weaknesses are significant when it comes to explaining the swift demise of empire after the Second World War. But, second, the strengths, the elements of steel in the imperial framework, are the historical context for the rapid replacement of the constitutional arrangements of the immediate successor states by single-party and military regimes. Finally, the interaction of Africa and the wider world in the period of imperialism cannot be encompassed solely in terms of political history. Missionaries and capitalists, both black and white, peasants and workers, as well as the organic intellectuals who steered their communities towards literacy and print capitalism, all contributed to the development of civil society in Africa. Ultimately neither the imperial regimes nor their authoritarian African sucessor states, despite the claims of both to monopolize the civilizing mission, could satisfy the demands for the practical implementation of imagined communities.

NOTES

1 A. H. M. Kirk-Greene, 'The Thin White Line', *African Affairs* 79 (1980), pp. 25–44.
2 Paul Bohannan and Philip Curtin, *Africa and Africans* (Garden City, NY, Natural History Press, 1971), p. 333.
3 Michael Crowder, *The Cambridge History of Africa* (Cambridge, Cambridge University Press, 1984), VIII, p. 9.

4 C. Young, 'The Colonial State and its Political Legacy', in Donald Rothchild and Naomi Chazan, eds., *The Precarious Balance: State and Society in Africa* (Boulder, Col., Westview Press, 1988), pp. 25–66 is a mine of information and ideas.

5 B. Berman, 'Structure and Process in the Bureaucratic States of Colonial Africa', *Development and Change* XV (1984), p. 196, like Young a seminal study.

6 Anthony Clayton and David Killingray, *Khaki and Blue: Military and Police in British Colonial Africa* (Athens, Ohio, Ohio University Press, 1989), p. 176.

7 *Op. cit.*, p. 243.

8 *Op. cit.*, p. 243.

9 Cited in Victor Kiernan, *European Empires from Conquest to Collapse* (London, Fontana, 1982), p. 185.

10 Clayton and Killingray, *Khaki and Blue*, p. 243.

11 W. F. Gutteridge, 'Military and Police Forces in Colonial Africa', in Lewis Gann and Peter Duignan, *Colonialism in Africa, 1870–1960*, (Cambridge, Cambridge University Press, 1970), pp. 302–3.

12 D. Killingray, 'The Maintenance of Law and Order in British Colonial Africa', *African Affairs* 85 (1986), p. 415.

13 David Omissi, *Air Power and Colonial Control* (Manchester, Manchester University Press, 1990).

14 Note the comments of the 1962 Nobel Prize for Chemistry winner, Dr Max Perutz, *Daily Telegraph* (7 September 1992).

15 Omissi, *Air Power*, p. 6.

16 *Op. cit.*, pp. 109–10.

17 Cited in Kiernan, *European Empires*, p. 200.

18 Omissi, *Air Power*, p. 56; D. Killingray, 'A Swift Agent of Government', *Journal of African History* XXV (1984), pp. 429–44.

19 Cited in Killingray, 'Maintenance', p. 414.

20 Killingray, 'Maintenance', p. 415.

21 The phrase 'print capitalism' derives from Benedict Anderson's very influential *Imagined Communities* (London, Verso, 1983).

22 Cited in Berman, 'Structure', p. 184.

23 *Op. cit.*, p. 184.

24 *Op. cit.*, p. 184.

25 Cited in Young, 'Colonial State', p. 148.

26 Roland Oliver, *The African Experience* (London, Weidenfeld and Nicholson, 1991), p. 184.

27 Oliver, *African Experience*, p. 148.

28 Cited in L. Vail, ed., *The Creation of Tribalism in Southern Africa* (London, James Currey, 1989), p. 13.

29 Vail, *Creation*, p. x.

30 John Iliffe, *A Modern History of Tanganyika* (Cambridge, Cambridge University Press, 1979), p. 356.

31 T. O. Ranger, 'Connections Between "Primary Resistance" Movements and Modern Mass Nationalism in East and Central Africa', *Journal of African History* IX (1968), pp. 437–54, 631–42.

32 Iliffe, *Tanganyika*, Chapter 12.

33 Henry S. Wilson, ed., *Origins of African Nationalism* (London, Macmillan, 1969), pp. 157–225.

34 *Op. Cit.*, pp. 131–50.

35 Iliffe, *Tanganyika*, pp. 218–20.

36 Iliffe's lapidary summary of Symes' impact, *Tanganyika*, p. 336.

37 R. E. Kendall, 'The Missionary Factor', in Emil Fashole-luke, R. Gray, A. Hastings and G. Tasie, eds., *Christianity and Independent Africa* (London, Rex Collings, 1978), p. 19.

38 Cited in Raymond Buell, *The Native Problem in Africa* (8 vols., New York, Macmillan, 1928), II, p. 81.

39 Michael Doyle, *Empires* (Ithaca, NY, Cornell University Press, 1986).

40 D. Bruce Marshall, *The French Colonial Myth and Constitution-Making in the Fourth Republic* (New Haven, Conn., Yale University Press, 1973), p. 39.

41 G. Wesley Johnson, Jr., *The Emergence of Black Politics in Senegal* (Stanford, CA., Stanford University Press, 1971), pp. 133–45.

42 J. Ayodele Langley, *Pan-Africanism and Nationalism in West Africa* (Oxford, Clarendon, Press 1973), p. 118.

43 Kalu Ezera, *Constitutional Development in Nigeria* (Cambridge, Cambridge University Press, 1960), pp. 24–5.

44 Brian Willan, *Sol Plaatje* (London, Heinemann, 1984).

45 A. F. Roberts, 'History, Ethnicity and Change', in L. Vail, ed., *Creation of Tribalism* (London, James Currey, 1989), pp. 193–214.

46 Iliffe, *Tanganyika*, p. 325.

47 Not all African peoples in South-West Africa were Khoisan but it is the pastoralist Hottentots and hunter–gatherer Bushmen, as they were then known, who loom large in the literature of colonial administration. Thus Lord Hailey's *African Survey* (London, Oxford University Press, 1938), p. 19, citing older anthropological writers. The African peoples generally were believed to have had their social structures pulverized by the German army's ruthless wars of pacification, further reinforcing the case for relegation to category 'C' (Hailey, *Survey*, p. 373).

3

The Great Depression

The Wall Street crash of October 1929 unleashed the greatest economic crisis the world had yet witnessed, sending shock waves through Europe and the European colonies in Africa and elsewhere. John Iliffe has shown that in Tanganyika, for example, the price of sisal followed the disastrous trends of the American economy almost exactly.[1] The joint appeal of capitalism and imperialism to the undeveloped world had been grounded in expectations of economic progress and career security; both were falsified by the onset of the Great Depression.

The sudden impoverishment of the industrial countries slashed demand for colonial agricultural products and minerals. World prices for the East African staples – sisal, coffee, maize and hides – fell by 70 per cent between 1929 and 1932, while the price of cotton fell by over 60 per cent. Raw cocoa from West Africa, which had sold for 81 shillings per cwt at Liverpool in 1920, dropped from nearly 38 shillings in 1930 to just over 23 shillings in 1939. By 1934 palm-oil from the Belgian Congo fell to less than one-fifth its value in 1929. For some crops it was even worse: the money paid to Belgian Congo rubber producers plunged by 90 per cent between 1929 and 1932. And if African peasants tried to preserve their incomes by increasing their output – as they were encouraged to do, sometimes quite forcefully, by colonial authorities desperate for revenue from duties on exports – this seemed merely to accelerate the fall in prices they received.

The cost of manufactured imports also fell but rarely proportionately. (Overall world prices for raw materials fell by 56 per cent, foodstuffs by 48 per cent and manufactured goods by 38 per cent.) With variations for individual colonies and different years, the trend for the Depression years of the 1930s is one of marked deterioration in Africa's net barter terms of trade: the quantity of imports available for a given quantity of exports. Africans learned the bitter lesson that – with their rulers devoid of policies for recovery – they were linked to the developed world, for the foreseeable future, by a contagion of impoverishment rather than prosperity.

Colonial governments, responding to the depression according to orthodox economic principles, pared expenditure to meet dwindling revenues. Plunging prices shrank customs receipts so that the revenue of the Gold Coast and Sierra Leone, for example, fell by about a third. But two large items on the colonial budget were very difficult to cut. First, the interest charges on the relatively large sums of capital borrowed overseas in more prosperous times to finance the building of ports, railways and the rest of the infrastructure for commercial development. Second, the money spent on the salaries and pensions of the governments' own officials, the highest individual items, of course, being paid to expatriates. It was the low-income, daily-paid employees with scant contractual rights whom governments found easiest to dispense with, for example, reducing them from 20,239 in 1929 to 12,572 in 1930 in the Gold Coast.

One route to retrenchment, cutting out overseas allowances by Africanizing the colonial administrative service, was ruled out by the British on racial grounds. (The administrative class in Britain and its colonies was the bureaucratic élite, generally recruited directly from the universities, though in Britain itself promotion between the classes was also possible.) In fact much of the work hitherto undertaken by expatriates was delegated to Africans whose salaries and conditions were frozen at the top of the junior staff grade. Promotion prospects waned and conditions of service deteriorated. In Tanganyika all promotion for African clerks was suspended as an economy measure in 1931.

Expenditure on development and welfare was slashed: in 1936–7 it was typically between 3 and 8 shillings a head in the British colonies of 'black' Africa, with Nyasaland, Tanganyika, Nigeria and Sierra Leone getting substantially less, and only Zanzibar, Bechuanaland and Swaziland getting more.

Such pinch-penny budgeting at the expense of their African subjects was adopted reluctantly as European rulers realized that their legitimacy was being undermined by depression. In 1934, for example, Britain's West African dependencies introduced customs duties discriminating against Japanese textiles, which were just beginning to invade markets hitherto dominated by Britain. (The 'Congo Basin' treaties, dating from the period of partition, which Japan had acceded to in 1919, stipulating free trade, checked similar protectionism in East Africa.) Imperial ideology had been based on the antithesis between European progress and African stagnation, between open market economies and closed, defensive subsistence-oriented communities. Now, with European capitalism itself stagnant and defensive, Africans were being cut off from the free market.

These haunting statistics of depressed agricultural prices, careers aborted and jobs lost, translated into the scaling down of individual life chances, meant that the Great Depression ranked with the two World Wars as one of the three great formative experiences of the first half of the twentieth century. Its meaning was swiftly appreciated and translated into political action in youth movements and student politics. All over the undeveloped world the Depression shaped the political consciousness of those on the threshold of adulthood, faced with making their way in a world where expectations of incremental improvement through collaboration with the Europeans were suddenly dashed. Students rioted against Western oppression in much of the Islamic world. Egyptian students emerged as an identifiable radical political grouping in the 1930s. The Young Egypt Society, founded in 1933, along with the Society of the Muslim Brethren, founded in 1928, the younger vanguard wing of the Wafd Party, and other smaller violence-prone youth formations, contested the British presence and the general notion of Western superiority. (Most of the generation of army officers, the generation of Nasser, who were to form the core of the Free Officer movement in 1949–52, whose coup forced the abdication and exile of King Farouk, became involved in these movements.)[2]

The Nigerian Youth movement, founded in Lagos in 1934 to demand better opportunities in higher education, set up a score of branches in provincial towns. Broadening its political interests, it established its own newspaper, the *Daily Service* and published the *Nigerian Youth Charter* in 1938 which called for the unification of Nigeria's tribes behind the common ideal of national consciousness leading to the goal of 'complete autonomy within the British Empire', while stressing that 'Our movement accept the principle of trusteeship as the basis of co-operation with the British Government in Nigeria.'[3] In the same year it wrested control of Lagos City Council, along with the Lagos seats on the Legislative Council, from older established politicians.

In the Gold Coast, Nigeria and Sierra Leone, the radical campaigning of the West African Youth League challenged not only British colonialism but the political decorum of their elders in the Congress of British West Africa. The Sierra Leonean, Isaac Wallace-Johnson, who was a founder member of the Youth League sharpened criticism of the colonial system by introducing Marxist concepts into West African journalism. The Marxist rhetoric of capitalist exploitation, adapted to the colonial situation, proved very effective in broadening the Youth League's appeal.

Wallace-Johnson had travelled widely as an army clerk in Africa and the Middle East during the First World War and as a seaman for Elder Dempster thereafter, when he appears to have joined the Communist Party. Consequently he brought a range of continental experience, a kind of practical Pan-Africanism, to his commentary on imperial policies. In 1930 he attended the First International Trade Union Conference of Negro Workers at Hamburg. He went on to study in Moscow where he got to know the Trinidadian, George Padmore, secretary of the International Trade Union Committee of Negro Workers and editor of its paper, the *Negro Worker*. Returning to West Africa in 1933, Wallace-Johnson used the *Negro Worker* to mount a sustained attack on the colonial system first in Lagos, then the Gold Coast. In both cases the colonial authorities responded to this aggressive journalism with legal harassment, forcing him to move on.

In 1938 he returned to his native Sierra Leone. Within three weeks of arriving in Freetown he had organized the West African Youth League's Sierra Leone branch there, and went on to found branches in the provinces. A village Krio from outside the Freetown establishment who threatened to unite those who felt disadvantaged from both Colony and Protectorate, Wallace-Johnson found conditions ripe for his fiery journalism and organizational skill. Government elementary school teachers were paid 10 pence a day, with no travel, accommodation or other allowances. The Sierra Leone Development Company (DELCO) iron mines, one of the chief beneficiaries of the 1929 Colonial Development Act, paid mine workers between 4 pence and 1 shilling a day. The local District Commissioner commented in 1939, after the fourth strike in seven years, 'The impression I get is that the company look upon their labour merely as an instrument for getting iron-ore out of that hill and shipping it home. The side issues, e.g. labour's welfare do not concern them.'[4] Workers for the United Africa Company (UAC) often got as little as 4 pence for an 11–14-hour day. Between September 1938 and the end of 1939 Wallace-Johnson established three unions – Postal Workers, Seamen, and the War Department Amalgamated Union – grouped in the Trade Union Congress, and was linked with strikes and sit-ins at the iron mines and the Mabella Coaling Depot.

Discontented civil servants leaked to Johnson a dispatch from Governor Jardine in which he declared that an African worker and his family could live on 15 shillings a month and that labour was plentiful at 9 pence a day, suggesting official complicity in exploitation. Jardine then instituted an inquiry which Johnson used as a platform to deride both British officialdom and the old Krio establishment. The Youth League swept to victory in both the 1938 Freetown City Council elections and the Legislative Council elections the following year. Dr Bankole Bright, the establishment Krio leader, stood down to avoid ignominious defeat.[5]

Even those who left behind plunging cocoa prices to seek education abroad could not escape the grip of worldwide depression. In 1935 Francis Nkrumah borrowed money from a generous family network to travel from the Gold Coast to the United States and work his way through Lincoln, a black university in Pennsylvania. The Depression had struck the United States particularly hard; with 12 million unemployed, industrial output halved and farm income worse than halved, the American dream became a nightmare for many Americans. But the experience of African Americans, from slavery onwards, had always tended towards the nightmarish, hence the success of the radical Jamaican, Marcus Garvey, in developing a black consciousness movement working towards restoring a black empire on ancestral soil. Doubly unfortunate, black and searching for menial casual work in the Great Depression, in competition with a mass army of fellow unemployed, Nkrumah became receptive to Garvey's black consciousness message while washing dishes in restaurant sculleries. By the time he emerged in Britain with a leading role in the 1945 Pan-African Conference he had reverted to his African name, Kwame Nkrumah.[6]

Such was the Great Depression in African experience. But, as Wallace-Johnson taught his followers in the Youth League, to make sense of it required transcending individual experience, however bitter, and understanding it as a systemic crisis of colonialism and capitalism. Not only Marxists were forced to such a conclusion. The rulers of Western capitalist states, and their non-Marxist economic advisers, were forced by their sheer failure to cope with it to diagnose the Great Depression as a profound structural crisis. Their understanding of its causes, and their recipes for avoiding its repetition, were to have profound consequences for the processes of decolonization.

Failure was the more traumatic because it was a general failure of the international political system, as well as international economics. The prospects of general economic cooperation in order to revive the international economy ended when the United States wrecked the 1933 World Economic Conference by announcing that it was going to ensure the restoration of equilibrium in its domestic economy before worrying about the international order.

But before this final international failure the powers had already begun to shift towards 'beggar my neighbour' policies of tariff protection and competitive devaluation. Even Belgium, famous for its free-trade policies, began to encourage imports of tropical goods from its own colonies. Britain, an even more celebrated exemplar of free-trade capitalism, had shifted towards imperial preference through the Ottawa agreements of 1932. Yet these agreements between Britain, its dependencies and the Dominions, promised more than they achieved. The imperial vision of a unified British world system, with a co-ordinated economic policy, proved almost as much a mirage as the hope of general international cooperation a year later. In both cases visionary schemes dissolved in hard bargaining.

While such grandiose plans for revitalizing world capitalism – or at least whole imperial systems within it – faltered the restructuring of individual economies and societies in the colonial mould slowed down. As new investments of effort yielded diminishing returns so both colonizers and colonized lost faith in the imperial vision. Europeans, cowed by the circumstances of the Depression, doubted whether their aims were attainable while Africans wondered whether they were desirable. The colonial regimes became increasingly conservative, and frequently repressive, as they struggled to defend their earlier achievements. Finally, this loss of creative energy by the colonizers meant that Africans progressively took the initiative. 'Liberation became the dynamic of change', in John Iliffe's neat summation.[7]

Basic to the Great Depression was the breakdown of coordination between agriculture and industry, as the prices of primary products fell much more steeply than manufactured goods. The Depression had begun in the United States and Canada where bumper crops flooded the market and prices dropped like a stone. Farmers were bankrupted when crop sales could not cover loan repayments. They brought over 5,000 United States banks – more than a fifth of the banks in the country – down with them. Such desperate domestic circumstances were behind the failure of the United States, by far the biggest economy, to act like a good internationalist: first, when President Hoover failed to veto the massive Smoot–Hawley tariff in 1930, setting off a chain reaction of retaliation; second, when President Roosevelt wrecked the 1933 International Conference.

The Great Depression brought similar failures of coordination between the European industrial metropoles and their primary producer satellites. From the mid-nineteenth century to the mid-1920s the interaction had, on balance, worked to their mutual advantage. Suddenly these complementary relations went wrong, badly wrong from the viewpoint of the primary producers, now that the mechanisms of the market worked against them. The cash-crop peasantries of the colonial world had no elected governments of their own, unlike American or Dominion farmers, to pressure into giving them the equivalent of Smoot–Hawley protection or to blame when things went wrong. Inevitably, their declining incomes and collapsed expectations led them to focus on the legitimacy of the whole relationship between industrialized imperial Europe and its dependencies. But the European imperial democracies, hard-pressed by mass unemployment and bankruptcy, were desperately seeking to stimulate home production and reduce imports.

There was, though, a strong strand of institutional continuity with that preceding period of complementary optimism, despite the ending of free trade – the prime ideological justification for the British world system – because of the Depression. That continuity was largely supplied by the survival of the British world system; indeed the Depression was marked by a strengthening of some existing trends.

Already in the late nineteenth century, as a truly international economy emerged with the spread of industrialization, Britain had evaded competition from the rapidly modernizing economies of Germany and the USA by concentrating on countries in Asia, Australasia and South America, as well as Africa, which lacked their own industries in textiles, iron or steel and which were already exporting foodstuffs and raw materials to Britain. With its strong pre-existing financial sector, Britain was stategically placed to act as banker, shipper and insurer, as well as railway builder, to the new global economy. Britain responded to increasing competition, therefore, not so much by modernization as by developing the possibilities of its existing situation.

The Great Depression strengthened this pattern. The fragmentation of the open world economy begun by the 1929 Wall Street collapse was completed by the Eastern European banking crisis of 1931. Before 1914 the pound was the 'top currency', in the words of sterling's historian, Susan Strange, because of Britain's mercantile supremacy, industrial primacy and capital accumulation. Many states, but particularly the colonial dependencies and the dominions, conducted their transactions and maintained their reserves in sterling, as well as looking to London as a source of loans.[8]

After the First World War Britain's overseas investments continued with the Empire and Commonwealth receiving a slightly higher proportion, about a quarter, of new capital issues in London. The pound, though, was no longer 'top currency'. Britain had borrowed heavily from American bankers during the war and United States investment in Britain was growing. Indeed, the United States was pre-eminent as the world's greatest financial and creditor nation with a larger output than the other six ranked great powers put together. But the dollar had not yet assumed the role of 'top currency'. The American economy was very different from that of Britain, less dependent on foreign trade and hence much less integrated into the world economy. It was inclined to protectionism – especially in agriculture – rather than free trade and lacked a full equivalent to the Bank of England. There was now no 'lender of last resort', comparable to Britain before 1914, offering long-term loans for the infrastructural development of the world economy and stabilizing temporary disjunctions in international accounts.

When both the USA and Britain abandoned the gold standard in 1931 the cosmopolitan world order fractured into rival currency blocs. A sterling bloc, based on British trade patterns, was consolidated by the 'imperial preferences' of the 1932 Ottawa Conference. The United States led a largely western hemisphere dollar bloc, to which Canada, though host at Ottawa, inevitably linked itself because of the economic interlocking of North America. France led a gold bloc and in the Far East there was a yen bloc headed by Japan.

The collapse of the unified world order of the gold standard, backed by a 'top currency' linked to a free-trading British world system, had three significant effects. First, it cleared the way for the rounds of competitive devaluation which were held partially responsible for the international anarchy which culminated in the Second World War. This line of thought became particularly strong among Anglo-American policy-makers and, therefore, affected their wartime planning of the postwar international order. Second: the origins of the postwar sterling area and the franc zone can be seen among the rival blocs. These currency arrangements by the two premier colonial powers in Africa were to be critically important during decolonization, especially given the chronic shortage of dollars at this time. Third: the creation and management of such separate currency blocs during the depths of recession was geared to preserving employment and staving off agricultural bankruptcy at home, in the metropole, rather than to the smooth functioning of those commercial networks which were so crucial to imperial relations. Democratic European states, whose economic policies were governed by their electorates' aversion to unemployment, were finding it increasingly difficult to hold together empires containing such a multiplicity of producer interests.

The era of the Great Depression merged into that of the Second World War. As soon as the colonial economies began to pull out of the worst of the Depression they were hit by a rolling wave of labour unrest which continued through the war to around 1950. Before the war there were major strikes on the Northern Rhodesian copper-belt in 1935, in the main city of Dakar in French West Africa in 1936, and the Kenyan port of Mombasa in 1939, as well as many lesser stoppages. In the West Indies a series of strikes and riots hit the oilfields of Trinidad and the plantations and urban areas of Jamaica. Britain responded with a Royal Commission under Lord Moyne to examine West Indian problems and with the Colonial Development and Welfare Act of 1940, promising to spend much more on development.

This was a vigorous and imaginative response to colonial crisis, in marked contrast to the way the Depression had been handled. Yet already by 1940 it was probably unrealistic to think of reviving the colonial empires by pumping in European capital. At a high-powered meeting to discuss 'Future Policy In Africa', during the early weeks of the war, Professor Keith Hancock, the imperial economic historian, pointed out that Britain, now a net importer of capital, was unlikely to fulfil the role of capital provider effectively given the massive investment needed. 'His views were neither shared, nor . . . understood', commented Kenneth Robinson, imperial administrator and fellow-historian.[9]

The period of the Great Depression revealed profound shifts in economic power that would soon have far-reaching effects on European empire. Even cotton exports, symbolic of Britain's long commercial domination of the undeveloped world, were affected. By 1929 Japan had surpassed Britain as chief supplier of cotton goods to East Africa; by 1938 it commanded 93 per cent of that market. Total imports from the United States already ranked second or third in British Africa during the 1930s. Above all, the United States economy, origin of the Depression, indicated even in the consequences of its failure the sheer magnitude of American power. Sooner rather than later, the European empires would need to take account of these radical transformations in the balance of economic power.

NOTES

1 John Iliffe, *A Modern History of Tanganyika*, (Cambridge, Cambridge University Press, 1979), p. 343. (Iliffe's table sets US percentage capacity utilization against Tanganyika sisal prices, 1929–39.)

2 P. J. Vatikiotis, *Nasser and his Generation* (London, Croom Helm, 1978), pp. 1–97.

3 James S. Coleman, *Nigeria: Background to Nationalism* (Berkeley, University of California Press, 1958), p. 225.

4 G. A. Sekgoma, 'The Second World War and the Sierra Leone Economy: Labour Employment And Utilisation, 1939–45', in David Killingray and Richard Rathbone, eds., *Africa and the Second World War* (London, Macmillan, 1986), p. 247.

5 L. Spitzer and L. Denzer, 'I. T. A. Wallace-Johnson and the West African Youth League', *International Journal of African Historical Studies* VI (1973), pp. 413–52, 565–601; Akintola J. G. Wyse, *H. C. Bankole-Bright and Politics in Colonial Sierra Leone* (Cambridge, Cambridge University Press, 1990), pp. 117–32.

6 Kwame Nkrumah, *Ghana: The Autobiography of Kwame Nkrumah* (Edinburgh, Nelson, 1961), p. 37, on being inspired by Garvey's writings; pp. 20–39, on his decade in America generally. Also David Birmingham, *Kwame Nkrumah* (London, Cardinal, 1990), pp. 1–5, is brief and perceptive on the years abroad.

7 Iliffe, *Tanganyika*, p. 342.

8 Susan Strange, *Sterling and British Policy: A Political Study of an International Currency in Decline* (London, Oxford University Press, 1971), especially pp. 4–36, for definition of 'top' currency.

9 K. Robinson, 'Margery Perham and the Colonial Office', *Journal of Imperial and Commonwealth History* XIX (1991), p. 188. Along with Hancock and Perham those present included the Colonial Secretary, Malcolm MacDonald, Hailey, Lugard, Julian Huxley, Professor Reginald Coupland, as well as the Parliamentary, Permanent and Deputy Under-Secretaries.

4

1936: Citizenship Betrayed

The year 1936 witnessed serious setbacks for that trend in colonialism which adapted to the consequences of the civilizing mission by co-opting the indigenous élite. In both Algeria and the Union of South Africa that élite's aspirations to equality of citizenship on the grounds of cultural achievement were dashed. There were, of course, sharp differences between the two cases which will emerge as they are considered in turn but the same basic issue, the extension or contraction of citizenship, underlies both crises.

ALGERIA: THE DEFEAT OF THE BLUM–VIOLETTE BILL

French imperialists argued that their Empire, though much smaller and poorer than that of Britain, was geo-politically superior. While the British Empire was condemned by geography to remain an accumulation of overseas territories remote from the United Kingdom, France possessed an empire on the southern shores of the Mediterranean which could be permanently integrated into the metropolis. Propagandists for 'Greater France' stressed that Algeria was 'so close' to France and so much like 'another Midi . . . that we think efforts towards separation are insane'.[1] Such geographical determinism was the more beguiling because it seemed to turn the tables on Britain, which by the same geopolitical logic had hitherto been able to capitalize on its insularity by claiming precedence over continental rivals in consolidating its status as a nation state, with 'frontiers against Europe', as Sir Lewis Namier remarked, 'drawn by nature'.[2] Contemporary racial determinism was similarly pressed into service as French imperialists identified an Iberio-Ligurian race spanning the Mediterranean whose North African branch was seeking 'progressively to merge itself with the people of France'.[3]

Maurice Viollette, a committed Jacobin, appointed Governor-General in 1925, was determined to assimilate Algeria into France by sweeping away restrictions on citizenship and implementing radical educational and social welfare programmes. He won strong Muslim support but in the face of intense settler hostility was recalled in 1927. Back in France and re-elected to the Senate he expounded his ideas in *Can Algeria Survive?* (1931). Condemning the settlers for sabotaging his reforms, he warned that Algeria would be lost to France unless the native Algerian élite was won over. He advocated they be allowed the privileges of naturalization while retaining Muslim personal status together with direct parliamentary representation for all ex-servicemen, elected officials and high-school graduates.

In June 1936 the Socialist leader Leon Blum formed his Popular Front government after sweeping left-wing gains at the April general election. He brought Viollette into the cabinet as Minister responsible for Algerian affairs. The French left celebrated victory in carnival and song as well as a massive 2 million strong factory sit-in. In Algeria the native élite responded promptly and enthusiastically to these metropolitan happenings by forming the reformist Muslim Congress. The same week that the new French government took office Muslims had celebrated the birthday of the Prophet. In Algiers the festival atmosphere continued; the mosques were crowded and at dusk Muslim families lit the traditional red, white and green candles. On 7 June, 'Algeria's Day', as the journal *al-Shibab* characterized it, over 5,000 people met at the Majestic Hotel, 'leaving their tasks to follow their hopes'. The meeting, cataloguing Muslim grievances but consistently friendly to France, evoked comparison with the States General of 1789.[4] 'Never was the Algerian people so unanimous in its hopes', wrote the Algerian leader Ferhat Abbas reflecting on this moment in colonial history.[5]

Three separate strands of Muslim opinion were drawn together by Congress. The first was the religious movement of reformist Muslim clerics, with Abd el-Hamid Ben Badis as spokesman, which wanted Muslims to absorb enough from the West to strengthen Islam without destroying it. Criticizing Islam in Algeria as backward and superstitious, they organized the Association of Reformist Ulama in 1931 and founded a network of Muslim schools independent of the French administration. Ben Badis had blamed the French for the decline of Muslim education and the consequent threat to the Islamic character of Algeria. The masthead of his movement's journal proclaimed, 'An independent, national newspaper acting for the happiness of the Algerian people with the aid of a democratic France.'[6] That belief in the good faith of democratic France was damaged when the administration closed several Ulama schools (schools run by Muslim clerics) and declared Arabic a foreign language. But at the Majestic hotel he hailed the advent of the Popular Front in courteous, scholarly Arabic, 'When French liberty was sleeping we kept silence. Liberty revived in France, and we intend to follow it.'[7]

The second strand, the most assimilationist, was personified by Ferhat Abbas, the most eloquent spokesman, in French, for the local élite in the Muslim Congress. Unlike Ben Badis, whose family traditions encompassed centuries of political and religious leadership, Abbas came from peasant stock. His father, though, had risen to be *Caid* (Arab local governor) and Commander of the Legion of Honour, a career which epitomized for Abbas the possibilities for

Muslim advance under enlightened French colonialism. He was educated at a French lycée at Constantine and at Algiers University where he became president of the Muslim Students Association. While there he entered politics as a champion of Muslim civil rights. Linguistically more at ease in French than Arabic, he divorced his Muslim wife then married a Frenchwoman. In short, he became the quintessential *évolué* – 'evolved one' – in that revealing French classification, assiduously rising through the ranks of legislative posts open to him, working closely with the Federation of Elected Officials, whose head Dr Bendjelloul chaired the Algiers meeting. Abbas expounded his political creed in 1936 in terms to gladden Viollette:

> Had I discovered the Algerian nation, I would be a nationalist and would not blush as if I had committed a crime. . . . However, I will not die for the Algerian nation, because it does not exist. I have not found it. I have examined History, I questioned the living and the dead, I visited the cemeteries; nobody spoke to me about it. I then turned to the Koran and I sought for one solitary verse forbidding a Muslim from integrating himself with a non-Muslim nation. I did not find that either. One cannot build on the wind.[8]

All his research had revealed was a series of imperial pasts, Arab and Muslim Empires now gone. Pushing aside what he described as nationalist 'clouds and dreams' he declared that Algerians must 'join their future to the French endeavours in this country'.[9]

Two months later Ben Badis riposted. He and the Ulama had also 'examined history' and discovered there was a 'Muslim Algerian nation' which 'has its culture, its traditions and its characteristics, good or bad like every other nation of the earth. And, next we state that this Algerian nation is not France, cannot be France, and does not wish to be France.'[10] Although rejecting incorporation in France, he did not point his followers in the direction of full political independence for Algeria. In 1936 he called for a free Algeria which would be linked with France as a dominion. But throughout Ben Badi's career politics was always secondary to religion. More than any other contemporary leader he illuminated the Algerian people's sense of communal identity – an identity that was Islamic and Pan-Arab – as well as Algerian and thus difficult to compress into the political arena of the modern state.

The third strand was unequivocally separatist. Only Messali Hadjj and his followers called clearly and consistently for national independence for Algeria. With some help at the start from the French Communist Party, he had founded a series of nationalist organizations, beginning in 1925 with the *Etoile Nord-Africain*. His nationalism had a strong proletarian character calling for the redistribution of French state and settler property. He won support from Algerian immigrant workers in France but had little success in Algeria itself. Two months after the initial meeting Messali appeared at a Congress rally to denounce the goal of assimilation as reformist and demand full Algerian independence but his appeal found little support. Dr Bendjelloul dissociated the

Congress from Messali's nationalism, proclaiming loyalty to France. Sheik El-Okbi, one of Ben Badi's closest collaborators, denounced Messali's activities as 'inimical to Islamic values'.[11] In the 1937 Algiers municipal elections Messali's slate of candidates failed to win a single Muslim seat. All 12 were won by mainstream Muslim Congress candidates.

The Congress eagerly welcomed the Popular Front's triumph and Viollette's appointment, urging the assimilation of Algeria to France through the extension of political and civil rights, calling for French citizenship with the retention of Muslim status and a single electorate based on universal suffrage. A formal petition also asked for a compulsory integrated educational system, with a Muslim parochial school system alongside. Congress also endorsed a land-reform plan which would redistribute charitable foundation land (*habous* land) to Muslim peasants while leaving settler property intact.

The immediate response of the Popular Front government was promising. It issued a series of decrees benefiting Algerian Muslims which included removing restrictions on the immigration of Muslim workers to France, authorizing a minimum wage and streamlining the application process for naturalization. But Blum was nothing if not legalistic. He overruled Viollette's Jacobin preference for swift executive action by insisting that changes in the political rights of Algerian Muslims should not be made by decree. They must be submitted to the French Assembly for its approval.

In December 1936 the Blum–Viollette reform bill was tabled by the Assembly. It embodied Viollette's passionate élitist assimilationism. His ideal, proclaimed in his friend Abbas's journal of the Association of Muslim Students, was that 'Muslim students, while remaining Muslim, should become so French in their education, that no Frenchman, however deeply racist and religiously prejudiced he might be . . . will any longer dare to deny them French fraternity.'[12] Its most significant provisions were the grant of citizenship, including full voting rights within a single electorate to Muslim ex-servicemen, elected officials and high-school graduates. These new citizens numbering 25,000 (out of some 6 million) Muslims, were to retain their statutory rights in Islamic law. The bill was enthusiastically welcomed by the Federation of Elected Officials and the executive committee of the Muslim Congress. But 302 out of Algeria's 304 European mayors jointly denounced it. Settlers formed armed militias and threatened civil war should the bill pass. Inside France the powerful settler lobby, notably influential within the Radical Party wing of the Popular Front, worked assiduously. Muslims and settlers argued their cases before parliamentary investigation committees. Muslim leaders declared their commitment to gradualism, their loyalty to France, and the crucial difference between maintaining their Muslim identity, which they insisted upon, and pursuing separatist objectives, which they renounced.

The Algerian debate dragged on while the Blum government was distracted by domestic and international crises. In 1937 the *Etoile Nord-Africain* was outlawed, but with no real concessions to the moderates the policies of the Popular Front foundered. The Muslim Congress expressed 'bitter disappointment' at the government's failure to enact the Blum–Viollette bill, warning of a nationalist upsurge if the reforms were defeated. Blum's government finally collapsed before the bill was enacted. When Blum resigned in the summer of 1937, to be replaced by another Popular Front government less committed to Algerian reform, 3,000 elected Muslim officials in the department of Constantine resigned vowing not to return until the Blum–Viollette bill was passed. Finally, in 1939 Viollette bitterly admitted defeat in the Assembly: 'When the Muslims protest, you are indignant; when they approve, you are suspicious; when they keep quiet you are fearful. *Messieurs*, these men have no political nation. They do not even demand their religious nation. All they ask is to be admitted into yours. If you refuse this beware lest they do not soon create one for themselves.'[13]

Viollette's prophetic warning was grounded in his understanding of profound shifts in key sectors of Muslim opinion in response to French inaction. In July 1938 Muslim cohesion was damaged when the Federation of Elected Muslims split into Bendjelloul's moderate 'Franco-Musulman Algerien' and Abbas's more intransigent 'Union Populaire Algerienne'. Immediately, the breach weakened the Muslim cause in the eyes of most Frenchmen, especially when it was contrasted with the obdurate solidarity of the settlers. In fact the points which Abbas now emphasized had been present in his position all along, though in the flush of optimism he had emphasized political assimilation. Now though he sought a new term to identify his position, '*rattachement*' ('connection') in place of assimilation: 'We want Algeria to preserve her own physiognomy, her language, her customs, her traditions . . .'[14] Like Viollette, right up to the outbreak of war, he continued to urge that the bill be passed, warning that its rejection would lead to disaster.

With benefit of hindsight those who have argued that France might have succeeded in integrating Algeria as a permanent part of the country, through skilful and determined state-building, have sought to identify the final lost opportunity. There is no consensus. Indeed some think that effective integration was always a forlorn hope. Some authorities believe that the period immediately before and after the First World War constituted the last chance for a generous policy of extending citizenship to head off separatism. Others consider that enduring integration could have been achieved after the Second World War or even later. A strong body of opinion, however, focuses on the failure of the Blum–Viollette reform bill as the last chance to incorporate Algeria into France.[15]

What is the place of these counterfactual speculations in a general history of African decolonization? At the simplest level they are a reminder that in 1936 the immediate cause of the defeat of the integration option, the programme of Viollette (and Abbas), was the resistance of the settlers, not Algerian nationalism.

Effective settler opposition prevented the integration option even being tried. Whether, if attempted, élite co-option would have worked is, of course, another matter. The settlers argued that it would not, whereas Viollette contended that their obstinate resistance was likely to produce the very Algerian nationalism and militant Muslim separatism that they feared.

The arguments some mid-twentieth-century experts derived from geographical and racial determinism to support integration have obviously proved fallacious. (The notion of an Iberio-Ligurian race was grounded in the belief that there was an objective biological race destined to dissolve the historically specific racism of the settlers along with metropolitan xenophobia. An anti-racist racialism, as it were!) Since the end of the Second World War, though, cultural determinism has become much more fashionable. Should we believe, on the evidence of the present-day existence of a strongly Muslim Algerian nation-state, that this outcome was culturally predetermined? Much nationalist history is indeed written to such a subliminal agenda of cultural determinism. Less, though, in Africa than elsewhere, for in that continent the processes of state-building in the usually brief colonial period and the even briefer postcolonial period have been transparently obvious. There such cultural determinism tends to be the prerogative of the chroniclers of ethnicity. Historians and social scientists have amply demonstrated both that state-making in Africa involved nation-breaking and that ideologies of ethnicity were crafted and adapted to changing circumstances by literati working to that subliminal agenda.

Similar demolition work on the myths which consecrate nationhood in older established states is somewhat less conspicuous. One of the most illustrious examples, though, is Eugen Weber's *Peasants into Frenchmen: The Modernization of Rural France* (1976) which examines the consolidation of modern France very much from the state-building perspective adopted by Viollette, maintaining that not until the 30 years either side of 1900 were the different regions and cultures that had come under the control of the French political apparatus integrated into a modern nation-state:

> The famous hexagon itself [the conventional shape of metropolitan France] can itself be seen as a colonial empire shaped over the centuries: a complex of territories conquered, annexed and integrated in a political and administrative whole, many of them with strongly developed national or regional personalities, some of them with traditions that were specifically un or anti French. . . . By 1870 they had produced a political entity called France – a kingdom, or empire or republic – an entity formed by conquest and by political and administrative decisions formulated in (or near) Paris.[16]

That Viollette was born in 1870, the starting point for Weber's study, is a nice coincidence. That he grew up in a period in which bourgeois Frenchmen could refer to provincial villagers in similar derogatory terms to those used by settlers and officials to describe Algerian peasants during his Governor-Generalship, while at the same time an *évolué* like Abbas could think of himself as Muslim,

Algerian and, potentially, French, manifestly conditioned his sense of what was politically possible.

SOUTH AFRICA: THE REMOVAL OF AFRICANS FROM THE CAPE COMMON ROLL

In 1936 the South African government removed Cape African voters from the common electoral roll. This had been on the political agenda since 1926 when General Hertzog's government had introduced a bill to that effect. Hertzog became Prime Minister in 1924 as head of a Nationalist–Labour alliance, sympathetic to the interests of white farmers and workers. His government was less disposed than that of his predecessor, General Smuts, to pursue co-optive policies towards blacks and more determined to enforce segregation. The franchise bill's enactment 10 years later was a major stage in the construction of a legally entrenched racial order throughout the Union. It was recognized at the time as a crucial defeat for South African liberalism. W. M. Macmillan, a leading liberal, lamented the perversion of the civilizing mission:

> Free 'White' South Africa, itself the latest achievement of the old Liberalism, headed the breakaway from the Roman tradition; its Africans can no longer boast as it were, *civis Romanus sum*. In 1936, by all but unanimous vote [169 to 11], the Union Parliament made the possession of a black skin a final disqualification for the privileges of citizenship. . . . 'Civilization' came to be not a gospel but a white monopoly. 'Defend white civilization' was a slogan in South Africa.[17]

African spokesmen, from conservative chiefs to urban radicals, agreed with Macmillan about the critical nature of the threat, hence they sought to organize on a country-wide basis to combat it.

In order to understand why the removal of the Cape African voters was considered so significant we need to look at the formation of the Union. In 1910 the colonies of the Cape, Natal, the Orange Free State and the Transvaal joined to form the Union of South Africa as a unitary state with parliamentary sovereignty. There was no bill of rights. The preceding constitutional convention, made up of prominent colonial politicians (all white) had to deal with the fact that the franchise laws of the four colonies differed substantially. In the old Afrikaner republics, the Transvaal and Orange Free State, all white men, and none but white men, were entitled to vote and stand for election. In Natal white men could vote provided they complied with quite low economic criteria, whereas the colonial government had eroded the political rights of non-whites so that in practice all but a very few were excluded. In the Cape, though, the franchise laws were non-racial in form. Any man could vote or become a member of parliament there, provided that he was at least barely literate and earned 50 pounds a year or occupied a house and land worth 75 pounds, outside the communal land in the African reserves. In practice, however no black man ever sat in the Cape parliament, and in 1909 while 85 per cent of the voters were white, 10 per cent were Coloured (mixed race), and only 5 per cent Africans.

After intense debate in the Convention the delegates reached a compromise. Membership of parliament was confined to white men and the franchise laws of each colony were to remain in force in its successor province, but, to protect the rights of blacks in Cape province, any bill changing those laws would require the support of two-thirds of both houses of parliament in a joint sitting.

Indirectly the circumstances which brought about the end of the Cape franchise can be traced to the Depression. The coming together of South Africa's two leading white politicians, General Hertzog and General Smuts, in a coalition government early in 1933 was prompted by economic crisis and the extremely volatile political situation before South Africa left the gold standard in December 1932. The Hertzog–Smuts coalition was endorsed by the white electorate later in 1933, to be followed in mid-1934 by the fusion of Hertzog's Nationalists with Smuts' South Africa Party into a single United Party. Once off the gold standard the South African economy rapidly revived, with gold mining leading the recovery. The new government eagerly returned white political attention to the 'Native Question' – the legal and constitutional status of the black majority – that had preoccupied the two previous Nationalist-dominated governments led by Hertzog. Now, though, Hertzog for the first time commanded the two-thirds majority of the joint membership of both houses of Parliament necessary to amend the entrenched clause of the Act of Union protecting the non-white franchise in Cape Province.

The Hertzog government's proposals were met by a storm of protest from black South Africans as well as liberal and radical whites. The government ignored calls for a national conference of African leaders on the proposed abolition in accordance with the Native Affairs Act of 1920. Instead it hurriedly organized a series of regional conferences to which chiefs and other selected Africans were invited. But even these hand-picked Africans endorsed many of the initial protests. At the United Transkeian Territories General Council, 30 March 1936, several speakers referred to the political rights granted them 80 years earlier by 'our Beloved Queen Victoria the Good' which the Cape delegates had sought to safeguard at the Act of Union. Councillor Bam, seconding a motion expressing grave concern at the government's proposed legislation, stressed that 'The vote . . . gave us the right of citizenship in this country. Citizenship we understand to mean this, that whether you are white or black you vote for a representative who goes to Parliament; and whether you are a European or a Native, if you are qualified you become a voter and because you are a common citizen of the country you gain all the privileges so that you can make progress.'[18]

The main focus of African protest, however, was the All African Convention (AAC), a new umbrella organization linking existing African political groupings. It brought together moderates, notably the Cape Native Voters Convention, which had previously remained somewhat aloof from national politics, with members of the African National Congress (ANC), the Communist Party and sometime activists in the Industrial and Commercial Workers Union (ICU), which at the peak of its celebrity in 1928 had claimed a membership of nearly 200,000. In December 1935 the AAC chose Bloemfontein, symbolic capital of black protest, as its convention site, where Africans had met in 1909 to oppose the terms of Union and where Congress had its beginnings three years later. Among the Coloured delegates were members of Cape Town Trotskyite study circles along with John Gomas from the Moscow-oriented Communist Party of South Africa (CPSA). A proposal by Gomas that mass protest meetings be organized across the Union was accepted unanimously. Dr G. H. Gool, also from Cape Town, urged that the AAC should become much more radical laying 'the foundations of a national liberation movement to fight against all the repressive laws of South Africa.' Delegates rejected Gool's revolutionary radicalism, but endorsed a proposal originating from Clements Kadalie, leader of the ICU, that the Convention remain in being beyond the immediate crisis as a base for further political action.[19]

Throughout their protests black South Africans were at pains to point out that they had discharged their side of the contract implicit in the civilizing mission. 'It is noteworthy', said the report of the proceedings, 'that the delegates included six graduates from the University of South Africa, six from the United States of America, one from the University of Budapest, one from Glasgow, two from Edinburgh, and two from the University of London.' They agreed 'that the exercise of political rights in a democratic state demands the possession, on the part of those who enjoy them, of a reasonable measure of education and material contribution to the economic welfare of the country.' This was certainly – and quite explicitly – bourgeois democracy. Their political philosophy was suffused with the creed of Cape liberalism, especially its desire for good race relations: 'In short, we believe that a civilization test such as was contemplated at the National Convention in 1909–10, is equitable; but that the criterion of race or colour, which is implied in these Bills is contrary to democratic government and is calculated to engender and provoke feelings of hostility and ill-will between White and Black.'[20]

The Hertzog legislation was passed removing Africans from the common roll, creating instead a new set of segregated political institutions for them, including white 'Native Representatives' in Parliament and an elected advisory 'Native Representative Council'. It also entrenched the unequal distribution of land. The Capetown left-wingers urged the AAC to boycott the new institutions, but established black politicians were reluctant to make a clean break. By December 1937 the AAC had come round to accepting the new institutions and accepted as official delegates six of the white 'parliamentary members' elected under the Hertzog legislation.

The force of AAC protest continued to be diluted with affirmations of loyalty to South Africa and the Crown. Reminders that Smuts' eloquence on behalf of liberty when abroad, as Rector of Saint Andrews, was hardly matched by his performance as Minister of Justice at home, were balanced by invocations of Queen Victoria and Cecil Rhodes's slogan, 'Equal rights for all civilized men'. The civilizing mission, modulated through Cape liberalism, was predicated on faith in progress; now its agents, forced on the defensive by aggressive Afrikaner nationalism, found themselves in the ironic posture of invoking a golden age set in the past. Respectable African politicians, equally nostalgic for an era of supposedly good race relations, were ensnared by the same progressive dilemma. Instead of advancing towards outright challenge to white domination, they remained trapped within the conventions of petition and protest.

CONCLUSION: AMBIGUITIES OF CITIZENSHIP

Citizenship, like democracy, has been an essentially ambiguous concept throughout much of the twentieth century. And not just in colonial states and settler societies. To cite just two of the most glaring anomalies: French women only gained the vote after the Second World War, while black men in the USA, although technically given the vote in the 1880s, had to wait until after the civil rights movement in the late 1960s for practical enfranchisement. Contemporary notions of race, class and gender in Europe and the United States meant that the term 'citizenship' still bore the stamp of its origins in ancient Greek city-states as a privileged status from which women, slaves and 'aliens' were excluded. Later, as we have seen, the Romans had adapted the Greek concept to co-opt native élites for purposes of imperial consolidation.

In South Africa its functions were manifold. It helped reconcile Afrikaner traditions of *herrenvolk* democracy with ideas of 'the pale of the constitution' and 'the civilizing mission', that were strongly held by the British and the African mission élite. (It is salutary to recall that the 1854 constitution of the Orange Free State was in part modelled on that of the USA.) More than that, citizenship was instrumental in the fine-tuning of segregation and, later, apartheid. Indeed such circumscribed but flexible institutions of citizenship were admirably adapted to regulate a world of migrant workers, rural homelands, squatters and 'foreign natives', preserving parliamentary respectability and a semblance of the rule of law, while facilitating rapid South African industrialization on the basis of cheap black labour shorn of its civil and political rights.

In Algeria, Viollette, from the French side, attacked the problem of citizenship with Jacobin clarity and conviction. Cape liberals, thrown on the defensive, whether white or black, were rarely so robust. In Algeria, moreover, the position was somewhat less complicated and therefore easier to treat in strictly political terms. Within Algeria there was nothing like the massive social engineering by the cyclical processes of segregation and apartheid, which sucked in black labour, then pumped it out again fast enough to prevent it settling into a charge on welfare and a political problem. Neither the Algerians or the French, therefore, had to wrestle with such paradoxical categories as 'foreign natives'. (Indeed, Algeria's equivalent to the Witwatersrand, as a magnet for immigrant workers, lay inside France in the slums and shanty towns of Paris, Lyons and Marseilles, where they scrambled for those physically demanding, low-paid jobs – especially in road and railway construction gangs – which the native French tended to reject. Particularly since Algerian independence in 1962, however, the issue of the citizenship rights of North African workers in France and other European Community states has become a major political issue displaying some interesting parallels with South Africa.) Nor was the issue of citizenship complicated for the Algerian native élite by pitching their claims in terms of the invaders' religion, Christianity, with all that implied in accepting missionary and other white liberal values and patronage. The Algerian élite and the Algerian masses were conjoined by their pride in a common Islamic civilization, mutually differentiating themselves from the French whether Christian or secularist.

Algerians also found the realities of their constitutional situation somewhat easier to understand than did black South Africans. The Union of South Africa had Dominion status within the British Empire and Commonwealth, with the Crown – in quick succession King George V, Edward VIII and George VI – as Head of State. African spokesmen, for example the afore-quoted Councillor Bam, properly addressed their petitions to the Crown. But they easily slipped from that constitutionally correct position into regarding South Africa as a British colony rather than a sovereign settler state. Partly this was wish-fulfilment, a way of screening out the awful reality of the way they had been betrayed at the formation of the Union by that same British liberalism to which they gave allegiance; partly an attempt to bring moral pressure to bear on the South African authorities through British and international opinion; partly an understandable wish to keep discussion within the English language – a world language and the language of their Bible after all – and the discourse of British liberal constitutionalism, rather than be trapped into the terms of debate set by Afrikaner nationalism. But it also reflected real uncertainty about the current constitutional position. (Nor was it only black South Africans who were beguiled by the prospect of dominion status within the Commonwealth. When Ben Badis challenged the assimilationism of Ferhat Abbas, claiming that independence was the natural right of every nation of the Earth, he hoped that France would model its colonial policy on that of Britain by treating Algeria to the same dominion status that Canada, Australia and the Cape Colony enjoyed.)[21]

All such manipulative approaches, incorporating local élites through citizen-ship, were vulnerable when eventually challenged by a battery of popular movements which sought to transform the struggle over citizenship into a democratic project. In the discourse of these challengers citizenship entailed the full participation of all adults regardless of 'race', creed, sex or ethnicity. Citizenship was also developed as a nation-building project, a way of incorporating culturally diverse groups within a single state by reaching beyond them to equip each individual with standardized rights and duties. For democratic nationalists the extension of citizenship to all adults became the prime means by which the 'nation' established its legitimacy both in the sight of its own inhabitants and that of the international community. They also believed that such inclusive 'national fronts' were necessary from a strictly practical viewpoint of mobilizing adequate political strength to force the imperial power to decolonize. (Hence in the early 1960s some newly independent postcolonial African, and Asian, states had full universal suffrage whereas in the USA it was still only partial, despite white American men having won the struggle for what they considered to be democracy as early as the 1840s.)

NOTES

1 Michel Deveze, *La France d'outre-mer* (Paris, Librairie Hachette, 1944).
2 Lewis B. Namier, *England in the Age of the American Revolution* (2nd edn., London, Macmillan, 1961), p. 7.
3 Jacques Stern, *The French Colonies: Past and Future* (New York, Didier, 1944), p. 258.
4 Jacques Berque, *French North Africa* (London, Faber, 1967), pp. 275–8.
5 Ferhat Abbas, *La Nuit Coloniale* (Paris, Juillard, 1962), p. 128.
6 Cited in Alistair Horne, *A Savage War of Peace* (London, Macmillan, 1977), p. 37.
7 *Op. cit.*, p. 37.
8 *Op. cit.*, p. 40.
9 Alf A. Heggoy, *Insurgency and Counterinsurgency in Algeria* (Bloomington, Ind., Indiana University Press, 1972), p. 14.
10 Horne, *Savage War*, pp. 40–1.
11 Ian Lustick, *State-building Failure in British Ireland and French Algeria* (Berkeley, University of California Press, 1985), p. 74.
12 Horne, *Savage War*, p. 37.
13 *Op. cit.*, p. 37.
14 Heggoy, *Insurgency*, p. 43.
15 Lustick, *State-building Failure*, p. 71.
16 Eugen Weber, *Peasants into Frenchmen: The Modernization of Rural France* (London, Chatto and Windus, 1977), p. 485.
17 W. M. Macmillan, *Africa Emergent* (revised edn., Harmondsworth, Middlesex., Penguin, 1949), p. 11. (originally published 1938).
18 T. Karis and G. M. Carter, eds., *From Protest to Challenge* (4 vols., Stanford, CA., Stanford University Press, 1973), II, p. 25.
19 *Op. cit.*, p. 7.
20 *Op. cit.*, p. 33.
21 Heggoy, *Insurgency*, p. 15.

5

The Second World War

Writers accounting for the end of the European empires in Africa differ significantly about the effects of the Second World War. Those who hold that the war heralded the end of empire observe that it proved immensely costly to the two major colonial powers in Africa, Britain and France, both materially and in terms of imperial prestige. Belgium, like France, suffered defeat and occupation. The imperial powers were, it is true, part of the eventually victorious United Nations but that alliance mobilized its own citizens, as well as enlisted the support from the peoples of its dependencies, in defence of freedom against the Axis' totalitarianism. And fascism, like colonialism, was both racist and authoritarian, hence the doubly corrosive impact of wartime propaganda. By 1945 the political balance on which European imperial supremacy rested was destroyed with the emergence of a new bipolar world order, dominated by the anti-colonial superpowers, the United States and the Soviet Union. This school of thought posits strong causal connections between such wartime upheavals and the sequence of decolonization. In 1957, just 12 years after the war ended, the Gold Coast became the first Sub-Saharan black colony to gain independence. Only three years later the world's press proclaimed 1960 to be 'the Year of Africa', as 17 colonies, including such large states as Nigeria and the Belgian Congo, surged to independence.

Exponents of the theory that the Second World War was the 'big bang' which demolished European colonialism can also point to a significant exception to prove – that is to say 'test' – their rule: Portugal, which managed to stay out of the war, although unquestionably less powerful, hung on to its African colonies longest. And there is one rather neglected case where the 'big bang' theory fits the chronology precisely: fascist Italy's African Empire was conquered by allied armies during the war and disposed of in the course of the peace settlement.

The view that there is a simple causal connection between the effect of the war and general postwar decolonization, especially the decolonization of Africa, is challenged by a number of writers who focus on the history of the largest imperial power, Britain. Questioning the notion of sudden catastrophe, they maintain that the British were already very conscious of the structural weaknesses of their imperial system during the interwar years – weaknesses which became especially apparent once it was subject to the prolonged stress of the Great Depression. Moreover, they argue that Britain exploited wartime emergencies to strengthen the colonial state, a process which was continued into the immediate postwar period creating a general intensification of colonialism, aptly dubbed 'the second colonial occupation' of Africa.[1] And in those areas where the British world system was characterized by informal imperialism, rather than formal colonialism, they discern a shift to force, as against influence, during the war years. In short, they argue that the chronology – and hence the causation – of the end of the British Empire, and by extension of other European empires, is more complex than the conventional focus on the Second World War allows.

Similar arguments can be made for the French and Africa. Indeed, French policy proclaimed at the Brazzaville Conference in 1944 specifically ruled out any possibility of decolonization. Africa had proved its value during the war and was expected to play a crucial role in metropolitan recovery. Both France and Britain thus planned that the economic development of their African territories would be vital to the reassertion of their status as great powers.

Such contrasting judgements on the significance of the Second World War, once shorn of the forensic and metaphorical exuberance with which they were originally advanced, have been effectively synthesized, however. It has plausibly been argued that the view that the Second World War, and the period of postwar reconstruction, witnessed the reinvigoration of imperialism *and* the view that the war was critically important in bringing about the end of European colonial empire in Africa, should not be regarded as mutually contradictory.[2] John Lonsdale's epigrammatic summary of modern Kenyan history – 'Colonialism was a social process that decolonisation continued'[3] – with its suggestion of powerful linkages and continuities, can be applied much more widely.

BRITISH COLONIAL REFORM AND THE ATLANTIC CHARTER

Article III of the 'Atlantic Charter' of August 1941 declared 'the right of all peoples to choose the form of government under which they live'. This proved an especial embarrassment to Britain when Afro-Asian nationalist leaders, including Nnamdi Azikiwe of Nigeria and other West African radicals, claimed that it should apply to the colonies in the form of responsible self-government. Both Winston Churchill, the British Prime Minister, and General Charles de Gaulle, the leader of the Free French, insisted that Article III should apply only to the European countries liberated from the Axis powers. President Roosevelt, on the other hand, declared that the right of self-determination should apply to all peoples and that the United States would actively support it. Such diversity is not surprising for the Atlantic Charter was essentially a press release rather than a formal document, since Roosevelt, for obvious domestic reasons, wanted to avoid anything that might be interpreted as an alliance. There was therefore scope for continuing debate about its proper meaning, which broadened into a general discussion about the future of colonies in the postwar world.[4]

The United States position fluctuated somewhat but American policy-makers generally held that existing colonies should be prepared for self-determination by coming under the supervision of some successor international organization to the League of Nations. United States policy, therefore, envisaged an extension of the mandate system to replace European colonial rule. Britain took the lead in seeking to counter this viewpoint. The British argued – and the French did not demur – that for self-determination to be meaningful it must involve economic and social, as well as political, development. This would best be achieved under experienced colonial administrators. Indeed the British policy of colonial trusteeship was held to exemplify just such an approach. But Lord Hailey who, after the publication of his encyclopaedic *African Survey* (1938), just before the war, held a semi-official position within the Colonial Office as an expert on imperial problems, proposed Britain should take the initiative away from its foreign critics by replacing 'trusteeship' with the term 'partnership'. His conception of 'partnership' involved greater involvement by the colonial peoples in their economic and social development, with corresponding political progress to enable them to fulfil this new, more active, role.

This wartime debate led the British, therefore, to emphasize colonial reform, opening the way for those administrators, both in the colonies and in the Colonial Office, with specific proposals for African political progress and economic development. In West Africa some Governors believed that substantial concessions to educated African leaders were necessary. Sir Alan Burns, appointed to the Gold Coast in 1941, insisted on appointing Africans to his Executive Council. So also did Governor Bourdillon of Nigeria. By late 1942 Burns was proposing an African majority on the Legislative Council, although only a few members would be directly elected, and the Governor, not the Councils, would hold ultimate power.

Despite this retention of gubernatorial power, Burns had proposed a quicker pace of political advance for the educated élite than Hailey's notion of 'partnership' envisaged. Hailey resisted such concessions to 'groups of politically-minded Africans' until 'the vast bulk of African cultivators living under tribal conditions' had significantly progressed in social development and political consciousness. In fact the cultivators of Asante, through the Asante Confederacy Council, were already in October 1943 submitting petitions which corresponded closely with the demands of the politically minded Africans, led by J. B. Danquah. The Colonial Office could only meet these petitions by accepting Burns' proposals for a new constitution with a substantial African majority in the Legislative Council, though it was to be mainly elected indirectly through regional Advisory Councils, which themselves would be formed through Native Authorities. This was granted, to African acclaim, in 1944, though not implemented till 1946.

In Whitehall the committed Fabian Socialist Andrew Cohen became head of the Africa division in 1943. Late in 1944 the Treasury agreed that the Colonial Development and Welfare scheme be extended, with £120,000,000 allocated for the period 1946–56. Funds were to be earmarked for the development of higher education. The Colonial Office had already in 1943 appointed two high-level Commissions to make recommendations, thereby ensuring that the development of African universities would play a key role in its long-term plans for decolonization. The Commission on Higher Education in West Africa, chaired by the Conservative MP, Walter Elliot, declared 'Somewhere in West Africa within a century, within half a century, a new African state will be born.'[5]

FRENCH BLACK AFRICA: FROM THE FALL OF FRANCE TO THE 1944 BRAZZAVILLE CONFERENCE

In Gaullist political mythology the 1944 Brazzaville conference features as a seminal event in the decolonization of Africa. But this reads history backwards, finding continuity between de Gaulle's return to power and events of the late 1950s and his earlier role as '*l'homme de Brazzaville*'. De Gaulle's peculiar view of history, combining reverence for a glorious past with compelling concern for a more or less distant future, was conducive to such teleological myth-making. Moreover, the Gaullist myth did affect the actual course of decolonization in Francophone Africa. But Brazzaville hardly seemed significant in quite that way to contemporaries. In fact the pronouncements of the conference were sufficiently ambiguous, even contradictory, to permit a variety of creative interpretations. After all, it was not meant to provide definitive and detailed colonial policies, but rather to offer suggestions for some future Constitutional Assembly when France was liberated. As the historian of French decolonization, Raymond Betts, has commented, 'Brazzaville was indeed a turning point; the immediate question was: in which direction?'[6] But to answer that question the conference has to be set in historical context.

After the fall of France in 1940, General Charles de Gaulle found asylum in Britain to resume the fight against Germany. The meaning of the constitutional relationship between the metropole and the French colonial empire, 'Overseas France', now became a matter of intense conflict between de Gaulle's Free French and the Vichy regime. Those who considered the relationship was one of colonial subordination to the metropole found it logical that the colonies should abide by the terms of the Armistice of 1940 and share the fate of metropolitan France. Many colonial officials took this view and therefore aligned their territories with Vichy. The Free French, on the other hand, were forced by the logic of their circumstances to clarify the opposing position. They pointed to a common sovereignty as the defining characteristic of 'Greater France', drawing the conclusion that the war should continue from the overseas territories regardless of the defeat suffered by the army in the metropole.

Whereas French North Africa stayed with Vichy, '*Afrique Noire*' or French Black Africa, was split. The Socialist Freemason Guyanese Governor of Chad, Félix Eboué, and his Catholic humanist Chief Secretary, Henri Laurentie, rallied to de Gaulle. In 'three glorious days' in late August a Gaullist coup brought Cameroon and French Equatorial Africa (AEF) to the Free French side with Eboué as Governor-General. On the other hand, Pierre Boisson, the Governor-General of French West Africa (AOF), kept within the orbit of Vichy by successfully defeating an attempted seizure of Dakar by de Gaulle and the British in September 1940.

Brazzaville therefore played a unique role as the sole territorial embodiment of 'Free France' in Gaullism's heroic origins. Rare among French officials, Eboué and Laurentie had a respect for traditional African institutions, which was heightened by their wartime cooperation with the British in Northern Nigeria. (They were apparently treated to a persuasive exposition of British policy towards traditional institutions by no less an authority than Lord Hailey himself.)[7] Rare, too, was their consideration for African *évolués*; unlike their European colleagues they addressed African civil servants by the respectful '*vous*',[8] although Eboué had no doubt that 'there is no common measure between even the most senior native civil servant and the chief.'[9] Such then were the bases of Eboué's much acclaimed new 'native policy': greater dignity accorded to individual *évolués* and paternalist encouragement of traditional African institutions, with a greater role for chiefs on the model of Northern Nigeria. Formulated in his circular of 8 November 1941, Eboué's policy was reprinted as a separate pamphlet by the French National Committee in London. Thousands of copies were distributed, targeting the British and Americans who had just signed the Atlantic Charter, to demonstrate that French colonial doctrine and practice were in line with – perhaps even in advance of – the Charter's provisions.[10]

Eboué's reputation has oscillated since the period when his Brazzaville administration was advertised by the Free French as the quintessence of enlightened colonialism. That postwar generation of Africanists which began their careers during the 'springtime of the nations', optimistically interpreting the development of African nationalism and the course of decolonization against the background of the struggle for civil rights in the United States, was impressed by the mere presence of a black man making imperial policy. And they were right to be so impressed; the contrast with British racial practice is striking. (Certainly the possibility that the presence of Eboué as the most prominent Free French proconsul contributed to Anglo-American coolness cannot be ruled out; doubtless some of the Americans and British who had dealings with the French did find Vichyite racial etiquette more congenial.)[11]

More recently Eboué's reputation has been somewhat tarnished in the eyes of those who were formerly so impressed. First, they discovered that he gave greater priority to prosecuting the war than reforming colonial administration.

Indeed de Gaulle and Eboué were determined to mobilize their territories for a major contribution to the war effort in production and manpower. This meant that Africans were subject to increased taxes, unpaid labour and compulsory delivery of crops. The Free French regime in Brazzaville, moreover, took an equally stern line with potential subversives as had its predecessor. Andre Matswa, the leader of the political-cum-messianic Amicalist movement died in prison in 1942.[12]

The other reason for the decline of Eboué's reputation was that the 'New Native Policy' seemed a good deal less radical on analysis than Free French wartime propaganda had claimed. Partly this was connected with the circumstances of his Governor-Generalship. (Some of Eboué's administrative pronouncements which supposedly embodied the 'New Policy' are concerned with the detailed specifics of wartime mobilization and must have made dull reading for Africanists in search of the springs of political change.) His tendency to borrow selectively from British procedures in Northern Nigeria – not exactly in the vanguard of enlightened colonialism when judged by postwar Africanist standards – has already been noted.

Eboué's ideas do, however, foreshadow certain crucial aspects of the actual course of decolonization. His recommendation that political power be shared with the chiefs was based on long-term political strategy as much as administrative theory:

> [I]nstead of allowing a mob of proletarians, more or less badly dressed, speaking more or less French, to grow up through contact with us, we would do better to create an élite, beginning with the chiefs and notables who, having been made by us personally responsible for power, will progress by their experience in dealing with the difficulties they encounter and, as they become attached to their work, will win their spurs on behalf of the country and within it. Is this not better than a crowd of soured individuals bringing in unsuitable slogans from who knows where?[13]

Guided by a strong sense of historical destiny, de Gaulle was determined to act according to '*une certaine idée de France*'.[14] To his 'Anglo-Saxon' allies – Churchill and, even more, Roosevelt – this frequently seemed pretentious play-acting, based on a notion of France that bore scant relation to the realities of his position. Their casual dismissal of France as no longer a great power rankled. It found expression in military operations in parts of the French colonial empire without consultation or Free French participation. The British invasion of Madagascar on 5 May 1942 was followed by the Anglo-American invasion of North Africa of 8 November 1942. British involvement in France's former mandates of Syria and Lebanon was seen by de Gaulle as a further evidence of predatory Anglo-Saxon imperialism. United States dealings with Vichy, as well as with Petainist officials and civilians in the colonies, prompted Free French fears of betrayal. In Dakar, after AOF had eventually swung to de Gaulle in 1943, following the Anglo-American success in North Africa, a social clique of Vichyites, from the services and commerce, formed around Admiral Glassford,

Roosevelt's personal representative, and his wife. British officers also tended to mix in these circles, spurning their Free French counterparts who naturally suspected such a coterie of reactionary, even collaborationist, politics.[15]

Each side, de Gaulle and the 'Anglo-Saxons', fed the hostility of the other. Certainly, the General – with his mystique of France, stiff-necked and standing on protocol – was a difficult colleague. On the other hand, both Churchill and Eden were seriously worried by Anglo-American Francophobia and usually sought to put the best light on the General's actions.[16]

The discourse of imperial relationships, even more than other forms of international intercourse, seems prone to racial, national and ethnic stereo-typing. The high-watermark of 'scientific' racism coincided with the greatest extent of Western domination. It was therefore taken for granted by contemporary imperialists that racial difference constituted a necessary and sufficient explanation of the imperial situation. Of course, Western imperialism was locked in a symbiotic relationship with intense nationalism, so that the supposed rightness of Western control was further enhanced by the fact that the actual rulers were American, British, French, Belgian, German, Portuguese and Afrikaner – each claiming, to their own satisfaction, to epitomize what was best in Western civilization.[17]

At the same time there were evolving notions of acceptable norms of international and imperial behaviour, dating back to the British crusade against the slave trade. These were further delineated by the provisions of the 1890 Brussels Conference – described by Lord Salisbury as the first that met 'for the purpose of promoting a matter of pure humanity and goodwill'[18] – in favour of free trade and against traffic in arms and liquor. Such norms culminated in the stipulations of the mandate system of the League of Nations and the United Nations that the ultimate goal of colonialism should be its own abolition.

The enunciation of such international criteria for acceptable colonialism also proceeded by scapegoating unacceptable behaviour, spotlighting, in turn, such scandals as the 'red rubber' of King Leopold's Congo Free State, Portuguese forced labour, slavery in Liberia in the 1930s, and, increasingly after 1948, South African segregation and apartheid. In the Second World War such stereotyping discourse was peculiarly volatile as wartime propaganda tended to picture the enemy as either criminally subhuman or comic buffoons, while at the same time notions of Western superiority were subverted by Japanese victories and the very concept of race, which underpinned colonialism, was called into question from the United Nations' side because of the pivotal role it played in enemy ideology.

Quite why Americans scapegoated French colonialism so vehemently during the war years has been adequately documented but hardly satisfactorily explained.[19] Why the British were sometimes complicit in this, can be explained, if hardly excused, by the opportunity it gave them to deflect American anti-colonialism on to the French, feeding off the sense of American exceptionalism

by bracketing the Commonwealth with United States self-liquidating colonialism in the Philippines. Moreover, for the British there was the problem of the
dominions, particularly Australia and New Zealand. If the dominions supported
the United States in its opposition to the restoration of French colonial rule, the
Foreign Office was clear that Britain would have to acquiesce, for, as one official
noted in 1943, 'Britain cannot be expected to fight for the future of the French
Empire at the price of splitting her own.'[20] Nor was de Gaulle himself above
fishing for American sympathy, stressing Anglo-French differences and playing
on France's current weakness to claim that France and the United States were
'the only two major powers without imperialistic ambitions'.[21]

Yet the North African invasion marked a critical stage in the transformation of
Gaullist mystique into political reality. It led to the German decision to occupy
all of France. Vichy thereby lost all sovereign territory while the Free French
moved closer to becoming an actual government. Leaving Britain for Algeria,
where he was to establish his provisional government, de Gaulle was received by
Anthony Eden, the Foreign Secretary, who, with the Foreign Office, had striven
to lessen the hostility of the Americans and Churchill towards the General.[22] In
recollection, de Gaulle savoured this encounter:

> 'Are you aware,' said Mr. Eden to me in good humour, 'That you have caused us
> more difficulties than all our allies in Europe?'
> 'I don't doubt it,' I replied, smiling as well, 'France is a great power.'[23]

De Gaulle established himself in Algiers on 30 May 1943. Very aware of allied
criticism of French imperialism, as well as a moral obligation to those
dependencies which had supplied Free France with its territorial base and had
contributed so significantly to its war effort, he soon directed attention to the
condition of France's African colonies. By July 1943, he deemed it imperative to
'modernize our methods and concepts of colonial rule and not maintain these
states in their present condition.' Rene Pleven, the Colonial Commissioner,
assisted by Henri Laurentie, who had been Chief Secretary in Chad, organized a
conference of governors from tropical Africa to meet in Brazzaville in French
Equatorial Africa in January 1944. At first sight it appears oddly remote from the
main theatres of military activity for a high-profile war leader to plan to spend so
much time there. But this was to be a characteristically carefully choreographed
Gaullist 'grand gesture'. At the time, the triumphal progress of the journey was
as important as the final destination. De Gaulle flew to Brazzaville in easy stages,
proceeding with 'deliberate solemnity', his own description, via the African cities
which had declared for him – Dakar, Conakry, Abidjan, Lome, Cotonou,
Douala and Libreville – serving public notice, especially to the Americans, of the
continuing significance of French colonial ties with Africa.

The British press ignored Brazzaville.[24] Not so the State Department, for
which the black American official, Ralph J. Bunche, supplied a balanced

assessment. Reporting against a background of sustained American denigration of French colonialism, which, especially on the part of Roosevelt, was much more scathing than that directed against its British and Dutch equivalents,[25] Bunche noted that the Brazzaville delegates had emphasized decentralization and declared themselves against excessive protectionism. So far, so good – from the standpoint of repairing Franco-American relations. Brazzaville had even stated that the natives should be brought, step by step, to manage their own affairs, although he observed that this was hardly new in French policy. Bunche concluded that, 'The implication was very strong that Brazzaville clung tenaciously to conventional French policy of integration and assimilation of the colonial territories and their peoples.'[26]

De Gaulle and his entourage thus achieved one immediate political goal of the conference: to send a clear signal to Washington, and the rest of the international community with pretensions to peacemaking, that France intended to resume its role as an African colonial power in the postwar world. More than that, Brazzaville came to symbolize, for American policy-makers, a shift in French colonial thought towards American, British and Dutch notions of imperial trusteeship – a sort of catching-up exercise, an implicit recognition of where France had gone wrong, even a willingness to learn from others. (Bunche did not labour Brazzaville's copious rhetoric about the unique French 'civilizing mission'.) Henceforth, even if Roosevelt still disparaged and distrusted France, the Americans grudgingly admitted that it might be more expedient to allow the French to resume control of their colonial empire than to bring it under international administration.

When de Gaulle landed at Brazzaville he was received by Felix Eboué, along with 20 other Governors-General, and some assorted observers. Eboué was the only black man present and there very much in his official capacity as Governor-General. Africans had not been invited, as the organizers took the view, impeccable in logic, that no single one could be considered competent to speak for the diversity of peoples in French Black Africa. Eboué took it on himself to present local *évolué* opinion, along with the ideas of Fily-Dabo Sissoko, a teacher and canton chief from French West Africa, which together tended to support his own anti-assimilationist views.

The conference, as well as being staged to impress international opinion, was the French equivalent of British officialdom's wartime planning for postwar development. After opening orations by Pleven, Felix Gouin, a veteran Socialist politician, and de Gaulle, its proceedings were dominated by experienced colonial administrators. They represented the voice of reform, liberal paternalism as expounded at the *Ecole Coloniale*, their more reactionary colleagues having excluded themselves through collaboration with Vichy, while the location insulated them from settler pressures. Advance preparation in offices that had to be improvised in Algiers meant that they functioned without the bureaucratic backup available to their British counterparts but this prompted them to revert to the colonial policies of the Popular Front rather than to embark on new and radical thinking of their own.

It was firmly stipulated in the preamble to the conference's recommendations: 'The goals of the task of civilization accomplished by France in her colonies rule out any idea of autonomy, any possibility of evolution outside the French bloc of the empire; the eventual creation, even in the distant future, of "self-government" [*sic*] for the colonies is to be set aside.'[27] The symbolic refusal even to translate 'self-government', isolated as a quaint Anglo-Saxonism from the body of the text, eloquently underlined the point that French discourse, especially Gaullist discourse, on Africa was quite distinct. Pleven's opening remarks elucidated the underlying ideology: 'In greater colonial France there are neither peoples to enfranchise nor racial discrimination to abolish. . . . There are populations which we intend to conduct, stage by stage, to a political personality, and for the more developed to political rights, but this will still mean that the only independence they will want will be the independence of France.'[28] Clearly the French were giving notice that what they envisaged by the development of 'political personality', and even 'political rights', was something very different from the British model of constitutional advance from colonies constituting part of an empire to voluntary membership of a Commonwealth via dominion status.

The most important recommendation of Brazzaville was to call for the inclusion of overseas representatives in the Constitutional Assembly that was expected to follow the end of the war. (It was assumed by the Free French that far-reaching constitutional reforms would be needed in order both to remove the repressive legislation of Vichy and to strengthen the feeble structures of the Third Republic.) How that would be coordinated with the development of a 'political personality' in each individual colony was unclear. Some, such as Laurentie, were beginning to envisage some form of federal solution. De Gaulle, speaking to the American press in July 1944, endorsed this in general terms. Indeed, before the end of the year he seemed to envisage going far beyond Brazzaville, speaking of France's aim to 'lead each of its peoples to a level of development which would allow them first to administer themselves and, later on, to govern themselves.'[29]

Such provisional pronouncements supplied the texts from which the legend of '*l'homme de Brazzaville*' was constructed. Eboué stressed that this involved a shift away from the assimilationist notion of democratic citizenship. But all the Governors at Brazzaville, no less than de Gaulle himself, were clear that the development of a 'political personality' in their territories would be in the hands of a political class thoroughly assimilated in language and culture, as the educational recommendations of the Conference made plain. 'Assimilation', as envisaged in French administrative discourse, may have been anathema to Eboué, but both in his practice and doctrine, as enshrined by Brazzaville, he pointed the way to that assimilation of the political élite by which French decolonization actually proceeded.

The French style of decolonization would not have been so successful if it had not been a two-way process. Included in the conference proceedings were depositions from *évolués* calling for 'the extension into Africa of western civilization', and specifying that it should be in the medium of French rather than the vernacular.[30] Nor was such commitment mere pious words. Houphouët-Boigny, who was to lead the Ivory Coast to independence, sent 150 scholars to France in 1946. Therese Brou who later became his wife was in the first batch.[31]

CONCLUSION

What of the question with which this chapter began: what was the significance of the Second World War in ending European empire in Africa? European imperialists tightened the grip of their administration to force farmers and miners to produce increased targets of foodstuffs and strategic minerals, as well as rubber, for the allied war effort. At the same time administrators and chiefs were required to supply personnel for public works to furnish the necessary infrastructure for such increased economic exploitation of colonial resources. And all this had to be done while building strategic roads, railways and airfields. This has been seen for the British and French colonies. Similarly in the Belgian Congo, the government intensified its pressure, especially in those widening areas which supplied labour to extract Katanga's crucial strategic minerals: copper, cobalt and uranium. While such intensified exploitation – 'the second colonial occupation' of Africa – was taking place, colonial rulers were subject to international pressure, especially from the United States, to reform their administrations in line with developing ideas of trusteeship, stipulating that African interests should be paramount. Colonial reformers within the British and French administrations found such international criticism instrumental in getting their own governments to accept their policies. In any case they were sure that political and economic development should go hand in hand. What they understood as economic development, however, frequently provoked grass-roots opposition which threatened to subvert their control over political events.

Such a generalized scenario varied from colony to colony. (In the important cases of the ex-Italian colonies – Ethiopia, Eritrea, Italian Somaliland and Libya – the simpler 'big bang' model works best.) The emerging African political élite differed in its origins and composition, strategy and tactics. And the colonial powers displayed distinct national styles in adjusting to wartime and postwar change. But it should be clear that the important question is not whether the war affected the process of decolonization, but how it influenced the outcome in any particular case.

NOTES

1 D. A. Low and J. M. Lonsdale, 'Introduction: Towards the New Order, 1945–1963', in D. A. Low and A. Smith, eds., *History of East Africa* (3 vols., Oxford, Clarendon Press, 1976), III, pp. 12–16.

2 'Whatever caused the end of empire, it was not the Second World War', John Gallagher, *The Decline, Revival and Fall of the British Empire* (Cambridge, Cambridge University Press, 1982), p. 141. Gallagher's revisionism is subtly incorporated into John Darwin's account of the 'vicious circle' of imperial decline in his *Britain and Decolonisation* (Houndmills, Macmillan, 1988), especially pp. 24–5.

3 J. Lonsdale, 'The Depression and the Second World War in the Transformation of Kenya', in D. Killingray and R. Rathbone, eds., *Africa and the Second World War*, (Houndmills, Macmillan, 1986), p. 135.

4 See Chapter 6, this volume.

5 [Elliot] Report . . . on Higher Education in West Africa (Cmd. 6655, 1945), p. 18, cited in John D. Hargreaves, *The End of Colonial Rule in West Africa* (London, Macmillan, 1979), p. 102.

6 Raymond F. Betts, *France and Decolonisation, 1900–1960* (London, Macmillan, 1991), p. 61.

7 Brian Weinstein, *Eboué* (New York, Oxford University Press, 1972), pp. 262–333.

8 John Kent, *The Internationalization of Colonialism: Britain, France and Black Africa, 1939–1956* (Oxford, Clarendon Press, 1992) pp. 34–59.

9 E. M'Bokolo, 'French Colonial Policy in Equatorial Africa,' in P. Gifford and W. R. Louis, eds., *The Transfer of Power in Africa* (New Haven, Yale University Press, 1982), p. 180.

10 *Op. cit.*, p. 184.

11 Kent, *Internationalization*, p. 110.

12 M'Bokolo, 'Colonial Policy', pp. 189–90.

13 *Op. cit.*, pp. 181–2.

14 D. Bruce Marshall, *The French Colonial Myth and Constitution-Making in the Fourth Republic* (New Haven, Yale University Press, 1973), pp. 75–143.

15 Kent, *Internationalization*, p. 110.

16 Warren F. Kimball, *Churchill and Roosevelt: The Complete Correspondence* (3 vols., Princeton, Princeton University Press, 1984), II, p. 257; III, pp.390, 392.

17 I have dealt with this issue generally in Henry S. Wilson, *The Imperial Experience in Sub-Saharan Africa since 1870* (Minneapolis, University of Minnesota Press, 1977), Chapter 6, 'Theory and Practice of Empire', especially pp. 115–17.

18 Suzanne Miers, *Britain and the Ending of the Slave Trade* (New York, Africana, 1975), p. xi.

19 H. D. Bruce Marshall, *The French Colonial Myth*, pp. 75–100, reveals the tensions between de Gaulle and the Americans. W. R. Louis, *Imperialism at Bay* (Oxford, Clarendon Press, 1977), and Christopher Thorne, *Allies of a Kind* (Oxford, Oxford University Press, 1978) are two classic accounts which elucidate, without explaining, American Francophobia. Perhaps as stereotyping and scapegoating are by definition irrational we should expect random, essentially inexplicable, elements to be present in any given case. Nevertheless, given recent significant advances by historians and social scientists in the study of such similar cultural themes as anti-Semitism – and indeed anti-Americanism – American Francophobia would surely repay further investigation.

20 Kent, *Internationalization*, p. 134.
21 Thorne, *Allies*, p. 383, citing James V. Forrestal's Diary for 18 August 1944.
22 Cited in Kent, *Internationalization*, p. 134.
23 Cited in Betts, *France*, p. 58.
24 Edward Mortimer, *France and the Africans* (London, Faber, 1969), p. 27.
25 Louis, *Imperialism at Bay*, especially p. 335.
26 *Op. cit.*, pp. 45–6.
27 Cited in Marshall, *French Colonial Myth*, p. 107.
28 Cited in John Chipman, *French Power in Africa* (Oxford, Blackwell, 1989), p. 91.
29 Cited in John Hargreaves, *Decolonization in Africa* (London, Longman, 1988), p. 65.
30 Cited by J. R. de Benoist, *L'Afrique occidentale française de 1944 à 1960* (Dakar, NEA, 1982), p. 28.
31 Paul-Henri Siriex, *Felix Houphouët-Boigny ou la sagesse africaine* (Paris, Les Nouvelles Editions Africaines, 1986), p. 88.

II

DECOLONIZATION ACHIEVED

6

Great Powers and Superpowers in a Bipolar World

On 8 May 1945, the war in Europe ended. Just over three months later, on 14 August, eight days after the Americans dropped the first atom bomb on Hiroshima and five days after they dropped the second on Nagasaki, the Japanese surrendered unconditionally. Next day, 15 August, the Allies declared victory and celebrated VJ day (Victory over Japan day). But the victors had already begun shaping the postwar settlement. This chapter, and the next, will be concerned with that settlement and especially with its ramifications for decolonization. Whereas Chapter 7 will deal with the development of nationalism in Africa and the initial responses of the powers and interstate organizations to its emergence, here the focus is on interstate relationships and the creation of an international organization, which took its title, the United Nations (UN), from that of the victorious allies, to regulate those relations. The Second World War, especially after the Japanese attack on Pearl Harbor on 7 December 1941, was much more truly global than its predecessor, which is sometimes described as Europe's self-destructive civil war – a war that continued into a further episode, 1939–41. Appropriately the span of the United Nations was also more universal than its predecessor, the League of Nations; for example, the United States was included from the outset. The UN was to assist the rise of new states, themselves the result of decolonization, which in their turn became involved in the international diplomacy of subsequent decolonizations.

SUPERPOWERS IN A BIPOLAR WORLD

In 1944 the term 'superpower' was coined by the American scholar William Fox to describe states with 'great power plus great mobility of power.'[1] He identified the three such superpowers which would be responsible for sustaining the postwar international order: the United States, Britain and the Soviet Union.

There was no mistaking the accuracy of Fox's designation when applied to the United States. It was certainly the pre-eminent economic power in the world. Unlike almost every other industrialized country, the USA escaped the war with its productive capacity unscathed. Indeed, from 1940 to 1944, industrial expansion rose faster – over 15 per cent a year – than at any time then or since.

The US Gross National Product (GNP) rose from $91 billion in 1939 to $220 billion in 1945. At the end of the war the USA owned half the world's shipping and almost two-thirds of its gold. By 1947 the US share of world trade amounted to one-third, compared to one-seventh in 1938. In 1948 the US produced 41 per cent of the world's goods and services. With much of the rest of the world either exhausted by the war or still in a state of colonial underdevelopment, US preeminence was to some extent artificially high and thus, at such a level, inevitably temporary. (It has been compared to that of Britain in 1815, at the end of the Napoleonic Wars, for example.)[2] Nevertheless, by any standard, the United States stood out from the rest of the pre-war great powers as the only one which had become richer, very much richer, rather than poorer because of the war.

The perception of American military strength also placed it clearly in the superpower category in 1945. With 1,200 major warships it far outstripped the Royal Navy, the only other significant maritime force. Its aircraft carriers and Marine Corps had effectively demonstrated the reach of its sea power. Even more impressive was its 'command of the air', manifest in the pounding of German and Japanese cities and, finally and most spectacularly, in its monopoly of the atom bombs which devastated Hiroshima and Nagasaki. Also, although the 12.5 million US service personnel at the end of the war were cut to a ninth of that amount by 1948, this was a matter of political choice, not loss of military potential.

Nor was there any intention among American policy-makers, even as they were preoccupied with demobilization and the switch to peacetime production, of abandoning their internationalism and repeating their country's retreat after the First World War. Indeed the construction of a postwar international order appropriate to American economic expansion was now their main aim. Nearly all US officials dealing with economic diplomacy believed that the 1930s era of closed economic blocs – Nazi Germany in Eastern Europe, Japan in the Far East, together with Britain and the Commonwealth countries, as well as the USSR – worsened international rivalries, eventually creating the conditions for world war. Their postwar planning, moreover, had an edge of urgency because most of them also feared that peace would bring recession in its wake, threatening a repeat of the pre-war cycle of depression, bilateralism and economic isolationism. In their eyes, therefore, US and world prosperity, lasting peace and democracy, depended on swiftly establishing a stable and open economic order.

Hence the series of international economic arrangements hammered out from 1942 onwards to create a new world order beneficial to the needs of Western capitalism. The International Monetary Fund (IMF) and the International Bank for Reconstruction and Development were created by the Bretton Woods Agreement of 1944, while the General Agreement on Tariffs and Trade (GATT) was signed by 23 countries in 1947. Less fortunate states wanting to get some of the money available for postwar reconstruction found themselves obliged to conform to American stipulations on open competition and the free convertibility of currencies, as the British did, despite wishing to preserve imperial preference.

The Soviet Union refused to comply with such conditions for assistance, although its economy was badly damaged by the war. To have done so would have affected its superpower prestige and undermined the strict internal discipline of the immediate pre-war period. Indeed Stalin reinforced his dictatorship, demanding even more stringent conformism. Partly he could resist American pressure because territorially the Soviet Union had done very well out of the war. In the wake of the rout of the German armies, Soviet boundaries had been greatly extended. The Red Army's advance had incorporated a belt of satellite states, a vast informal empire, stretching far into central Europe. Although that whole area was shattered by war, there were still some useful economic pickings.

Although the Red Army was reduced by two-thirds, the Soviet Union maintained the world's largest military forces, comprising 175 divisions, with 25,000 front-line tanks and 19.000 aircraft. It was committed, moreover, to modernizing its forces, bringing the formidable Mig-15 jet-fighter into service by 1947–8 and creating a long-range stategic bomber force in imitation of the Americans and the British. In 1949 the West was shocked to learn that the Soviets had already successfully tested an atom bomb. The Soviet navy was also transformed by developing a fleet of ocean-going submarines and new heavy cruisers, although it was not until the 1970s, with Brezhnev's naval build-up, that it could support wars of national liberation in distant areas, a major factor in the chronology of decolonization. To sustain these powerful forces the output of heavy industry was almost doubled between 1945 and 1950.

Britain, the third member of Fox's trio, found it increasingly impossible to live up to his designation – hence its compliance with America's conditions for financial assistance. Under Churchill there was no doubt that it was one of the 'big three', the only major state which had fought through the war from beginning to end. But the cost of this sustained mobilization was the loss of two-thirds of its export markets and the sacrifice of at least a quarter of its foreign stocks to pay its bills. Britain, moreover, was deeply in debt. Keynes commented bitterly on the price of victory in May 1945, 'we and we only end up owing vast sums, not to neutrals and bystanders, but to our own Allies, Dominions and Associates.'[3]

Yet in May 1945 British troops were encamped on the Elbe and three months later Churchill was lording it over Germany with Stalin and Truman at Potsdam, apparently on equal terms. Nostalgia for wartime glories as an undisputed member of the 'big three' lingered on into the peace. Even when the electorate threw Churchill out in July, the Labour ministry which followed assumed Britain would continue to function as a great power.

France, defeated and occupied, was not one of Fox's notional superpowers. Plundered for four years by Germany, then devastated by months of major fighting in 1944, it had suffered vastly greater economic damage than Britain. Its national income was only half that of 1938, itself a bad year. France had no stocks of foreign currency and inflation was rampant. Fixing the franc at 50 to the dollar in 1944 proved sheer guesswork, within a year it had slid to 119 and by 1949 it was down to 420 to the dollar.

Yet the remarkable run of military successes by the Free French was the basis for de Gaulle's claim to great-power status. Besides those Free French who followed him into exile, he had raised a colonial army of eight divisions amounting to 300,000 men which triumphed over the pro-Vichy forces in West Africa, the Levant and Algeria and fought in many of the great allied campaigns. The resistance (Forces Française de l'Interior, FFI) was incorporated into the regular army and fresh troops mobilized once the Free French were back on French soil. By the time of the armistice France had an army of some 18 divisions with a distinguished record of hard and protracted fighting during the closing stages of the war in Europe.

The British were keen to see France develop as a major European military power as a counter to Russia, now that Germany had collapsed. They also wanted a restoration of French imperial control in Indo-China, a policy which the Americans, too, eventually adopted though only after a good deal of heart-searching hesitation. Although French military successes, backed by Churchillian pleading, did not win France a place at the peace talks at Yalta and Potsdam – to de Gaulle's lasting indignation – it did acquire permanent membership of the United Nations Security Council and an occupation zone in Germany. It still possessed the second largest colonial empire in the world and, though failing to regain its former mandates in Syria and Lebanon, it was determined to retain the rest. De Gaulle bitterly resented being thus beholden to British diplomacy and American hand-outs – even as he pressed his allies for more of the same – while he strove to restore France to the status of a great power.

Despite the efforts of the British and French governments to the contrary, however, historical statistics register the passing of 'the European age'. While the American GNP had surged by 50 per cent in real terms during the war, that of Europe outside the Soviet Union had fallen by 25 per cent. Europe had increased its share of the world's population from about 20 per cent in 1800 (190 million) to around 25 per cent by 1900 (420 million), despite sustaining very high rates of emigration to other continents which peaked just before the First World War. By the mid-twentieth century, however, its share of the total world population had fallen 15–16 per cent and was continuing to drop. The population of South Asia (India, Pakistan, Bangladesh, South-East Asia) was more than double that of Europe in 1960 and had more than trebled by 1985. In 1950 Africa's population was still just approximately 57 per cent of that of

Europe but by 1980 it had almost drawn level. In 1985 it had drawn ahead with 555 million to Europe's 492 million.

Before the war, Britain and France had looked to the wealth and extent of their empires to redress the balance against German, Russian and American domination. In 1945, encouraged by the urgent wartime demand for tropical products, especially those with strategic potential which were in short supply, they turned to their empires to redress the balance once more. Viewing the whole sweep of postwar history social scientists and historians of all stripes – experts in military history, diplomatic and international relations, imperial and national history – have virtually unanimously condemned this as folly. For postwar France and Britain Empire proved to be a brilliant mirage disguising for a few critical years the extent to which the geopolitical landscape had been trans-formed by the war. Their imperial overstretch gave an illusion of great-power status, which hastened the decline that imperialism was intended to avoid.[4]

Why was the illusion so widely held? How were these optimistic expectations deflated? What were the consequences of disillusion? Even the briefest preliminary explanation must note that the euphoria of victory hardly helped dispassionate analysis. Nor, of course, were contemporaries equipped with the hindsight and statistics to set that victory in historical perspective. For the French, 'France Overseas', at any rate in Africa, had developed a special material and sentimental significance during the years of defeat and occupation. For the British, the attraction of persisting in their imperial role, with the triple menace of Germany, Japan and Italy removed, was even greater. If Britain's pretensions to world power were challenged by the manifest military superiority of the Russians and Americans, it was equally obvious that for the time being Britain ranked much above the rest. In 1945, moreover, while the traditional enemies of the British Empire were devastated, the Dominion forces of Canada, Australia, New Zealand and South Africa had earned considerable military stature within the winning alliance. This clutch of Commonwealth countries, ranking as 'middle' rather than 'smaller powers', was expected to feature equally effectively in peacetime international affairs. Fortified by such considerations of relative power, the British remained optimistic about the survival of their world system; indeed, suitably modernized, they expected it to play a crucial role in postwar reconstruction.

Two smaller powers, Belgium and Portugal, controlled sizeable African empires. Each, for its own reasons, believed they contributed significantly to its international standing. For the Belgians the Congo, Ruanda and Urundi, had similar importance to 'France Overseas' in the years of defeat and occupation. Belgian Africa's strategic minerals, especially cobalt and uranium, promised to be even more crucial to Western defence, moreover, than they had been to the allied war effort.

Portugal had kept out of the war and a Soviet veto kept it out of the United Nations until 1955. Dr Salazar's increasingly dictatorial *'Estado Novo'* ('The

New State') regime, with its affinities with fascism, was out of tune with the dominant political doctrines of the postwar world. The country was thus to some extent insulated from the growing pressures of anti-colonial ideology. But ideological isolation did not imply the absence of a Portuguese world view, rather the reverse. The ultranationalist ideologues of '*Estado Novo*', like the writer and diplomat, Franco Nogueira, regarded an Atlanticist world outlook as essential to survival. Portugal's colonies, and its claim to a distinctive science of colonization, Lusotropicology,[5] were therefore regarded as crucial components of its historic national identity, the guarantee that it was more than just one among several Iberian regions which would eventually succumb to the pressures of geo-political logic and become part of its greater neighbour, Spain. Overseas possessions in strategic locations meant that, even when outside the United Nations, Portugal's wish for international recognition of its world role gained some credence from Western military planners. During the war the United States and Britain made use of the Portuguese Azores as an air base and postwar agreements extended some of these privileges. The old Portuguese–British alliance continued. Portugal participated in the Marshall plan and became a member of the North Atlantic Treaty Organization (NATO). Such acceptance by the Western states was vital to '*Estado Novo*'s' self-image of its world role as defender of Western Christian civilization.

THE UNITED NATIONS

The United Nations movement culminated in the great international meeting in the San Francisco Opera House in April 1945 to draw up a charter. President Roosevelt, in particular, was determined that this time the appropriate international organization should be created before the end of the war, to avoid its origins becoming entangled in the wrangles of detailed peace-making with a possible consequent revulsion against internationalism by the American public. A preliminary informal great-power conference was held at Dumbarton Oaks in Washington in August 1944 and was remarkably successful in reaching agreement on the basic structure. Consideration of the League's mandates and of colonial territories in general, however, was deliberately postponed at this stage in view of British sensitivity as the major colonial power as well as American uncertainty about the future of the Japanese Pacific islands.

At the unhappy Yalta summit conference in February 1945 'the big three' – Roosevelt, Churchill and Stalin – had their final chance to set the stage for San Francisco. They squeezed the future of the mandates into a crowded agenda. American anti-colonialism, especially on the part of Roosevelt, had been the decisive force behind the drive for a comprehensive system of international trusteeship for all non-self-governing territories, with a view to their eventual political advancement. But Roosevelt's concept of trusteeship proved flexible. The Secretary of State, Cordell Hull, curbed the radical plans of his officials by limiting the projected trusteeship system to the former League mandates and Axis colonies. Such pragmatism still left the problem of the Japanese islands in the Pacific, some of them Japanese mandates, conquered by American forces at great sacrifice. The naval and military Chiefs of Staff deemed their retention as US bases essential to national security. Roosevelt was doubtful about the navy's capacity to rule dependent areas and suspected its wish for peacetime jobs. But the presidential concept of trusteeship was sufficiently elastic to cover such contingencies. In the end the American state, war and navy departments agreed on the device of designating the Japanese mandates 'strategic trust territories', to the sardonic amusement of their allies.

Neither the proponents or the opponents of international trusteeship got everything they wanted from Yalta. British opponents, who included Churchill and were prominent in the Colonial Office, hoped that the United States could be persuaded to abandon as impractical such schemes to expand the scope of the old League mandate system. Indeed their ultimate aim was to sweep away the mandate system itself in a general reconstruction of the postwar international order. In its place they set forth their own version of the proper internationalization of colonial issues in what has been dubbed the Poynton–Robinson project after the two key officials involved, Sir Hilton Poynton and Kenneth Robinson. Poynton and Robinson proposed a series of 'Regional Commissions' and 'Functional Agencies' to organize international technical cooperation on such matters as health, communications, agriculture and forestry in order to foster the development of all non-self-governing territories. Originally they planned 'Regional Commissions' for both West and East Africa but when the future of the Italian colonies became critical it was decided that there should also be a separate commission to deal with north-eastern Africa, comprising Italian, French and British Somaliland, Ethiopia and the Sudan.

The 'Functional Agencies' would call on the expertise of such existing international bodies as the International Labour Organization (ILO) in colonial development. This was an astute move. Far from adopting a provocatively reactionary stance on general problems of international organization the Colonial Office deliberately courted an influential body of opinion on either side of the Atlantic which advocated what was known as 'the functional approach' to problems of international organization. The leading advocate of this approach, David Mitrany, was a relatively early – and very distinguished – example of the academic as governmental adviser and international expert, a breed which would subsequently proliferate in the lush pastures of decolonization and development. Born in Romania and educated in Germany and Britain, he had developed truly transatlantic institutional affiliations and connections, doing war work for the Foreign Office, becoming adviser on international affairs to the Anglo-Dutch multinational Unilever, while hobnobbing with old Fabian Society cronies and maintaining his connection with the Institute of Advanced Study at

Princeton, to which he had been recruited, along with Einstein, as one of the founding scholars.[6]

The international functionalists pointed to the ILO as a model of practical international cooperation. The only League of Nations organization that the USA had agreed to join, the ILO, weathered the débâcle of the League by shunning controversial political issues and concentrating on universal social and economic needs and problems. Indeed, it achieved much success in raising labour conditions worldwide and survived the war with its structure intact. The international functionalists argued that a web of such technical organizations could be created which would gradually envelope the whole field of international relations, eventually achieving world government piecemeal, without ever having to confront the sovereignty of existing states directly.

International functionalism projected a global vision that was peculiarly attractive to imperial bureaucracies in an age when overseas empires had to coexist with new forms of international organization while simultaneously withstanding the doctrinal challenges of nationalism and Marxism. As far back as 1919 Mitrany had questioned the received wisdom of orthodox 'liberal–radical opinion', represented by the Labour Advisory Committee and Bal Gangadhar Tilak, the Indian nationalist leader. Mitrany suggested that instead of advancing towards 'the glories of independence' by the route of parliamentary self-government, which would simply exacerbate communal conflict, India should progress by functional stages so that 'as soon as there should be Indian technical and administrative personnel capable of running a particular service – railways, posts, agriculture and so on – that service should be handed over to an autonomous national authority . . . above all, such technical advance would help bridge the religious division.'[7] Whether dealing with the problems of individual colonies, riven by communal and tribal division, or with world affairs, international functionalism proclaimed the significance of expertise. As in Marxist theories of imperialism, it identified powerful economic forces subverting the traditional nation-state, but, whereas Marxism pivoted on the inevitability of conflict, the basic theme of functionalism was the inevitability of cooperation. Ultimately it promised a new and harmonious world order with administrators and technocrats as philosopher-kings.

International functionalism operated at more than one level. At its most theoretical, as expounded by Mitrany and elaborated by later proponents,[8] it was both descriptive and prescriptive, again like Marxism, analysing the main currents in modern history while prescribing appropriate courses of action to bring about a better world. But a rudimentary functionalism had also seeped into public consciousness as a commonsense appreciation of recent history – two World Wars, punctuated by the Great Depression – which again, was both descriptive and prescriptive. The beggar-your-neighbour economics and politics of the interwar years seemed a proven recipe for disaster and despite America's avowed isolationism it had found itself involved in both World Wars.

'Interdependence' became the catchword encapsulating this popular function-alism – and godsent repartee to beleaguered imperial representatives confronted by demands for colonial 'independence' during international assembly!

Although few national leaders accepted the full optimistic logic of functional-ist theory, many were persuaded by functionalist advocacy of specific proposals. The United Nations established the Food and Agriculture Organization (FAO) in 1943 while its Monetary and Financial Conference at Bretton Woods in July 1944 eventuated (in December 1945) in the two international lending agencies: the International Bank for Reconstruction and Development and the Inter-national Monetary Fund (IMF).

One of the attractions for the British of associating the ILO with the Colonial Office plan was that, in Poynton's words, it monitored 'labour conditions the world over – sovereign states and Colonies alike.'[9] The Poynton–Robinson project was carefully crafted to counter the assumptions behind what became known after the war, in a phrase usually credited to Poynton, as the 'salt-water fallacy', the notion that exploitative imperialism was unique to maritime empires, ignoring continental overland expansion exemplified by the USA and the USSR. In February 1945, commenting on a Canadian telegram stating that international functional agencies would affect the native Indian tribes of Canada and the United States, Poynton noted, 'That's exactly why they're so relevant.'[10] At this stage in the unfolding argument over discriminating between formal colonial territories and 'internal colonies', it is important to note that Poynton's American counterparts agreed with him that it would be important to develop universal international agencies concerned with the welfare of dependent peoples caught up in both situations. As far as they were concerned he was not being controversial, merely clarifying the issue.

By the end of 1944 the Poynton–Robinson project 'On International Aspects of Colonial Policy' appeared to have won general acceptance within British governing circles as the basis on which the postwar colonial world should develop. Regional development through economic and social progress should be the aim of these international agencies creating strong interdependent units within existing colonial empires. Once this was achieved then sound political progress would follow as a matter of course. There was general satisfaction that Britain, through the Colonial Office, had devised a well thought out policy to divert institutionalized international interest in the development of the world's non-self-governing territories into channels that would prove acceptable to the colonial powers.

Unfortunately the Foreign Office failed to realize that the Colonial Office's grand design was based on abolishing the mandate system. No Colonial Office man went to Yalta. Eden, the Foreign Secretary, signed the Yalta agreement committing Britain, along with other members of the Security Council, to converting the existing mandates into United Nations' trusteeships. Churchill, although sharing the Colonial Office's attitude to mandates, had not read the

Poynton–Robinson paper. He was persuaded, grumbling, to go along with the American blueprint for what became the Trusteeship Council of the United Nations.

The master plan to develop the whole of the colonial world, in the words of William Roger Louis, 'along British lines and according to British ideals',[11] was thus initially discarded because of British bureaucratic bungling rather than superpower bullying. (Naturally some at the Colonial Office suspected Foreign Office chicanery.) Henceforth, the British had lost the initiative, finding themselves, with damaged morale, more often reacting to events rather than plotting them.

Yet the Foreign Office could claim that squaring the British national interest with the creation of a new world order was more complicated than the Colonial Office planners had allowed. If the purport of the Colonial Office programme was misunderstood, then the Foreign Office exercised creative caution in misinterpretation. As the only colonial power among the 'big three', the British assumed that they were charged with securing the joint interests of those of their European allies – France, Belgium and the Netherlands – who were members of the colonial club. (The British had failed to get France invited to Yalta but had succeeded in having it admitted as a permanent member of the Security Council.) If, however, the force and clarity of their arguments identified them too obviously as spokesmen for colonialism they were likely to provoke the USA and the USSR, along with China, the Latin American, Asian and Arab countries, into lining up against them.

Throughout the war the balance of power in the Anglo-American relationship had shifted steadily, leaving Britain more dependent than its leaders always cared to admit, even to themselves, let alone their lower echelons. Nor did the American guarantors of Lend–Lease care to spell out the full implications of a transformation which would involve them in massive global responsibilities. Failure to coordinate policy between the Colonial Office and the Foreign Office was an incidental cost of the wishful thinking and mutual ignorance sustaining the Anglo-American alliance.

In the approach to peace, just as in war, neither Churchill or the Foreign Office took the United States' new globalism for granted. They were always conscious that the cumulative frustrations of Republicans excluded from the highest levels of policy-making by Roosevelt's long presidency might find expression in a resurgence of isolationism. It was not only a matter of keeping on the right side of the White House; American opinion generally had to be appeased. If the British negotiators ever seemed in danger of forgetting this, American internationalists urgently reminded them. In January 1945 the *New York Times* went public, describing the President as warning Churchill that 'The American people are in a mood where the actions of their Allies can precipitate them into whole-hearted cooperation for the maintenance of the peace of Europe or bring about a wave of disillusionment which will make the isolation of the nineteen-twenties pale by comparison.'[12] Until the Senate finally endorsed the US commitment to the United Nations no one in London could be absolutely sure that 1919, when America renounced its own brainchild, would not happen again.

For both Churchill and Roosevelt, but especially the former, the life-and-death struggle with Germany had priority; indeed for Churchill, his cabinet and the whole nation it filled every waking hour. Historians whose principal concern is with other parts of the world than Europe should make due allowance for this. The fate of the mandate system tended to be raised within the context of the Pacific war and that of the future global organization to replace the League of Nations, frames of reference in which the British were more than usually likely to defer to the Americans. With a strong hand anyway, Roosevelt, the master manipulator, held the top trump, the threat of recurrent American isolationism.

Even fellow European colonial powers, smarting from defeat and occupation, were likely to resent British pretensions to leadership. The French, in particular, had their traditional suspicions of perfidious Albion's designs on their territories reinforced by wartime frictions in Africa and the Middle East. British diplomacy had to tread cautiously. When the French eagerly took up the idea of a regional conference in West Africa, in the lead up to the San Francisco meeting, the British quickly backed off lest they should be drawn into a demonstration of Anglo-French colonial solidarity against the United States.

There was, moreover, the problem of the Commonwealth. Three Commonwealth leaders in particular complicated the British approach to the postwar order. First, there was Smuts. Britain did not wish to be too closely associated with South Africa in anything concerning the principles of colonial government because of that country's avowedly racialist policies. On the other hand it could not afford to alienate or weaken Smuts for fear of consequences a good deal worse. South Africa's strategic position, its relative strength as the dominant regional power, as well as its economic resources and potential market, made it a most useful ally for postwar Britain, militarily overextended and strapped for dollars. And Smuts, who had played a significant role in the creation of both the League and the United Nations, had better credentials than most Commonwealth leaders as a world statesman. Indeed, he served at San Francisco as chairman for the commission on the General Assembly. He had also participated in the general allied discussion about the postwar colonial world, recommending in the American magazine *Life* in December 1942 that there should be regional groupings of colonies in which the metropolitan countries would continue to be responsible for administration but 'the ultimate control of the general or common policy would come under a regional commission or council representing all countries with economic or security interests in the region', including the USA in the case of Africa.[13] The future of the South African mandate over South-West Africa and the question of South African participation in the various international commissions which Britain had mooted for dealing with postwar Africa meant that such awkward and contradictory general considerations had to be taken into account.

Then there were Dr Herbert Vere Evatt, the Australian Attorney-General and Minister for Foreign Affairs, and Peter Fraser, the Prime Minister of New Zealand. Both of these antipodean leaders believed that the principles of trusteeship should be applied to all colonies and that there should be accountability to the future international organization. They were a powerful combination. Fraser became chairman of the United Nations Trusteeship Commission at San Francisco. Evatt, in particular, raised the hackles of the Foreign Office with his undiplomatic language, prickly temper and undoubted mastery of his brief. He certainly irritated the Americans, even though his ideas on international trusteeship corresponded to theirs rather than to those of the British. What both the British and Americans feared was that Evatt, if not handled adroitly, would stand forth in the new United Nations organization as the robust, even demagogic, champion of the smaller nations against the great powers.

This was the irony of the British position. What distinguished them, in their own eyes, from other colonial rulers was the Commonwealth; to them its very existence was proof of their enlightened colonialism, supplying their credentials for advising other colonial rulers and providing general guidelines for the future development of the undeveloped world. They believed that they had solved the problem of imperial disintegration through nationalist insurrection by allowing for the phased progress of each unit from colony to Commonwealth membership. It was in the Commonwealth context that they offered 'self-government' in place of the American preference for 'independence'. And, presumably thinking of the exemplary Smuts rather than the insular De Valera, they further expected that the attractions of Commonwealth participation would lure nationalist leaders along paths of wisdom and moderation to world statesmanship. But once they sought to formulate ground rules for a postwar international order which would facilitate this controlled transition they were constrained by the independent foreign policies of that self-same Commonwealth.

British imperialists had demanded that the interwar Imperial Conferences should be revived in order to ensure a similar level of coordination to that achieved at the 1918 peace conference when the British Empire delegation and the Dominion representatives worked closely together. But a series of informal meetings made it clear that such harmony was now impossible. In particular Mackenzie King of Canada was against any suggestion of a Commonwealth bloc.

In April 1945 Britain called an informal Commonwealth meeting in London as an immediate prelude to the San Francisco conference. Oliver Stanley, the Colonial Secretary, patiently explained the Poynton–Robinson project, but was faced by determined resistance from both Evatt and Fraser. They pressed Britain to set the other colonial powers a good example by placing its colonies under international trusteeship. Only Smuts joined Britain in general opposition to the mandate system. Ominously, Sir Ramaswami Mudaliar placed India firmly on the side of Fraser and Evatt, arguing that following a British lead, the 'pressure of world opinion would oblige such states as France, Belgium and Portugal to follow suit.'[14]

From Britain's standpoint the meeting was a failure. Immediately after his confrontation with Evatt and Fraser, Stanley, stricken with nervous tension, retired to his bed on the orders of his doctor. The best Cranborne (the future Lord Salisbury), the Secretary of State for the Dominions, a skilled chairman, could manage was some degree of negative consensus. All accepted, for example, that single-power mandates were preferable to multinational mandates; Sir Firoz Khan Noon, from India, comparing 'the former to a cow belonging to one person and the latter to the cow that was communally owned by the village, milked by all and fed by none.'[15]

At least the British could take wry pleasure as the Commonwealth leaders, once assembled at San Francisco, punctured foreign illusions. 'On the whole we are a pretty good Empire party here', Eden reported to Churchill from San Francisco. 'Smuts has been the most helpful at every point. . . . Evatt is the most tiresome and Fraser the most woolly. But between them they are making it clear to the Americans and all concerned that we do not control their votes.'[16]

In the end the British reconciled the multiple roles on which their international status rested: membership of the 'big three' and the Security Council; possessor of the world's largest 'salt-water' empire and self-appointed spokesman for the European colonial club, and, finally, leader – or at least coordinator – of a Commonwealth of jealously independent states. But the price of reconciliation was circumspection. In place of the bold Colonial Office blueprint for a future international order they settled for carefully uncontroversial proposals emanating from the Foreign Office, glossed further in the interests of safety-first by colleagues from the Dominions Office.

Under threat of being overtaken by an end to the fighting, the 'Big Three' – expanded to the 'Big Five' with the addition of France and China – hustled to erect the basic structures of a postwar international order. Accordingly, the charter-drafting San Francisco Conference began on schedule on 25 April 1945, despite the sudden death that month of President Roosevelt.

The San Francisco Charter did change the relationship of the new international body to the colonial world from that which obtained under its predecessor. Article I of the UN Charter stipulated that the general purpose of the organization was 'to develop friendly relations among nations based on respect for the principle of equal rights and self-determination of peoples . . .' The League had established a Permanent Mandates Commission composed of nine, later 10, independent experts, who were in no way official spokesmen of their governments, and four of whom were always drawn from mandatory powers. The Commission was advisory to the League Council in which ultimate responsibility was vested, although in practice the League Assembly frequently expressed views on mandates. The United Nations, on the other hand, lodged ultimate authority with the General Assembly, but, in effect, transformed the Mandates Commission into a separate organ under the title of the Trusteeship Council. Unlike the old League Mandate Commission, the Council was to consist not of experts but of representatives of member states, comprising all the administering powers, together with all the non-administering members of the Big Five, plus as many members elected from the General Assembly as were needed to make the numbers of trusteeship and non-trusteeship states equal. Just as in the case of the League, oversight was only to be exercised by agreement with the state holding the trusteeship and moral pressure was to be the Council's only weapon. But unlike the Mandates Commission, the Trusteeship Council was given the right to receive petitions and also to visit territories if invited by the administering authority. Such changes appeared to grant the United Nations little more formal power than the League. Many of those opposed in principle to colonialism were sharply disappointed. Expectations that the United States would adopt a crusading anti-imperial stance, which had been raised by Roosevelt and many in his entourage, were dashed.

The key figure in aligning the United States with the other colonial powers at San Francisco was Harold Stassen, ex-Governor of Minnesota. When the Soviet Union and China proposed on 12 May that the term 'independence' be included in Chapter XI of the United Nations Charter, the Declaration Regarding Non-Self-Governing Territories, they provoked a fundamental ideological rift. France, the Netherlands and South Africa all objected. Stassen intervened, arguing that 'self-government', the term the colonial powers preferred, was sufficient, since self-government could lead to independence. Stressing that the future of the world lay with *interdependence* rather than independence, he compared the colonial empires to the federal system of the United States.[17]

It was a position he was forced to argue subsequently within the American delegation, against those who regarded any compromise over independence as a betrayal of the ideals of the dead President and the 1776 Revolution. Stassen prevailed, coolly rebutting the proposition that the United States endorse 'independence' with similar arguments to those he had advanced in the Trusteeship Committee but clinching his case with one that he had diplomatically withheld in such an open international forum, 'We . . . did not wish to find ourselves committed to breaking up the British empire.'[18] Henceforth, Anglo-American cooperation became a central feature of the rest of the conference, proving very effective in bringing the smaller states as well into line. American pressure also persuaded the Chinese to withdraw 'independence' from the general colonial declaration, while the Soviet Union also proved amenable to be sure of a seat on the Trusteeship Council.

Leo Pavlovsky, a State Department official with an eye to public relations, played an important role in blurring the Anglo-American stand over the distinction between 'independence' and 'self-government'. He wanted to 'dress up' Stassen's position so that the United States would appear to endorse independence, whereas in practice supporting self-government. Accordingly, he devised a formula acknowledging independence as a possible outcome of self-government. It was agreed to urge the British to go along with this. Despite their aversion to 'independence', they agreed, relieved that the Americans had sided with them over the general declaration on colonies. The upshot was that the term 'independence' was included in Chapter XII which dealt with trusteeship, whereas it was omitted from Chapter XI dealing with non-self-governing territories. Meanwhile, Cranborne, as well as Stassen, pronounced for the record that self-government need not preclude independence.

Chapter XI proclaimed that all colonial powers should recognize that the interests of the inhabitants of non-self-governing territories should be paramount and accept as a 'sacred trust' their obligation 'to develop self-government, to take due account of the political aspirations of the peoples . . . to assist them in the progressive development of their free institutions, according to the particular circumstances of each territory and its peoples and their varying stages of advancement.'[19] Chapter XII, dealing specifically with trusteeship territories, specified the obligation to promote their 'progressive development towards self-government or independence as may be appropriate to the particular circumstances of each territory and its peoples and the freely expressed wishes of the peoples concerned.'[20]

The League had entrusted principal responsibility for its mandates, as well as economic and social questions, to its Council, an inner circle or 'cabinet', largely consisting of great powers, while the full membership operated as a form of 'world parliament' during its annual meetings. The UN Charter, however, while strengthening the great powers by equipping them with the veto in their capacity as permanent members of the Security Council, then virtually restricted the Security Council to matters of 'peace and security', giving the General Assembly an exclusive ultimate authority in other fields. In fact the lesser powers had criticized the Dumbarton Oaks proposals for giving too much control over the organization to the great powers, which, provided they got the Security Council they wanted, were prepared to make concessions to the General Assembly elsewhere. The smaller powers were able, therefore, to get the economic and social functions of the organization expanded, upgrading the Trusteeship and Economic and Social Councils to the level of 'principal organs', and amplifying those clauses which prescribe UN obligations in those fields. The nature of the bargain was conditioned, first, by neither of the superpowers possessing overseas empires so that trusteeship became a prime area for concession. Second, 'international functionalism', both as a doctrine and as embodied in the growing numbers of administrators and technocrats bent on an international career, reinforced the smaller states' preoccupation with global welfare. The preamble to the Charter blended these concerns proclaiming a determination 'to promote social progress and better standards of life' and 'the economic and social advancement of all peoples'. Altogether, it added up to a warm, if rather woolly, commitment by the UN to 'welfare internationalism', quite different from the precision that the great powers insisted upon in those political clauses which they considered were matters of life and death. But it created the environment in which the ideas and institutions of internationally sponsored development could prosper and thus vitally affected the processes of decolonization.

The conflation of race, culture and social development enshrined in Article XXII of the League's Covenant, which had underwritten the mandate system, was scrapped. The trusteeship system which replaced it was not based on implicit racism, ranking 'A', 'B' and 'C' peoples, but on the general United Nations premise of racial equality. Few of those who were involved in the San Francisco Conference believed, though, that this now committed them to rapid decolonization. Even Evatt himself, whom the British and Americans considered the arch-radical, for all his anger at the substitution of 'self-government' for 'independence' and the restriction of trusteeship to the old mandates, still thought in terms of gradualist progress.

Some gradualists, though, were more gradualist than others. Cranborne's parting words to the Conference warned that, 'We are all of us in favour of freedom but freedom for many of these territories means assistance and guidance and protection'. He found ample scope for old-fashioned colonial paternalism within the United Nations remit:

> Do not let us rule out independence as the ultimate destiny of some of these territories. It is not ruled out. . . . But to have it as the universal goal of colonial policy would, we believe, be prejudicial to peace and security. Nor am I sure it is in the minds or desires of the vast majority of colonial peoples themselves.
>
> What do these people want? They want liberty. Let us give them liberty. They want justice. Let us give them justice. . . . Let us help them to climb the ladder of self-government. That is the purpose . . . so that ultimately dependent or independent they may play their full part in a peaceful, prosperous and independent world.[21]

Contemporary opinion differed sharply as to what the likely consequences of the San Francisco decisions on trusteeship would be. Charles Taussig and Benjamin Gerig, for example, had worked together throughout the war years on US policy towards dependent territories. But they took diametrically opposed views when Stassen aligned America with Britain, and against the Soviet Union and China, over the issue of 'self-government' as against 'independence'. Taussig believed that, 'Independence as a goal for all peoples who aspire to and are capable of it has been the traditional and sacred policy of this Government.'

By retreating from it the US was throwing away the 'opportunity to make a profitable gesture on behalf of the peoples of the Orient as well as Africa and the Caribbean.' Dire consequences would follow; the Soviet Union, especially, and China would capitalize on their role as the only great powers committed to independence and he reminded his fellow delegates of Roosevelt's belief that to 'deny the objective of independence . . . would sow the seeds of the next world war.'[22] Benjamin Gerig, on the other hand, believed the trusteeship system would bring swift benefits to colonized peoples. The UN trusteeships, scattered as they were throughout the colonial world, would act 'as a world laboratory of colonial administration', now that the imperial powers had been made accountable to international opinion.[23]

In the controversial arena of East Africa there was keen interest in the San Francisco decisions. In a treatise on the mandates in international law published in 1935 Dr Evatt, the radical opponent of the Anglo-American standpoint, had focused on the view set forth by Britain in the Kenya White Paper of 1923 as an appropriate model for international trusteeship: 'We are the Trustees of many great African Dependencies, of which Kenya is one, and our duty is to do justice and right between the various races and interests, remembering, above all, that we are *trustees before the world for the African population*' (Evatt's emphasis).[24]

Tanganyikan Africans also focused on Kenya, but rather as an example of the deprivations they were likely to suffer should they lose the protection of international surveillance. The threat of South African expansionism and white-settler schemes for bringing Britain's East African territories into closer unity, combined with the obvious grudging reluctance with which Britain gave way to American pressure for a United Nations trusteeship over Tanganyika, gave a sharp edge to their concern as uncertainty persisted until the trusteeship arrangements were completed in 1947. Tanganyika's African Association, convened at Dodoma on the eve of the San Francisco Conference, bracketed the continuation of the mandate along with 'no East African Federation' and no European settlement in its demands to government. At its 1946 conference at Dar es Salaam, which marked the transition of Julius Nyerere from student leader to the national stage, the Association urged that Tanganyika come under trusteeship, with Britain undertaking to develop it speedily 'until the Africans reach the point where they can manage their own affairs', when 'the Trustee power should grant them their independence without any unnecessary delay.' And, the Conference added, they should proceed to 'independence or self-government as Tanganyika Africans and not as East Africans.'[25] Clearly East Africans felt that Britain had failed to live up to the letter of its own doctrine of trusteeship, at least in that exemplary case, selected by Evatt, of Kenya. They expected, though, that once that concept was enshrined in the UN Charter, and had specific reference to themselves as Tanganyikans, the British would be forced, morally and politically, to comply.

COLD WAR COMPLICATIONS

The immense discrepancy between the might of the superpowers and all the other states is the dominant characteristic of postwar international politics. Britain and France, despite being permanent members of the Security Council and the major possessors of overseas empires, were well aware of this disparity. Faced by the proximity of Soviet power they depended on their alliance with an even mightier superpower, the United States. De Gaulle had been often reminded of the costs of depending on what he took to be the arrogance of 'Anglo-Saxon' power. The British hoped that they would benefit from the 'special relationship' that the term 'Anglo-Saxon' implied. They did, as, for example, their close working relationship with Harold Stassen at San Francisco indicates. Nevertheless, the British government was made vividly aware by the terms of the postwar settlement that America was now the senior partner. The crippling dollar debt in 1945 was to be paid off by the import of US goods; hence the American insistence on the convertibility of sterling. A stampede to convert sterling holdings into dollars in 1946 depleted Britain's gold and dollar reserves and caused a crisis. Convertibility was suspended in 1947, after this demonstration of sterling's vulnerability, thus Britain's remaining pretensions to global rivalry with the United States were quickly killed off. (Some British policymakers frantically searched for ways of redressing the balance within the Western alliance – for example, Ernest Bevin during his more sanguine moments about schemes for 'EurAfrican' development[26] – but consulting the national accounts sooner or later effected a return to sobriety.)

The bipolar structure of international power, increasingly apparent as the Cold War progressed, however, meant that the United States often had to compromise with its feebler allies. American sterling–dollar diplomacy may have brutally demonstrated British inferiority in 1946–7, but, paradoxically, the sheer weakness of America's Western European allies, once established, proved one of their strongest bargaining cards. And by 1947 the economic weakness of Europe and the growing threat of Communist expansion seemed patently obvious to the Americans. The ideological appeal of the Marxist myth of inevitability was still strong, with upwards of a quarter to a third of French and Italian electors voting Communist. Containment of Soviet power, the Truman doctrine on aid to Greece and Turkey in March 1947 – prompted by Britain's inability any longer to supply them with the requisite military aid – and the Marshall plan for European recovery in June, signalled a new coordinated strategy.

The shift from what has been characterized as rather tight-fisted to relatively open-handed American predominance had important consequences for the European colonial powers.[27] The United States stopped insisting on convertibility, easing the economic pressure on Western Europe, especially Britain. In order to speed Western European recovery from the war and reduce its susceptibility to Communist ideology, Americans tolerated discrimination against US goods, including possible American exports to European colonial markets. The 'Open Door', that classic principle of American foreign policy and an article of faith with US postwar economic policy-makers, was thus compromised by the constraints of the bipolar power structure. Similarly, American concern about Communist expansion led the United States to ease its pressure on the European allies to decolonize.

In fact when the Marshall plan for European recovery was implemented American officials connived at the use of funds to strengthen European colonial structures with a view to production for metropolitan prosperity, and US strategic needs, rather than local welfare or preparation for ultimate decoloniza-tion. France used a substantial proportion of its aid to develop raw material production in Africa. In 1950 European colonies supplied the United States with 82 per cent of its bauxite, 68 per cent of its cobalt (critical in the manufacture of jet engines) and 23 per cent of its manganese ore.[28]

The solid links between Western security and European recovery were emphasized when Belgium granted the United States and Britain first option for a number of years on a rich uranium source in the Belgian Congo. The United States and Britain paid Belgium well for this atomic-energy fuel; proceeds from a special tax on the ore substantially funded the development of the Belgian atomic-energy programme. In 1955 the Belgian Socialist leader, Paul-Henri Spaak, attacked those who argued that Belgium's traditional neutrality was compromised by such close cooperation and that the interests of their small country would be submerged in a large treaty organization such as NATO, 'The atom bomb leaves no room for neutrality or separate national policies. The West is condemned not only to wage war together but to create policy together. . . . The Atlantic Alliance is a great thing.'[29] In 1957 he was able to put his principles into practice when appointed Secretary-General of NATO.

The United States could reconcile the relaxing of pressure on its European allies to decolonize by arguing that time must be taken to do the job properly. The timetable Roosevelt had agreed with Filipino nationalists in 1934 was carried through, despite the intervening Japanese occupation. The Philippines became independent on 4 July 1946. Here was the proof, Americans proclaimed to the non-European world, that they had not lost their traditional anti-colonial idealism. But, as early as November 1942, Roosevelt had used the US–Philip-pines relationship to refine the doctrine of American anti-colonialism: Philip-pine history, since the US occupation at the turn of the century, indicated, first, the necessity of a 'period of preparation' through the expansion of education and economic and social development; second, the need for a 'period of training for ultimate independent sovereignty' through the evolution of self-governing institutions. Even the United States, he noted in sly diplomatic tribute to his British imperial ally, passed through 'preliminary stages' with a 'whole process of political training and development', beginning in the town meetings and local assemblies of the colonial period.[30] This was to be the oft-repeated distillation of American–Filipino wisdom, a message for imperialists and nationalists alike. Roosevelt's successor, Harry Truman, drew essentially similar lessons almost 10 years after the Philippines' independence when he said in his memoirs, 'We accepted the principle of political freedom as our own and believed that it should apply elsewhere as well. The real problem was that of procedure and method.'[31]

Behind Truman's stress on the exemplary decolonization of the Philippines, with its phased hand-over to a stable anti-Communist government, lay his awareness that the Soviet Union, the other superpower in this bipolar world, also claimed anti-colonial credentials and seemed to offer nationalists aspiring to be rulers of postcolonial states an intriguing model for rapid industrialization. In response, Western Cold War rhetoric posed the US and its allies in democratic opposition to Bolshevik tyranny over Eastern Europe as well as the Soviet Union, much as the wartime United Nations had resisted German and Japanese fascism. Europe and its colonies were thus ranged together on the side of self-determination and individual freedom, so long as they combined schemes of economic and social development with training for democratic government. It was a far cry from simple anti-colonialism.

Even the Soviet Union's approach to nationalism and colonialism was somewhat complicated, however. On the one hand, Lenin's terse analytical treatment, *Imperialism, the Highest Stage of Capitalism*, written in 1916, was a powerful ideological weapon, which posited an organic relationship between capitalism and imperialism, thus putting the socialist Soviet Union firmly on the anti-colonial side. Moreover, according to Lenin, if imperialism was the highest stage of capitalist development it was also the last, further reinforcing that claim to historical inevitability which proved one of Marxist-Leninism's main ideological attractions.

Soviet ideas on nations and nationality, though, as propounded by Stalin and elucidated in later Marxist-Leninist texts, offered scope for flexibility. They developed from the basic Marxist theory of social evolution, making a fundamental distinction between the earlier forms of political identity, clans and tribes, and nations. Clans and tribes were associated with precapitalist economic formations, regarded as mere 'ethnographic categories'; nations, on the other hand, were considered to be 'historical' because they belonged to 'the epoch of rising capitalism'.[32] Even among nations only those with a clear territorial base and a certain size were recognized as possible candidates for self-determination in later Marxist-Leninism.[33] (Marxist-Leninism thus transposed into materialist terms the traditional invidious distinction between 'historic' and 'non-historic' nations in central and Eastern Europe, the former boasting an aristocracy and a literary tradition, the latter being basically peasants, with an essentially oral folk culture.)

Such categories, though theoretically universal, had originally been devised to explain the politics of the multinational Tsarist, later Soviet, state. Nationalism has been a recurrent theoretical problem for Marxists who associated it with capitalism and expected it to be transcended by socialism.[34] But it was also a practical problem for the Soviet government. Unlike the capitalist United States, or Communist China, where nationalism reinforced social cohesion, the Soviet Union experienced nationalism as a corrosive force. (The Russian population of the Soviet Union was only 57 per cent of the total in 1950 and the Soviets were uneasily aware that the higher birthrate of some of the other nationalities would make them a minority around the turn of the century.)[35] The Soviets were partly shielded from criticism by the 'salt-water' theory of imperialism[36] – and widespread acceptance of their Leninist linkage between capitalism and imperialism – but awareness of their vulnerability to nationalism at home, as well as subtracting from their overall strength, modified the single-mindedness of their ideological assault. The positions of Communist parties in imperial powers, particularly France, moreover, sometimes left colonial peoples, like the Algerians, bitterly disillusioned.

Juxtaposing the origins of the United Nations with the transformations of world power during the Second World War and the onset of the Cold War illustrates the complex interplay between the international system and the international organization. The image of the United Nations which inspired the founding fathers at Dumbarton Oaks and San Francisco was very different from the actual international system to emerge from the Second World War. The Charter assumed, indeed required, there would be a concert of great powers, the Big Five, which would be responsible for peace and security through the Security Council, a modern version of the nineteenth-century Concert of Europe. The bipolar world of the late 1940s, which plunged into the Cold War, and was also wracked by tension and conflict between colonizers and colonized, bore scant resemblance to this optimistic vision. The United Nations survived the breakdown of great-power consensus by imaginative *de facto* revision of the Charter, with both the General Assembly and the Secretary-General improvising their scripts to take advantage of the impaired role of the Security Council.

The transformation of the United Nations was based on an image of the world at least as different from reality as the original image of the United Nations. It imagined a fictitious world community which would make of the United Nations an instrument to represent and enlarge the common interest of humanity. Once more it created illusions and disillusion. But in postulating a common humanity it prompted the organs of the United Nations to be concerned with human rights and development worldwide, creating a propitious international environment for the many relatively poor and weak states that resulted from decolonization. And once these postcolonial states were admitted, however small and weak, they had equal voting rights in the General Assembly and the prospect of being voted onto the Security Council.

At the same time, as we have seen, the Cold War and bipolarity constrained the superpowers. Those involved in the processes of decolonization – colonizers and colonized alike – had to adapt, therefore, to a bipolar international system and an international organization, the United Nations, both of which complicated the workings of each other. But it was a two-way process, in adapting they also adapted both international system and organization in subtle ways. Decolonization itself, by progressively increasing the number of actors on the international stage, significantly transformed the United Nations and further modified the bipolar system.

NOTES

1 William T. R. Fox, *The Superpowers: The United States, Britain, and the Soviet Union* (New York, Harcourt Brace, 1944).

2 By Paul Kennedy, *The Rise and Fall of the Great Powers* (London, Fontana, 1988), p. 460.

3 J. M. Keynes, 'Overseas Financial Policy in Stage III', in D. Moggridge, ed., *Collected Works of J. M. Keynes* (Cambridge, Cambridge University Press, 1979), XXIV, p. 280.

4 The phrase 'imperial overstretch', now in general use, derives from Kennedy's best-selling and very influential, *The Rise and Fall*.

5 For Lusotropicology see entry in Key Terms.

6 David Mitrany, *A Working Peace System: An Argument for the Functional Development of International Organisation* (London, Royal Institute of International Affairs, 1943), while his *The Functional Theory of Politics* (London, London School of Economics and Political Science, 1975) is indispensable for the development and diffusion of these ideas. Karl W. Deutsch, *The Analysis of International Relations* (Englewood Cliffs, Prentice-Hall, 1968), pp. 166–8 provides a brief critique. (Mitrany's functionalism, with its focus on international politics, needs to be distinguished from the now better-known functionalism of well-known anthropologists, such as Malinowski and Radcliffe-Brown, which influenced colonial administration. See entries in Key Terms.

7 Mitrany, *Functional Theory*, p. 32.

8 Inis L. Claude, Jr., 'Economic Development Aid and International Political Stability', in Robert W. Cox, ed., *International Organisation: World Politics* (London, Macmillan, 1969); Ernst B. Haas, *Beyond the Nation-State* (Stanford, Stanford University Press, 1964).

9 William Roger Louis, *Imperialism at Bay* (Oxford, Clarendon Press, 1977), p. 385.

10 *Op. cit.*, p. 396.

11 *Op. cit.*, p. 463.

12 Robert Dallek, *Franklin D. Roosevelt and American Foreign Policy, 1932–1945* (New York, Oxford University Press, 1979), p. 505. (The occasion of this public warning was in fact British support for one side in the Greek civil war but FDR and the newspaper were making a general point.)

13 Louis, *Imperialism at Bay*, pp. 209–10.

14 *Op. cit.*, p. 510.

15 *Op. cit.*, p. 508.

16 *Op. cit.*, p. 520.

17 *Op. cit.*, p. 535.

18 *Op. cit.*, p. 537.

19 Chapter 11, Article 73. Herbert. G. Nicholas, *The United Nations as a Political Institution* (2nd edn., London, Oxford University Press, 1962) prints the Charter pp. 198–226 with this extract on p. 216.

20 Chapter 12, Article 76, Nicholas, *United Nations*, p. 217.

21 Louis, *Imperialism at Bay*, p. 547.

22 *Op. cit.*, pp. 536–7.

23 B. Gerig, 'Significance of the Trusteeship System', *The Annals of the American Academy of Political and Social Science* 255 (January 1948), pp. 42–4. Cited in Scott L. Bills, *Empire and Cold War* (London, Macmillan, 1990), p. 16.

24 Louis, *Imperialism at Bay*, pp. 108–9.

25 John Iliffe, *A Modern History of Tanganyika* (Cambridge 1979), pp. 423–32.

26 See the account of the Ground Nut scheme pp.149–50, and, more generally, Javier Gonzalo Alcade, *The Idea of Third World Development: Emerging Perspectives in the United States and Britain 1900–1950* (New York, University Press of America, 1987), especially pp. 191–7.

27 Robert O. Keohane, *After Hegemony* (Princeton, Princeton University Press, 1984), p. 142.

28 Thomas G. Paterson, *Postwar Reconstruction and the Origins of the Cold War* (Baltimore, Johns Hopkins University Press, 1973), p. 234.

29 P. H. Spaak, 'The Atom Bomb and NATO', *Foreign Affairs* 33 (April 1955), p. 359.

30 In a radio address on 15 November 1942, the seventh anniversary of the Philippines Commonwealth, quoted in Bills, *Empire*, p. 26.

31 Harry Truman, *Memoirs* I: *Year of Decisions* (Garden City, NY, Doubleday, 1955), pp. 237–8. Quoted in Bills, *Empire*, p. 205.

32 Cited from *Fundamentals of Marxist-Leninist Philosophy* (Moscow, 1974), p. 394, in I. M. Lewis, 'Introduction', in I. M. Lewis, ed., *Nationalism and Self-Determination in the Horn of Africa* (London, Ithaca Press, 1983), p. 11.

33 H. Wiberg, 'Self-Determination as an International Issue', in Lewis, *Self-Determination*, p. 53.

34 B. Anderson, *Imagined Communities* (London, Verso, 1983), pp. 12–16.

35 Paul Dibb, *The Soviet Union: The Incomplete Superpower* (London, Macmillan, 1986), p. 48.

36 For the 'salt-water' theory see p.77.

7

Nationalism, Pan-Africanism and Pan-Arabism

By the mid-twentieth century the right to self-determinatiom for 'all peoples' was accepted as the basic principle of international relations and law. National self-determination, tentatively advanced as the central legitimizing principle of international society by the League of Nations, was conclusively accepted by its successor, the United Nations. In 1945 the principle of 'equal rights and self-determination of peoples' was enshrined in the purposes of the UN in Article I of the UN Charter.[1] In 1948 it was expressed with greater rhetorical force in the Declaration of Human Rights endorsed without dissent by the UN General Assembly.[2] The principle thus came to enjoy international consensus with no state officially making explicit objections. Yet, as with so many other international norms, the consensus depended in practice on a considerable degree of ambiguity. The proponents of African and Arab nationalism, Pan-Africanism and Pan-Arabism, all sought to resolve that ambiguity to their own advantage. So, too, did the various European imperial powers, each of which devised projects for revamping its colonial structures to take account of postwar international norms. What constituted a 'people', and what could be construed as 'self-determination', had been critical political issues for Europe since the French revolution; after 1945 the public cant of the new internationalism meant that they were bound to become key political questions in Europe's African empires as well.

At the end of the Second World War African nationalists were attacking existing European imperial systems as outdated, oppressive, inefficient and artificial. But to their European rulers such nationalism still appeared somewhat nebulous. They had a point. The aims of the nationalists stretched all the way from the political claims of ethnic solidarity, via independence as citizens of nation-states fashioned from existing colonial territorial structures, to assorted varieties of Pan-Africanism. And such diversity was not, at this stage, much clarified by internal debate within nationalist circles; rather, individuals seemed to oscillate unpredictably between assertions of ethnicity, territorial nationalism and Pan-Africanism. Imperial bureaucrats, trained to think in terms of tidy administrative solutions to governmental problems, found it difficult to take such manifest inconsistency seriously. Indeed they believed, plausibly enough, that the nationalists' flickering focus reflected a failure, likely to continue for the foreseeable future, to locate a solid constituency base. They were mistaken.

Johnstone Kenyatta discovered his original constituency as the founding editor of the first Kikuyu newspaper, the monthly *Muigwithania* ('The Reconciler'), which operated on the assumption that the tribe was both the repository of traditional African wisdom and an appropriate instrument for communal modernization and individual self-improvememt. Here was the opportunity to develop the public agenda of what was involved in being Kikuyu. (G. W. F. Hegel had observed that newspapers were modern man's substitute for daily prayers.) In 1929–30 Kenyatta visited London in an effort to defend Kikuyu interests in discussions over the political future of East Africa. He returned to Europe in 1931 (aboard a ship named *Mazzini*) for what became a protracted stay.

At the London School of Economics (LSE) in 1936–7, Kenyatta participated in Bronislaw Malinowski's celebrated seminar for social anthropologists. In 1938 he published a study of the Kikuyu social system, *Facing Mount Kenya*, under a new first name, Jomo, with a preface by Malinowski. But Kenyatta expounded Kikuyu ethnography in the service of African nationalism as well as ethnic solidarity. His book was deliberately intended to challenge 'those who monopolize the office of interpreting . . . [the African] mind and speaking for him. To such people, an African who writes a study of this kind is encroaching on their preserves. He is a rabbit turned poacher.'[3]

With a zest for controversy, and an eye for the rewards of scandalizing, and titillating, the progressive metropolitan bourgeoisie – at which sport his patron, Malinowski was a master[4] – Kenyatta focused attention on female circumcision, a staple for missionary condemnation. He argued that Europeans were arrogant and mistaken to condemn this custom as barbaric. Condemnation was based on the attempt to apply some universal standard to all social practices. But the practice only had its meaning, its rationale, in the context of its own unique integrated community: 'No single part [of the integrated culture] is detachable; each has its context and is fully understandable only in relation to the whole.'[5] Inside that community significant meaning was attached to the way in which the passage from female adolescence to womanhood was marked, and that in its turn was a basic component of the sexual and social structure of Kikuyu society. Only from within that frame of reference could judgements be made.

Kenyatta had attached himself to Malinowski, the most celebrated of the functionalist anthropologists. Basic to their ideas was the concept of 'equilibrium'. Every society, certainly the society of the tribe, was able to function because it had achieved a degree of equilibrium. Changes introduced from outside into a tribe were likely to upset that equilibrium. Everything in that society (for example, in the case of the Kikuyu, female circumcision) could be justified as contributing to that equilibrium. Underlying the notion of equilibrium was an organic conception of society, whereby externally induced change was stigmatized as unnatural. Deviations from the natural state of a particular human unit – in this case the Kikuyu tribe, but essentially the same argument had been advanced by European nationalists, such as the Germans and Czechs with regard to their own customs – were, by definition, unnatural and, therefore, bad.

Kenyatta had learned Malinowski's message well and adapted it to his own political circumstances. The functionalist anthropology which underwrote Indirect Rule was now pressed into the service of African nationalism. (Although it is worth noting that a functionalist defence of African societies against Western, especially missionary, condescension and disruption, was originated, even as the process of partition began, by Edward Blyden, and elaborated by him and younger West African writers, such as Mensah Sarbah and Casely Hayford, during the period of consolidation of European rule.[6] Such texts were around, especially, for example in the African-American universities to which Africans in search of higher education gravitated – their ideas were available, as it were, whenever fashionable Western thought and the political situation in Africa, and elsewhere, caught up with them!)

Other nationalists similarly launched themselves into the political arena by mobilizing an ethnic following as the solid core of their constituency. Chief Obafemi Awolowo began by trying to make the Nigerian Youth Movement an effective political force during the war years, then, while in London as a law student in 1945, he joined with other Yoruba students to found the Yoruba cultural organization Egbe Omo Oduduwa (The Society of the Descendants of Oduduwa – Oduduwa being the mythical ancestor of the Yoruba people). In 1947 he declared Nigeria to be a 'mere geographical expression'. In 1948, on his return, he joined with prominent Yoruba from Lagos, to launch the Egbe Omo Oduduwa society into Nigerian public life, with the political commitment, along with its cultural aims, 'to accelerate the emergence of a virile modernised and efficient Yoruba state within the Federal State of Nigeria . . . [and] to unite the various clans in Yorubaland and generally create and actively foster the idea of a single nationalism throughout Yorubaland'.[7]

Such forceful assertions of Yoruba patriotism were prompted by the ascendancy of the National Council of Nigeria and the Cameroons (NCNC), led by Dr Nnamdi Azikiwe, an Ibo, in Nigerian nationalist politics during the mid-1940s, and consequent apprehension about the political orientation of Yoruba youth. But Azikiwe, too, could play the ethnic card. In 1949, addressing the Ibo State Union, he made his famous declaration that 'it would appear that the God of Africa has specially created the Ibo nation to lead the children of Africa from the bondage of the ages. . . . The martial prowess of the Ibo nation at all stages of human history has enabled them not only to conquer others but to adapt themselves to the role of preserver.'[8]

Western journalists, political scientists and, not least African nationalist leaders in their postcolonial role as 'founding fathers' of newly independent states, have combined to focus attention on ethnicity in the context of nation-building. The promotion of ethnicity was identified as hindering national integration and denounced, when exhibited by one's political opponents, as 'tribalism'. Indeed, the uninhibited assertions of ethnic pride by both Awolowo and Azikiwe in the immediate postwar period were to prove politically embarrassing when quoted against them by rivals at a later date. Awolowo's 1960 campaign autobiography, for example, provided a rather strained justification for his role in launching a Yoruba cultural solidarity movement on such nation-building grounds that 'the Yorubas . . . had become effete and decadent . . . it was widely bandied about that the Yorubas were no longer capable of leadership. . . . I thought it was in the best interests of Nigeria that the Yorubas should not be reduced to a state of impotence, into which they were fast degenerating.'[9]

But the historical study of nationalism has been bedevilled by failure to distinguish between nationalist politics and national integration. And not just the academic study of nationalism. Imperial officials from such old-established and relatively well-integrated nation-states as Britain, France and Portugal, tended to equate the absence of recognizable conditions of territory-wide nationhood within their African colonies as evidence that the new nationalist political movements lacked substance. But anti-colonial nationalists argued precisely the reverse. It was just because sociologically objective conditions of nationhood were absent that the idea of the nation as a project became supremely relevant, with unity having to be fashioned in the struggle for independence and consolidated in the new era of freedom.

Indeed, paradoxically, in the 1940s and 1950s the competitive mobilization of ethnicity was one of the most important means by which rival political leaders 'nationalized' the political process within a given colonial framework. The colonial town or city provided the arena within which the drama of competitive ethnic mobilization was initially played out. New immigrants were made abruptly and intensely aware of wider ethnic – as against purely local – identities when they left their home villages to seek work, education and general adventure in teeming, polyglot, highly competitive urban centres. They set up welfare organizations to ease their adjustment and the plight of those who had fallen on hard times. They gave fierce loyalty to their own sports clubs, especially soccer teams, and in the process they publicized new competitive spectator sports throughout the land. When Muslim they built their mosques in a competitive display of ethnic piety and in the process transformed the skyline of a city like Freetown, colonial capital of Sierra Leone, into a visible manifestation of the power of Islam. Their passion for improvement reached back to their rural homes as they set up organizations of the 'Sons Abroad' to promote welfare and scholarship schemes. Sooner or later these organizations began influencing politics back home, sponsoring those candidates for local office who displayed the proper blend of attachment to traditional loyalties and enthusiasm for modernization and improvement.

And they backed their ethnic heroes for provincial, even national office. Politicians like Awolowo and Azikiwe, or Kande Bureh, the schoolmaster leader of the Ambas Geda dance society among the Temne in Sierra Leone, became leaders of very effective vote-winning machines. (Ambas Geda is credited, first, with gaining the post of Temne tribal headman in Freetown for Bureh, the 'young men's candidate'; then, with being instrumental in wrenching control of Freetown from the local Krio-led political organizations and delivering it to the Protectorate-based Sierra Leone Peoples Party.)[10] It was all highly competitive and the collective process of competition stimulated more and more groups to stake their claims at every level of politics – but especially at the highest colonial, now increasingly 'national', level.

Privileged ethnic groups aimed to avoid such competition. This was most obvious in the case of European-settler regimes which sought to restrict citizenship on the basis of race or culture. Where such racial stratification existed right across colonial society, the sense of being exploited was both deeper and, above all, wider than in non-settler colonies where white privilege was less omnipresent. The task of putting together a broad national coalition was therefore somewhat eased when all Africans, whatever their ethnic identification, suffered exploitation as *Africans*, 'sons [and daughters] of the soil' robbed of their ancestral lands. On the other hand, the settler colony was usually much stronger than the average colonial state, with correspondingly more resources to buy the collaboration of certain selected groups from those who fell below the horizontal line of pure-white privilege. And, equally, it demonstrated scant inhibitions about curtailing such limited privileges, insecurity being the supposed guarantee of good behaviour in the collaborator system. With constitutions based on the premise of entrenched racial and ethnic privilege, the name of the political game was always 'divide and rule': witness the treatment of the 'Coloureds' and the whole development of segregation and apartheid in South Africa.

The immediate problem confronting Britain in East and Central Africa at the end of the war was the demand of the white settlers for greater freedom. But metropolitan powers confronted by such aspiring 'South Africas' as the settlers of Southern Rhodesia, Kenya and even – if the terms for incorporation into France were not right – Algeria, increasingly faced the delicate task of dealing with competing nationalisms. There was still some scope for manœuvre, with the metropolitan power employing its own delaying tactics of 'divide and rule', but much less than was realized at the time. With the competing nationalisms of settler and native proving mutually inflammatory, the sheer cost of maintaining metropolitan control rapidly threatened to become prohibitive.

There were also African peoples who claimed a privileged position, entitling them to detach themselves from the competitive coexistence of the emerging nationalist coalition within a given colonial territory on the basis of separatist self-determination. The classic case is that of the Baganda. When the British imposed control on Uganda in the late nineteenth century they followed their usual strategy of seeking out local collaborators. In the Baganda they found a people with a well-organized state system whose leaders willingly cooperated. The positions of the ruler of Buganda, the Kabaka, and the Baganda élite were guaranteed and, indeed, enhanced by the British. Many Baganda converted to Christianity, giving them a head-start in education and therefore in appointment to the new jobs created for Africans to staff colonial rule. Their help became instrumental in the extension of British control beyond Buganda, even down to supplying the ethnic terms by which the British labelled and controlled the other peoples of Uganda, prompting one writer to refer to Bagandan 'sub-imperialism'.[11] And they fully indulged colonialism's enormous condescension, referring to their mission to civilize the Bakedi, 'the naked ones', as they contemptuously referred to the surrounding peoples.

The special status of the Baganda was recognized formally in the Uganda Agreement of 1900, a treaty which gave them a remarkable degree of authority and autonomy within the British protectorate of Uganda. Buganda almost amounted to a state within the colonial state with its own monarch, the Kabaka, and its own parliament, the Lukiko, as well as a class of notables determined to preserve their prestige and authority. This favourable position was resented by the non-Baganda élites which emerged with the consolidation of colonial rule and the spread of mission activity. As they developed their own political organizations they focused on the Baganda as a common political enemy. The British also found it inconvenient to have such a powerful group of favoured collaborators inhibiting the development of a colony-wide collaborator system. Consequently the Baganda found themselves squeezed from both above and below.

The Baganda were especially suspicious of British postwar plans for economic development with the threat of more European and Asian intruders who would be given political status at least equal to their own. Above all they feared they would be submerged by amalgamation in British schemes for a Greater East Africa Federation. They responded by citing their legal entitlements under the 1900 treaty, arguing that it was subject to the principles of international law and that it signified that they were independent of, and equal to, the British. In effect they were claiming the right to determine their relations not just with the proposed federation but with the rest of colonial Uganda, even if that meant virtually complete autonomy. This somewhat optimistic reading of the Agreement was not shared by the British who could be ruthless with discarded collaborators.

The crisis in Anglo-Bagandan relations culminated in the Kabaka demanding that Buganda revert from Colonial Office to Foreign Office control, pending the implementation of a strict timetable for Buganda's separate independence.

Governor Sir Andrew Cohen responded with a brisk show of force, deposing and deporting the Kabaka in 1953. Such martyrdom simply strengthened the bonds of Buganda nationalism, obliging the British to retreat from their commitment to a unitary state for postcolonial Uganda. The Kabaka returned to his kingdom in 1955 amid the tumultuous rejoicing of his people. Although theoretically a constitutional monarch under the new Agreement of 1955, the Kabaka now wielded greater personal power than he or his father had ever done before.

Some Sierra Leone Colony Krios sought to counter the development of political parties based in the Protectorate by similar resort to legalities. The Sierra Leone National Council was formed to protest against the constitution drawn up by Governor Stevenson in 1947 which committed Britain to self-government, giving ultimate power to the majority of voters, who were drawn from the Protectorate. In September 1950 the National Council petitioned King George VI as 'British Subjects and Descendants of the Settlers, Maroons, and Liberated Africans for whom this settlement was acquired in 1787, and legally confirmed in 1788', protesting 'that it would be an abrogation of the democratic ideal to permit the illiterate masses of the Sierra Leone Protectorate [the petition claimed a 96 per cent illiteracy in the Protectorate] to overwhelm the advanced element of the Colony . . . on the mere grounds of population, even if British Protected Persons had a right to become members of Council.'[12] Krios traditionally prided themselves on the Colony's educational statistics, quoting them in favour of constitutional advance: thus James Africanus Horton pointed out in 1869 that 22 per cent of the population was involved in education, as against 16 per cent in Prussia and 13 per cent in England.[13] But in the mid-twentieth century 'fancy franchises', based on education and property, were associated with colonies of settlement. So, unabashed, the petition cited the precedent of the recent East African elections where the British had disregarded 'the overwhelming majority of indigenous masses of Africans', and therefore their professed democratic ideal, to allow 'a small minority of European settlers [to] control the legislature.'[14]

The British rejection of the Krios as preferred collaborators dated back at least to the proclamation of the Protectorate in 1896, with the shift towards Indirect Rule through the chiefs and the monopolization of higher-level posts by Europeans. (Although many Krios had availed themselves of the lower-level job opportunities provided by the expansion of colonial rule in Sierra Leone and elsewhere.) Like the Baganda they were squeezed between British distrust and Protectorate envy. Unlike the Baganda, however, they lacked a secure political base, as Bureh and the SLPP soon proved in Freetown itself. Nor did they have anything as effective as the Buganda monarchy through which to mediate their ethnic identity and their claims to legal entitlement, as well as rendering it more comprehensible and attractive to the British.

With no realistic chance of deflecting British constitutional policy, the National Council petered out, eventually to be replaced in the politics of nostalgia by the Settlers' Descendants Union. A rearguard legal campaign was mounted by elderly lawyers on behalf of true-blue 'Settler' – that is to say Krio – organizations. Younger Krio politicians increasingly worked within the new political parties, however. In the era of decolonization and independence, moreover, many Krios displayed a similar flair for survival, even promotion, through their indispensable bureaucratic expertise, as that exhibited by their predecessors under colonialism. Ironically, the apparently more secure, obviously more privileged, European settlers of East Africa, cited by the National Council in its 1950 plea that citizenship should be based on educational qualifications would soon need to demonstrate comparable versatility.

However awkward and unfashionable its stance, the National Council had a serious point. The implementation of the idea of 'self-determination', it held, should not simply be a matter of transferring control from the imperial power to a local successor government without proper constitutional safeguards for individual liberty, minority rights and free elections. Such views had a respectable pedigree, though they were usually expressed in the rhetoric of liberal optimism rather than legalistic conservatism. Woodrow Wilson's Fourteen Points had spoken of granting the peoples of Austro-Hungary the 'freest opportunity for autonomous development' at the end of the First World War, rather than automatically transforming the nations of the former Empire into nation-states. Hans Kohn's highly influential historical interpretation of nationalism distinguished between those nationalists whose concept of national self-determination was based on democratic claims – 'the inalienable rights of man' – rather than the purely national claims of 'freedom from foreign government'. (Kohn identified 'Western' concepts of national self-determination, deriving from the USA and Western Europe, as liberal-democratic, while 'Eastern' concepts, deriving from Germany and central and Eastern Europe, were essentially anti-foreign. As well as the general merits of his work, which were considerable, it could be construed as providing persuasive justification for the Allied war effort.)[15]

The most forceful expressions of the liberal-democratic concept of self-determination in postwar Africa came from the Union of South Africa and 'Overseas France'. Africans – along with Coloureds, Indians, and their liberal white allies – demanded equality of citizenship within the Union, challenging the ethnic and racial exclusiveness of Afrikaner nationalism, which Dr A. B. Xuma, President of the ANC likened to the philosophy of 'Dr Rosenberg in Hitler's Germany.'[16] The clarity and force of the ANC's demand for multiracial citizenship was partly impelled, though, by pressure from the Congress Youth League, formed in 1944 under the charismatic leadership of Anton Lembede who recommended that only the contrary strategy of a racially assertive African nationalism would produce mass mobilization.

Many of the emerging African political leaders of 'Overseas France' pursued the purely democratic concept of self-determination in the early postwar period. They were responding to the bold vision proclaimed in March 1945 by Paul Giacobbi, Minister for Colonies in the provisional government – which was then actually governing France – that they should be incorporated into the French Union as equal citizens while remaining citizens of their individual countries. Robert Delavignette, the prominent liberal colonial theorist hailed Giacobbi's speech as comparable to the Emperor Caracalla's edict of AD 212 conferring Roman citizenship on all free inhabitants of the Roman Empire.[17] Not only Leopold Senghor and Felix Houphouët-Boigny, but even Sekou Toure and Mobido Keita (both of whom were later to become defiantly anti-French) believed for a time that the nationalistic excesses of Fascists and Nazis aswell as increasing economic interdependence rendered national independence or 'separatism' a progressively outmoded concept. (General de Gaulle did much to popularize the terms 'separatism' and 'separatist' as negative equivalents of the positive term 'self-determination' in contemporary Francophone discourse; even more disparaging in Gaullist rhetoric were the denunciations 'secession' and 'secessionist'.) These African leaders sought self-determination in the democratization of the French Empire and participation as full citizens in the political life of France. In fact well into the late 1950s Africans served in the French National Assembly, Council of the Republic, and the Cabinet, as well as representing France internationally through serving as delegates to the United Nations. Certainly no other European empire achieved anything equivalent in the way of political incorporation.[18]

In a sense this was the culmination of assimilation. But it was the assimilation of an élite. The logic of that Francophone African political élite transcended national self-determination through embracing democratic self-determination. African leaders demanded local self-government, equality before the law, equal pay for equal work, equal welfare benefits, 'one man, one vote' – occasionally even 'one person, one vote' – on behalf of the Africans of France Overseas. West African labour leaders rapidly adapted their bargaining procedures to take up the cause 'of a universal industrial man – with common behaviour patterns and, surely, common needs. "Your goal is to elevate us to your level; without the means we will never succeed", said one union leader at a bargaining session [in January 1946], leaving his opposition speechless.'[19] Such aggressive egalitarianism was difficult enough to cope with at the colonial level; hard-pressed imperial officials hoped that the responsibilities of office would force African leaders to curb their rhetoric. The implications for metropolitan France were even more radical: to follow this democratic logic to its conclusion would have meant transforming the French nation-state into a multinational, multiracial state in which the native French were a minority. The fatal paradox of democratic self-determination was that, in France, that always remained an élite vision whose implications were never systematically explained to the ordinary citizens of the Fourth Republic. The vision of a Franco-African Empire *une et indivisible*, 'one and indivisible', eventually faded through piecemeal retreat, rather than any grand confrontation, prompting African disillusion in the late 1950s and early 1960s.

In Algeria, where 10 years earlier assimilationism through extension of citizenship had seemed possible, French overtures were rejected outright. Muslims were offered equal rights with French citizens and increased representation in local government by the provisional government. Abbas and the Ulamas (Muslim clerics), as well as Messali, denounced this as inadequate. 'Too little, too late', commented the historian of the Algerian Revolution, Alistair Horne.[20]

As a corollary of enfolding the Sub-Saharan Francophone political élite in the structures of the Assembly and the metropolitan political parties, French officialdom displayed sharp suspicion of alternative influences. Pan-Islamic ideas and Marxism were designated subversive, not only because of the thrust of their ideas, but also because they threatened the primacy of Paris. So also with Pan-Africanism: it was doubly suspect because it threatened Francophone assimilationism with the countervailing loyalty of racial and continental solidarity but also because Paris feared its 'Anglo-Saxon' and 'African American' connections. At the outset the insulation of Francophone Africa from these alien influences was largely successful. When Nkrumah and Kenyatta organized the fifth Pan-African Congress at Manchester in 1945 only two out of the 90 delegates came from French West Africa, both from Guinea. But why should Francophone Africans have bothered to attend? Some Manchester delegates, such as Wallace-Johnson and Awolowo had already made their mark in colonial politics; several more went on to play a prominent role in the independence politics of various states, with Hastings Banda as well as Nkrumah and Kenyatta becoming heads of state; whereas Senghor and Houphouët-Boigny, who were not present, were members of the French Assembly before becoming leaders of independent Senegal and Ivory Coast. To these sophisticates of the Parisian Assembly, the Manchester Congress, passing resolutions by delegates nobody had elected, with no effective powers to see them carried through, must have seemed a rather makeshift extension of student politics on the part of Anglophone Africa, cobbled together as a substitute for the realities of metropolitan parliamentary participation.

According to the British Colonial Secretary, Creech Jones, the Manchester Congress was also scarcely noticed by the Colonial Office. In 1945 the objectives of educated Africans were generally thought by British officialdom to be hopelessly unrealistic and therefore were not taken completely seriously. The Congress affirmed 'the right of all Colonial peoples to control their own destiny. All Colonies must be free from foreign imperialist control, whether political or economic.' Although the people of Africa were peaceful, the use of violence was not ruled out. 'We are determined to be free. . . . We are unwilling to starve any longer while doing the world's drudgery, in order to support by our poverty and ignorance a false aristocracy and a discredited imperialism.'[21]

Pan-Africanism had great ideological significance. The assertion of Pan-Negro solidarity and black pride was obligatory given the predominance of European racism. Generally, it helped black Africans repudiate various claims about Western superiority – cultural and technical as well as purely racial – in a period when it was not easy to do so. Its intercontinental character brought publicity and the idea of collective political action to remote areas of Africa. It provided a geopolitical context which transcended local colonial horizons so that Africans could perceive the moral and political fragility of the European empires in Africa. It helped leaders, like Kenyatta, to subsume local – 'tribal' – issues as grievances of 'the African' and gain colony-wide, sometimes even international, publicity, at a time when colonial structures tended to focus African politics at a parochial level.

In 1945 the colonial powers took Arab nationalism more seriously than its African counterpart. Arab states were already recognized as part of the international community at the United Nations. Indeed, already a few had been admitted to the League which, in any case, through confining Class A mandates to Arab countries effectively categorized them above Africans in claims to self-determination. In 1944–5 several Arab states, inspired by a common 'Arab spirit' and Islam, had formed the Arab League to coordinate their political activities.

Arab nationalism also enjoyed the prestige of similar scholarly treatment to that of its European counterpart. Hans Kohn's *Nationalism and Imperialism in the Hither East*, was published in New York in 1932, (originally in German in 1930), and George Antonius, a Lebanese Christian, serving the British administration in Egypt, published *The Arab Awakening: The Story of the Arab National Movement* in 1938. Both were essentially analytical histories of ideas, very similar in treatment to the pioneering classic studies of the development of nationalism in Europe by Carleton Hayes, *The Historical Evolution of Modern Nationalism* (1931), and nationalism generally by Kohn himself, *The Idea of Nationalism* (1944). From such accounts 'the rise of Arab nationalism' soon filtered into the conventional wisdom, quickly becoming an indispensable formula for understanding the course of modern history in the Middle East and North Africa.

The contrast between Antonius and Kenyatta is illuminating. Both published in 1938, but Kenyatta's book, like virtually all serious writing on African societies at that time, took the form of an ethnographic treatise, immediately identifying it as a study of primitives. The materials were certainly available in 1938 for a general study of African nationalism, especially one concentrating on the history of ideas, analysing the development of such writers as James Africanus Horton, Edward Blyden, Casely Hayford, Sol Plaatje, W. E. B. Dubois and Kobina Sekyi, as well as the African press, for example. But the dominant scholarly perspective on Africa was functionalist: Africans lived in tribes and so were proper subjects for anthropological study to discover their culture which programmed them to fit into tribal life without friction. There was a circularity about functionalist logic which trapped Africans in endless cycles of tribal culture. Subliminally, such scholarship denied the possibility of African intellectual history.

Arab nationalism, by contrast, was taken so much more for granted in the interwar period that Western observers did not regard it as requiring a modification of the analysis they had originally devised to explain their own nationalisms in Europe. There were special problems about the concept of 'Arab nationalism' when deployed by such outside observers, however. By customary Western nationalist definitions the Arabs were already a nation bound together by language and, to some extent, religion. But it was more difficult to reconcile Arab and Islamic political ideas with the conventional model of a modern nation-state than was generally realized. Much confusion stemmed from the lack of any exact Western translation of '*ummaya*', the total community of Islam (and by extension of all Arabs) and '*wataniya*', loyalty to and identification with the individual homeland. Westerners stuck to the term 'Arab nationalism' when 'Pan-Arab' or 'Pan-Islamic' would have been equally appropriate designations, further adding to the confusion caused by their basic failure to discriminate between nationalist politics and national integration.

Paradoxically, some of the strength of 'Arab nationalism' as a factor in world politics, derived from the perception of unity in the eye of the Western beholder. The unity the West perceived – and feared – was based on its traditional image, lumping all Arabs together on the basis of race and religion, even if in practice Arab politics tended to fragment through leadership rivalries.

The power of that image also derived from Western fascination with the pre-industrial, precolonial Islamic city, giving cover to urban mobs reminiscent of the Gordon rioters of 1780 London or revolutionary Paris. And such cities were expanding at an enormous rate, projecting an image of change careering out of control, prompting Western fears of being swept away by the swelling demographic tide. But the politicized crowd, as well as generating fear by tapping the generalized Western myth of Islam and the Arabs, and seeking to redress traditional distress at Western arrogance, could have quite specific aims derived from local circumstances. Cairo in particular exemplified this as, with wartime industrialization, its population shot up from almost 1.3 million in 1937 to over 2 million by 1947. Its turbulent crowd politics of mass demonstrations against the British, and those perceived as their Egyptian collaborators, culminated in the large-scale riots of February 1946 in which scores of people died, forcing the Nuqrashi government to resign. Arab politics – embracing nuances of Egyptian nationalism, Pan-Islamicism, and Pan-Arabism – were simplified by being lumped together under the single label 'Arab nationalism', in order to render them comprehensible and predictable.

Ironically, too, what gave Pan-Arabism its power and persistence in the postwar era was its most spectacular defeat, its failure to halt the Jewish immigration into Palestine between the wars, which swelled to flood-tide in the aftermath of the holocaust, then to prevent the catastrophic disinheritance of the Palestinians with the creation of Israel and the narrow recognition of the new Jewish state by the United Nations in 1948. But such a sequence of defeats clearly indicated the need to make cultural unity and common outrage politically effective. Above all it united the Arabs in abhorrence of their common enemies: Israel obviously, but also Britain, which had discharged its Palestinian mandate so feebly from an Arab standpoint. Also, possibly, the USA, which had combined crucial sponsorship of Israel with discriminating support for the rest of Britain's crumbling imperial position. Then what about France . . .? But the list could be extended almost indefinitely, according to circumstances. What Pan-Arabism could, and did, fix on was Western liberal opinion's inconsistency in renouncing colonialism in general while condoning the fate of the Palestinians. Zionist conspiracy and British hypocrisy featured as the most prominent actors in that tragedy.

The British, for the most part, naturally viewed their surrender of the Palestine mandate less critically. They agreed that it had ended in débâcle, in contrast to the decolonization of India and Pakistan which occurred almost simultaneously to general international approbation. They believed they had been reasonably even-handed but had come to see that neither side, Arab or Jew, was prepared to tolerate mere even-handedness. It was a hard lesson to learn for dedicated proconsuls committed to the view that they could legitimize themselves in the eyes of their subjects by providing disinterested public service. In Palestine they were to be denied even the dignity of quitting by arranging the phasing of their own decolonization. Hesitation about the forcible suppression of Jewish terrorism, because of concern about American opinion and the traditional sympathy of the governing Labour Party for Zionism, made postwar Palestine ungovernable. When the United Nations' special committee on Palestine recommended partition, the British believed that its implementation would lead to an Arab rising. As the mandatory power, should they attempt to repress this, their whole Middle Eastern position would be undermined by antagonizing the Arab states. Hence their decision to quit.

The unheroic ending of the mandate and the contrast with the negotiated decolonization of the Indian subcontinent, combined with the difficulties experienced by the French in Vietnam and the Dutch in Indonesia to ram home the message to the British that nationalism, once embattled – and certainly when embattled against another people claiming to be natives of the same land – was virtually impossible to cope with. Once a serious case of nationalism was diagnosed, then decolonization seemed the obvious, indeed the only, remedy. The skill lay in treating the patient before the disease got out of control. Self-government within the Commonwealth was the wonder drug to be supplied in judicious doses to suitable cases, while simultaneously soothing metropolitan nerves distressed by loss of empire. Compared to what had confronted them in Palestine, or earlier in Ireland, or even in India and Pakistan, the British still seemed to be faced with eminently reasonable, even patient, peoples in most of their African colonies. Moreover, Britain's position in Sub-Saharan Africa rested on the solid foundation of colonies and protectorates, rather than on treaty arrangements as was the case in so much of the Arab Middle East. Decolonization through phased progress to self-government within the Commonwealth was possible for Africans, whereas for most Arabs the retreat of British power simply meant the abrogation of existing treaties. The cultural ties of Christian conversion and education through the medium of the English language were further expected to strengthen the post-imperial connection in ways that were impossible with Muslim Arabs.

Even patient and reasonable peoples were caught up in the processes of modernization, however. The combined impact of the colonial state, capitalism, and the monotheistic missionary religions of Christianity and Islam, involved an enormous increase in scale and specialization of function. In politics, economics and religion such changes frequently entailed tension with the values encapsulated in local African society. Within the colonial state a system of political authority appropriate to the expanded scale of modernity faced a series of relatively small-scale and unspecialized local societies. Indirect Rule had been one way in which colonial and local authority adapted to each other. Now, in postwar Africa required to come to terms with modernization, new forms of mutual adaptation seemed required.

Nationalism appeared the obvious candidate. The 'upward' movement of local conflicts within African society to the territorial level of the colonial state increasingly 'nationalized' indigenous politics while, simultaneously, the colonial state reached downward through its collaborator system, as well as increased bureaucratic intervention, into local African society. Nationalist politics developed as an appropriate way to negotiate with the modern colonial state at both central and local levels. On the strength of its claim to have developed forms of politics suitable for a modern state, nationalism based its title to supersede colonialism. It condemned the colonial state as an essentially transitory phenomenon unable to make the transition to full modernization. But nationalist organizations claimed to be more than just modern political machines intent on wresting control of state power. The politics of nationalism, infused with traditional symbolism and idiom, fiercely defended indigenous society against alien encroachment. John Breuilly neatly sums up this capacity to embrace both local tradition and modernity: 'Nationalism thus always combines . . . incompatible concerns with modernity (in the form of statehood) and tradition (in the form of expressing the unspecialised culture of indigenous society).'[22]

In the postwar world some very influential imperial officials also chafed at the limitations of the colonial state. Sir Andrew Cohen, both as Colonial Office planner and, later, Governor of Uganda, for one. By definition the colonial state was stunted and incomplete: it was not self-standing; sovereignty was located in the metropolis; and the state's overarching bureaucratic command structure had to be adjusted to take account of such local citadels of power as Buganda, where the Governor's writ could be frustrated by the Kabaka and Lukiko. Such deficiencies made the colonial state very much less effective than the modern nation-state, which, operating on its home territory, featured in contemporary political and administrative theory – and which was exemplified in the political actuality of Britain, France, Portugal or Belgium, where imperial officials were born and educated, and to which they would probably retire. So long as 'Let sleeping dogs lie' was the maxim for successful colonial rule the discrepancy scarcely mattered; the colonial state's ambitions were suitably scaled down to its capacities. But once 'development' became central to imperial policy then its weaknesses were soon apparent. The new breed of activist colonial officials and the nationalists were hardly working to the same agenda but their programmes often converged sufficiently for them to form effective working alliances.

'Development' encapsulated a robustly optimistic approach to postwar reconstruction; an updating of the 'Dual Mandate', whereby the colony *en route* to becoming a nation-state, the metropolitan country and the world economy would all participate in the benefits of expansion. It was an amalgam of the confidence in planning which carried over from wartime victory into postwar British socialism and French reconstruction, together with the US 'Can do' approach that problems were there to be solved and the belief in incremental progress that sustained the international functionalism of the United Nations. Above all it represented a new crest of confidence in the capacities of states and interstate organizations to formulate ambitious but realistic policies and carry them through effectively.

Nationalism and internationalism combined to incite such hubris. The terms 'development' and 'modernization' offered a conceptual framework for ranking states in a hierarchy of wealth and power. Such a hierarchy, devised by Western social scientists and putting Western states top, was hardly culturally neutral; it proved internationally acceptable, even compellingly attractive, nevertheless. It particularly appealed to the rapidly growing army of diplomats, international bureaucrats and technocrats, which had to deal with inequalities of wealth and power between states, including colonial states and mandates, while eliminating the condescending terminology of racism and imperialism from its official vocabulary. Certainly 'modernization ' and 'development' were a radical and necessary improvement on 'primitive', 'tribalism', 'the natives', and the all-pervading concept of racial hierarchy, in explaining inequality in the increasingly intercontinental and multiracial world of international officialdom. (For example, the career of the African-American Ralph J. Bunche, who worked during the war in the State Department's Dependent Areas division and afterwards became an outstanding United Nations' trusteeship affairs official, exemplifies the changes in personnel which prompted a new etiquette of international race relations.) Also developmentalism proposed that rich and poor collaborate for their mutual benefit. As in both the West and the Socialist bloc, the emerging political leaders of Africa, and Asia, came to believe that their states could remould society through meticulous planning. 'Development', leading to liberation from dependence, became the essential corollary of decolonization.

The United Nations Declaration of Human Rights which was approved by the General Assembly in 1948, stimulated a crucial debate on the guidelines for state goals, especially through the economic and social rights which it embraced, in large part due to the pressure of the poor, ex-colonial states. Where earlier independence documents had concentrated on the formal constitution of authority and the relationship with the former imperial ruler, India and Israel set the fashion among the stream of newly arriving postcolonial states for also stressing economic and social justice and 'development'.[23] And the social sciences, especially through the rapid growth of development economics and the new-found preoccupation of political science with nation-building, sustained this sanguine approach.

Such optimism was cumulative. By the early 1950s, indeed, many social scientists considered the possibilities of policy and planning were almost limitless. Western leaders and social scientists, along with the anti-colonial nationalists, had convinced themselves that modernization and development, once initiated, were self-propelling processes. There was scant analytic consideration of the actual properties of the colonial or postcolonial state or how the state's capacities would be transformed by the transition to independence. It was simply assumed that this would happen. Indeed, the term 'state' was not much used; 'politics' was the current vogue word. This did not mean that the concept of the state was absent from the way in which social scientists thought about their policy recommendations, rather that it was uncritically taken for granted. Social scientists from all disciplines tended to advocate state activism, acquiring a vested interest, emotional and professional, in development.

What gave some added coherence and attraction to these rather loose-knit perspectives on the role of the state in development, was the simultaneous emergence of nationalism not only as the primary object of scholarly inquiry but the pervasive paradigm for self-consciously Africanist scholarship. Quite quickly, in the 1950s, nationalist interpretations displaced imperialist interpretations in giving over-all meaning and shape to African history and contemporary reality.

Two contrasting visions of Africa date from 1956: Lord Hailey's thorough updating of his *African Survey*, first published in 1938, a monumental work of well over 1,600 pages, and Thomas Hodgkin's pocket-sized, 200-page, *Nationalism in Colonial Africa*. Contrasting classics in style and substance, as well as size and weight, they epitomized the old and the new approaches. Hailey preferred the term 'Africanism' to 'nationalism', considering it more inclusive. Yet what he meant by 'Africanism' was in fact close to Hodgkin's use of protest as an organizing concept which embraced all forms of anti-colonial action as aspects of nationalism. Where they differed was that Hailey considered that 'Africanism' could be divided into a 'more constructive' phase, akin to European nationalism, aiming at 'a government dominated by Africans and expressing in its institutions the characteristic spirit of Africa as interpreted by the modern African', and a 'less constructive phase' which was simply a reaction against European dominance in political and economic affairs.[24] Hailey devoted 10 pages, tucked into one chapter of his encyclopaedic study of colonial objectives and structures, to a lucid summary of the 'Rising Spirit of Africanism'. His account, written from an essentially administrative viewpoint, concluded dryly that 'it has so far shown little coherence, and . . . to all appearances it lacks any one pattern or any common objective'.[25] Hodgkin's book, on the other hand, is suffused with the excitement of nationalism in action and delights in the variety and ingenuity of African protest politics.

In African studies the new paradigm of African action rapidly displaced the old preoccupation with colonial structures. Like Hodgkin, the vast majority of the new breed of Africanist scholars identified strongly with the movement for African independence. They became preoccupied with what they categorized as the processes of nation-building. In African religious history, for example, they fastened on the emergence of a mission-educated 'Westernized' or modernizing élite whose political ambitions transcended the purely local focus of Indirect Rule, as well as the development of separatist churches whose breakaway from mainstream mission Christianity was interpreted as proto-nationalist.

Modernization and nationalism were regarded as aspects of a single unilinear process, while both the modernization and nationalist approaches to African realities were alike in focusing on progress by the community as a whole rather than conflict within it. The large-scale social trends, such as urbanization, which, collectively, were labelled 'modernization and development' by Western social scientists, statesmen and proconsuls, were the precise forces on which the would-be nationalist rulers confidently expected to ride to victory.

The viewpoint of those a little lower down the colonial hierarchy – or of missionaries with pastoral responsibilities – was frequently less sanguine. Rapid urbanization, for example, which to the optimists appeared such a vital component of modernization and nationalism, was fraught with intractable social problems. Just as in North Africa and the Middle East, the flight from the countryside to the shanty-towns which grew up in the interstices of the cities and the urban periphery of Sub-Saharan Africa, suggested uncontrollable and dangerous social change as the pre-industrial 'mob' merged into the modern 'masses'. The bland words 'urban unemployment' signified a struggle for survival at the lowest levels of subsistence. Officials struggling with the consequences of modernization at this level snatched at decolonization as a solution to the problems of colonialism more in desperation than optimism. Ironically, those forces which made the nationalist accession to power appear inevitable could, from a slightly different perspective, be interpreted as social disintegration rather than modernization. But as subordinates in a well-oiled bureaucratic machine, by definition, the critics were aware of the perils of insubordination and normally kept their doubts confidential. Thus the visible processes of decolonization were carried through with ceremonial self-confidence.

CALCULATIONS OF CONTAINMENT

This chapter and its predecessor have been concerned with the adaptation and accommodation of the imperial powers, and the evolving international order, to the rise of Arab and African nationalism. But adaptation and accommodation involved a two-way process; those nationalisms also adapted to the emerging postcolonial international system.

The movements which Europeans and North Americans, as well as Africans, understood as 'nationalist' in postwar Africa subsumed complex and diverse processes. Only some of the forces involved were accommodated, to their own satisfaction, in postcolonial state structures. While the international system accommodated African and Arab nationalism, the new rulers, under the pressure of events, redefined and contained that nationalism. Such containment frequently began before formal independence – indeed became an essential component of the process of decolonization.

Not only rulers but scholars, too, eventually became involved in redefining nationalism. The separatist or independent churches are a case in point. Few scholars would now find the proto-nationalist label very useful, partly because postcolonial states have found many such religious movements at least as awkward to handle as did their imperial predecessors. Indeed some of the best-known erstwhile exponents of the proto-nationalist classification have more recently argued that such a reductionist approach – that is one that 'reduces' essentially religious events to aspects of political and economic processes – is seriously misleading.[26] Women's movements also found themselves frequently marginalized in the postcolonial order.[27] Peasants and urban workers often felt excluded. Indeed Pan-Africanism itself, the inspiration for nationalists in waiting, was similarly marginalized by nationalists in power.

NOTES

1 Cited in Herbert G. Nicholas, *The United Nations as a Political Institution* (2nd edn., London, Oxford University Press, 1962), p. 197.

2 Cited in H. Wiberg, 'Self-Determination as an International Issue', in I. M. Lewis, ed., *Nationalism and Self-Determination in the Horn of Africa* (London, Ithaca Press, 1983), p. 43.

3 Jomo Kenyatta, *Facing Mount Kenya* (London, Mercury, 1962), p. xviii.

4 Manifest in Bronislaw Malinowski's flair for eye-catching titles: *Argonauts of the Western Pacific* (London, Routledge, 1922); *Crime and Custom in Savage Society* (London, Kegan Paul, 1926); *Sex and Repression in Savage Society* (London, Kegan Paul, 1927); *Sexual Life of Savages* (London, Routledge, 1928).

5 Kenyatta, *Facing*, p. 309.

6 Henry S. Wilson, *Origins of West African Nationalism* (London, Macmillan, 1969), deals with these writers.

7 James S. Coleman, *Nigeria: Background to Nationalism* (University of California Press, 1958), p. 344.

8 *Op. cit.*, p. 347.

9 O. Awolowo, *Awo: The Autobiography of Chief Obafemi Awolowo* (Cambridge, Cambridge University Press, 1960), p. 166.

10 Michael Banton, *West African City* (London, Oxford University Press, 1957), deals with Ambas Geda generally. For the electoral politics see Martin Kilson, *Political Change in a West African State: A Study of the Modernization Process in Sierra Leone* (Cambridge, MA., Harvard University Press, 1966), pp. 227–80.

11 A. D. Roberts, 'The Sub-Imperialism of the Baganda', *Journal of African History* III (1962), pp. 435–50.

12 C. Fyfe, *Sierra Leone Inheritance* (London, Oxford University Press, 1964), pp. 326–9.

13 Cited in Wilson, *Origins*, pp. 173–4.

14 Fyfe, *Inheritance*, p. 328.

15 Hans Kohn, *The Idea of Nationalism* (New York, Macmillan, 1944).

16 T. Karis and G. M. Carter, eds., *From Protest to Challenge* (4 vols., Stanford, CA., Stanford University Press, 1973) II, p. 276.

17 Edward Mortimer, *France and the Africans* (London, Faber, 1969), p. 55.

18 *Op. cit.*, p. 20.

19 Cited in F. Cooper, 'From Free Labor to Family Allowances: Labor and African Society in Colonial Discourse', *American Ethnologist* XVI (1989), p. 754.

20 Alistair Horne, *A Savage War of Peace* (London, Macmillan, 1977), p. 43.

21 R. D. Pearce, *The Turning Point in Africa* (London, Frank Cass, 1982), p. 136, for Jones, the Colonial Office and Congress resolutions.

22 John Breuilly, *Nationalism and the State* (Manchester, Manchester University Press, 1985), p. 193.

23 A. P. Blaustein, J. Sigler and B. R. Beede, eds., *Independence Documents of the World* (Dobbs Ferry, NY, Oceana, 1977).

24 Lord Hailey, *An African Survey, Revised 1956* (London, Oxford University Press, 1957), pp. 252–3.

25 *Op. cit.*, p. 254.
26 T. O. Ranger, 'Religious Movements and Politics in Sub-Saharan Africa', *African Studies Review* XIX (1986), pp. 1–69, especially pp. 1–5.
27 S. Geiger, 'Women and African Nationalism', *Journal of Women's History* II (1990), pp. 227–37.

8

Accelerated Decolonization – North Africa and the Horn

The territories running through the Mahgreb, Egypt and the Sudan to the Horn of Africa can be conveniently grouped together. Despite the variety of peoples, the presence of Islam provides a generally unifying cultural influence. Moreover many of the inhabitants, especially in the north, were Arabs, and as such, by conventional definition, prone to 'Arab nationalism', a concept formulated before the Second World War which was considered increasingly descriptive and predictive of the subsequent course of events in North Africa and the Middle East. Italy's defunct African Empire – comprising Libya, Eritrea, Italian Somaliland, and, briefly, Ethiopia – was also located here. That, too, gave the region a certain geopolitical coherence both in the plans of wartime strategists and in the postwar presence of the victorious British armies. Finally, it meant that a large part of the region was scheduled for changed political status, perhaps even rapid decolonization, through the processes of the postwar peace settlement.

Some such generalized concept as 'Arab nationalism', and by extension 'Islam', seemed especially relevant to the British given their primary interest in preserving their world system across the whole area, through a series of treaties and informal arrangements, rather than retaining control over any specific colony. In June 1946 J. S. Bennett of the Colonial Office pointed out the contrast with France:

> I believe it is now a choice between treating the Arab world as a whole (in which case we can look for good relations with it), or having a series of 'bridgeheads' along the Mediterranean coast into a hostile Arab interior. You can't play both policies at once. The French and the Zionists (and previously the Italians) frankly go for the 'bridgehead' policy. I don't believe that, with our wide Middle Eastern interests, we can afford to.[1]

The 'bridgehead' option was closed, fortunately as Bennett believed, for there were no North African equivalents of the Rhodesias or Kenya, to compete with the large French settlements in the Mahgreb, and deflect Britain from formulating its policy with primary reference to the Muslim majority. (Bennett was making a general point, but he was also specifically concerned that Britain deter a mass return of Italian settlers to Cyrenaica and thus saddle itself with another potential Palestine.)[2]

The French presence in North Africa was substantial and unquestioned, a matter of the solid, unbudging presence of the settlements in the Mahgreb. The most powerful of these, Algeria, moreover, was bound to the metropolis by the conception of France as an indivisible Republic which had incorporated Algeria as an integral part of its being. Disassociation – dubbed 'secession' – would therefore present apparently insuperable, virtually inconceivable, problems of legitimacy involving the constitutional basis of the Fourth Republic. Britain's presence in North Africa and the Middle East, by contrast, was a matter of choice, of decision-making consequent on the interaction of groups of policy-makers seeking to protect British interests in a rapidly changing international environment.

In 1945–6 Britain's power and prestige in North Africa and the Middle East was at its peak with a large military presence throughout the area in the aftermath of the successful North African campaigns. The pivot of British imperial strength was the world's most elaborate military complex, the Suez base, occupying over 750 square miles, with 10 airfields and facilities for flying boats, equivalent provision for land and sea forces, its own assembly plants and factories, docks and railway system, as well as barracks, hospitals and recreational facilities. At the end of the war there were over 200,000 British troops there. By 1951 the Labour government had succeeded in reducing this, at least for statistical purposes, to 38,000, but this was still nearly four times the 10,000 allowed by the Anglo-Egyptian Treaty of 1936.

Britain sought to translate this swollen military presence into postwar regional predominance, by winning lasting goodwill as the wartime sponsor of Arab co-operation – Bennett's 'treating the Arab world as a whole' – through encouraging the major states in the region to form the Arab League in March 1945. With atheistic Soviet Communism defined as the main threat to Islam, Arab nationalism, guided gently but firmly, was thus expected to develop in ways that did not threaten the continued British presence.

Why did the British seek to keep their wartime grip on the Middle East? The option of retreat was specifically raised at the time by none other than the new Labour Prime Minister, Clement Attlee, who also held the office of Minister of Defence. Traditionally the British viewed the Middle East as crucial to their imperial strategy because it constituted the bridge to India. In February 1946 Attlee argued that, with Indian independence well on the way, the value of the Suez Canal to Britain was much less obvious. 'We should be prepared to work round the Cape to Australia and New Zealand', he argued. In March he suggested withdrawing from the Middle East altogether to 'a line of defence across Africa from Lagos to Kenya', thus placing 'a wide glacis of desert and Arabs between ourselves and the Russians'.[3]

Foreign Secretary Ernest Bevin was interested in such defence proposals for British tropical Africa, but envisaged them underpinning, rather than replacing, the British position in Egypt. Indeed, Bevin, somewhat typically, transformed Attlee's proposals for strategic withdrawal into a scheme to coordinate the economic development of tropical Africa and the Middle East, not least because it might attract a larger South African contribution towards 'our manpower, financial and industrial requirements.' He looked to 'a thorough development of the Middle East trade area, particularly in the belt extending from West to East Africa, [which] could offset the cost of the small defence commitment in the Mediterranean', and proposed that an interdepartmental committee study 'the political, industrial, commercial and strategic implications of developing East and West Africa, and the development of a Lagos–East Africa trunk road.'[4]

The Chiefs of Staff were concerned by Bevin's suggestion that the Middle East might be defended at no great expense but agreed wholeheartedly with him that Attlee's notion that it should be abandoned was wrong-headed. Attlee himself was no defeatist. He believed that the British Empire had been based upon sea power, hence in the new epoch of the atom bomb, with air and sea power interlinked, Britain must recast its defence strategy. In particular, he considered the Mediterranean fleet would be vulnerable. In 1946, with the commitment of the United States to defend Western Europe apparently very uncertain in view of America's hasty demobilization, he believed that it behoved Britain, which was so committed, to concentrate its forces. Once Bevin and the Chiefs of Staff made their opposition plain, however he concentrated on holding down costs.[5]

Bevin was not the only Commonwealth statesman to see Britain's position in the Middle East as pivotal to Commonwealth strategy and the survival of the British world system. In 1946 the leaders of Australia, New Zealand and South Africa all regarded the eastern Mediterranean as vital to their security. Smuts, with the authority of his military background and experience of shaping the post-1918 world order, called on the Empire-Commonwealth to hold the balance between the Soviet Union and the United States. He painted an ominous scenario of potential Soviet expansion into Africa, and beyond, through gaining control of the eastern Mediterranean and the Red Sea.[6] Such ideas corresponded to Bevin's own belief, shared by some top officials at the Foreign Office, that Britain's immediate postwar weakness was serious but not chronic. Moreover, through taking the initiative in organizing a 'Third Force', 'Euro-Africa', based on British leadership in both Europe and the Commonwealth, Britain would both compensate for its immediate weakness, relative to the United States and the Soviet Union, and create the conditions for economic recovery and parity with the two superpowers.

The notion of a 'Third Force', organizing the middle of the world from Scandinavia to the Cape, culminating in a Euro-African grouping which would counterbalance United States' predominance in the western hemisphere and Soviet domination to the east, had a strong geopolitical appeal to a generation of Europeans educated by their colour-coded maps to a vision of the world revolving around London and Paris rather than Washington and Moscow.

Decolonization was central to this grandiose conception of Euro-Africa. In November 1947 British governors of African dependencies were informed of 'the very special importance' Britain attached to colonial cooperation because of its value in relations between the Western powers and the 'practical benefits which it might bring to Africa' with the aim that when the African colonies reached self-government, they would 'form part of Western and above all European civilisation'.[7]

The idea of a British-led 'Third Force' was short-lived, foundering on the economic and political realities of the postwar world. The brief appearance of an anglophile Socialist government in France in early 1947 facilitated the signing of the Dunkirk Anglo-French treaty of alliance in March. But by then the freezing cold and blizzards of that winter had virtually closed down the factories and mines for several weeks, creating an economic crisis in which the Chancellor, Hugh Dalton, warned the Cabinet that 'we are racing through our United States dollar credit at a reckless, and ever accelerating, speed.'[8] Internationally, rapid withdrawal from India, Greece, Turkey and Palestine during 1947 meant that in practice Britain had abandoned the role of world balancer between East and West. By October 1948 the Foreign Office abandoned the prospect of leading a 'Third Force' and opted for the 'Special Relationship', a privileged British role in an American-led Atlantic Alliance. Nevertheless, in the critical years of peacemaking the 'Third Force' concept influenced British policy towards Africa, and Bevin himself only finally rejected it after the October 1949 devaluation crisis.[9]

United States policy was also evolving, simultaneously closing old options while offering fresh possibilities to its allies. The Truman doctrine hastily improvised to cope with Britain's retreat from Turkey and Greece in March 1947, the Marshall plan for European reconstruction in June 1947 and, finally, the formation of the North Atlantic Treaty Organization in April 1949, signified the United States' unequivocal assumption of Western leadership. Concepts like the 'Third Force' and the 'Special Relationship' do influence events, especially immediate events. When ideas are based on a true appreciation of past and present trends – which the 'Third Force' manifestly was not – they may powerfully mould the future. But even then they are always simplifications, and therefore to some extent distortions, of history; with the consequence that future events will bring them into question, and produce changes of perception and policy. Thus British policy towards the Middle East evolved, as present ideas incorporated much intellectual baggage from the past, with the notion of the 'Third Force' imperceptibly merging into the 'Special Relationship'.

Henceforth Britain's role in the Middle East was identified as the key to the 'Special Relationship' and, therefore, to its continued status as a great power. The Chiefs of Staff put the point forcefully in November 1949, with reference to the implications of Libyan independence:

> Today, we are still a world power, shouldering many and heavy responsibilities. We believe the privileged position that we, in contrast to the other European nations enjoy with the United States and the attention which she now pays to our strategic and other opinions, and to our requirements, is directly due to our hold on the Middle East and all that this involves.
>
> If we surrendered that hold and the responsibilities which it entails, we would automatically surrender our position as a world power, with the inevitable strategic and economic consequences. We should join the ranks of the other European powers and be treated as such by the United States.[10]

To the Chiefs of Staff and Bevin, Egypt's special importance derived from proximity to both the Soviet Union and the Middle Eastern oilfields, considered crucial both for Western defence strategy and postwar reconstruction. (The Soviet occupation of northern Persia till mid-1946 highlighted the danger.) From Suez and lesser bases Britain could organize the defence of the oilfields and strike with its bombers into Soviet territory. The oil argument became increasingly persuasive as Britain, from the early 1950s, grew progressively dependent on Middle Eastern oil for its own economy and, even more, to sustain the sterling area and Britain's exchange earnings in Europe. Moreover, as neither King Farouk or the Wafdist Party were equivalent in either local legitimacy or pro-British reliability to Congress and Pandit Nehru, rapid decolonization through transferring power to a strong nationalist party and leader, on the Indian model, was ruled out.

Britain was now trapped in a vicious cycle. Bevin himself sought a nationalism based on peasants not pashas but Britain's world role made this impossible. The hollowness of British-sponsored nationalism and Pan-Arabism, increasingly apparent after the Arab League failed to prevent the creation of the state of Israel, led to the continuing perceived need to preserve a strong military presence in order to defend British interests and sustain the 'friends' of Britain in office. But such 'friends' were always vulnerable, while they, in turn, were tempted to seek nationalist legitimacy by stressing their anti-Western credentials. (Thus Bevin was continually harassed at the United Nations by Egypt over the Suez base.) This, though, is to anticipate that cycle of mistakes, misunderstandings and provocations, that culminated in Britain's involvement, with France, and in conspiracy with Israel, in the Suez débâcle. The immediate postwar problem in North Africa and the Horn – and the occasion of so many pronouncements on Britain's role in the postwar world[11] – was the disposal of Italy's African Empire.

THE DISSOLUTION OF THE ITALIAN EMPIRE

General accounts of African decolonization frequently scant, or omit altogether, the dissolution of Italy's African Empire. Given its timing, out of phase with the major sequences of decolonization in British and French Africa, this is understandable. Because it came so much earlier, as a by-product of the defeat of Fascist Italy and the subsequent peace settlement, the international political context is somewhat different, making it difficult to fit into the predominant patterns of postwar decolonization. But for those regions which were involved – the areas of the Horn and of North-East Africa, both along the Mediterranean littoral and, at the opposite extreme, where the southward thrust of cultural expansion had never been entirely checked by European colonial rule – the early timing of Italian Africa's independence was to be crucial. In addition, both the Horn and North-East Africa were considered areas of special strategic significance and attracted great-power scrutiny.

For one great power, Britain, struggling to maintain its position in the first rank against the postwar predominance of the United States and the Soviet Union, the disposal of the Italian colonies had an especially poignant significance. These territories had been fought over – indeed, Cyrenaica had seen some of the fiercest tank battles of the Second World War – and because these wars in the desert and the Horn were won by British and Dominion forces British soldiers and statesmen assumed that they had earned the right to some say in their disposal. There were solid as well as sentimental consequences of wartime glory: British military personnel and British bases were deployed across this huge arc of former Italian territory, only intersected by the Anglo-Egyptian Sudan, stretching from Cyrenaica to the Horn.

In these postwar times of institutionalized anti-imperialism, moreover, the British enjoyed the security of being present with international approval. When the 'big five', plus 16 of their smaller allies, failed to reach agreement on the future of the Italian colonies at the 1947 Paris Peace Conference, they were left under British military rule, with the proviso that if no other arrangement was reached within a year they would be turned over to the United Nations General Assembly. No such arrangement was made, so – pending the General Assembly's decision – the British military supplied administrative continuity. (At substantial cost as Attlee never ceased to point out.)[12] In the countdown to the Assembly's decision, with his soldiers offering expansive advice, and his Prime Minister counselling financial caution, Bevin manœuvred to influence the outcome. As a first brush with African decolonization, it seemed a suitable scenario for implementing the traditional British policy of sustaining their world system by informal treaty arrangements. But this time, as both Attlee and Chancellor Dalton insisted, that really would have to mean – what Britain's foreign critics had often dubbed it – 'imperialism on the cheap'.

The Italian conquest of Ethiopia lasted a mere five years from 1935 to 1940. It never commanded international legitimacy. So decolonization in this case was especially swift, though not without complications.

After the Italian defeat, with British military forces in effective control of the country, Haile Selassie returned to his throne in 1941. Britain recognized Ethiopian independence by the Anglo-Ethiopian Agreement of January 1942, although it imposed irksome limitations on Ethiopian sovereignty, including provisions that no foreign advisers should be appointed without British consent and that cases involving foreigners should be heard by a British judge. As peace approached such irritants were removed in a second agreement of December 1944, though not before provoking bitter Ethiopian resentment.

Of more lasting significance was that the British retained control of the Somali-inhabited areas of Ethiopia. This meant that Britain now – for the first time – ruled the vast majority of the Somali people through its military administration in Ethiopia and former Italian Somaliland as well as British Somaliland, and the colonial administration of Kenya. (Only French Somaliland remained outside the British orbit.)

As early as 1941 the British had floated ideas of a Greater Somalia, perhaps under joint Anglo-Ethiopian trusteeship. Some senior officials in the Military Administration had worked among the Somali in the pre-war colonial service. They were committed to rectifying the anamolous situation of the Somali which arose from the partition of this pastoral people, with their strong, if fractious, sense of identity, ecologically committed to ranging with their herds across imposed boundaries. Officials had been seconded from units which had routed the Italian forces before the United States entered the war and they assumed that Britain was fully entitled to introduce such boundary changes unilaterally in the best interests of the inhabitants involved.

Lord Moyne, the Cabinet member resident in Cairo, recommended that it was 'desirable to unite the whole Somali population under one administration'.[13] In London there was support for prompt action on Moyne's proposal but such a wartime *fait accompli* was ruled out by the War Cabinet's directive that any arrangement with Ethiopia should await the final peace settlement. The band-waggon British lobby for 'Greater Somalia' had crashed into what was developing into a major issue in East–West relations. The Western states were involved in diplomatic argument with Stalin over recognition of his acquisition of the Baltic states and other territories in Eastern Europe and had bound themselves to leave the settlement of postwar frontiers until the final Peace Conference. Plainly the future of the Ogaden could not be treated as a special case. Pending the general peace settlement, Britain sought American support for the Greater Somalia project. The response was discouraging. Drew Pearson, a well-known anti-British columnist, suggested there was a conspiracy between the State Department and Britain to see that Ethiopia was denied the Ogaden. The British Ministry of Information commented sombrely: 'The story is of a kind which is likely to be believed by virtually all his readers, both official and lay.'[14] At the Anglo-American conference in Quebec in 1944, Secretary of State Cordell Hull handed Churchill a memorandum stating bluntly that 'since the Ogaden is an integral part of an independent sovereign state and ally any change in its status should not be considered.'[15]

Ethiopia had already consolidated its international standing during wartime. Its unique history guaranteed a sympathetic response, especially in the United States. Ethiopia had emerged from the scramble into the colonial period in the singular position of a black Christian state, with a royal lineage, claiming descent from the legendary son of King Solomon and the Queen of Sheba, which not only survived but actually profited from European partition. Like the European empires in Africa, Ethiopia was a conquest state. Its core people were the politically dominant Semitic-speaking Amharas. Socially the Amharas comprised a loose three-tier hierarchy with military aristocrats and clergy living off the surplus production of a cereal-growing lay peasantry which also reared cattle. Amhara stratification contrasted sharply with the traditional egalitarianism of the nomadic Cushitic-speaking pastoralists. The Muslim Somalis, now numbering around 4 million, for example, were organized in segmentary lineages, led by assemblies of elders rather than formally appointed chiefs. Many of the other pastoralist peoples, especially the numerically dominant Oromo, were gradually assimilated as they moved northward in search of better grazing, becoming Muslim in Somali areas, while converting to Christianity and adopting Amharic in the well-watered highlands. Such assimilation was eased by the Amhara kinship system which gives almost equal emphasis to maternal and paternal ties. Indeed Amharaized Oromo, and other assimilated groups, played prominent roles in the expansion of the Amhara Empire to the south and east. Unlike the European empires in Africa, or the European-settler states, therefore, the core of the Ethiopian Empire was an indigenous centralist nationalism, a local political élite, capable of assimilating – as well as dominating – some individuals and groups from neighbouring, less stratified and centralized peoples.[16]

Amhara conquest and expansion reached its furthest extent under the Emperor Menelik, an astute and forceful participant in the 'scramble' who exploited European competition for predominance in the area to modernize his army and routed the Italians at Adowa in 1896. The Ethiopians, as much as their European competitors, stressed their sacred civilizing mission to bring the benefits of Christian rule to benighted heathen subjects. In a series of treaties Menelik awarded trading rights to Britain, France and Italy together with recognition for their various spheres of influence along the coast, while in exchange they supplied the international recognition to legitimize his recent conquests. Consequently Eritrea and three-quarters of the Somali people were brought under European rule, while the remainder (the Ogaden), Harar and the southern Oromo areas were assigned to Ethiopia.

Ethiopia was immensely significant as a brilliant symbol of black achievement, especially to Pan-Africanists. The manner of its eventual loss of independence, after a ruthless invasion by Mussolini, ensured that its lustre was further enhanced as the Allies mobilized against fascism. Marcus Garvey's 'Back to Africa' movement demonstrated that this was Pan-Africanism with mass appeal. On a popular level, also Emperor Haile Selassie became a charismatic figure especially among Caribbean communities both within and outside the West Indies. The Rastafarian movement took its name from Haile Selassie's title before his imperial coronation. (For Rastafarians Haile Selassie remains the Black Messiah and Ethiopia heaven on earth, even though he was deposed by the Ethiopian Revolution in September 1974 and died in captivity a few months later.)

In December 1943 Roosevelt received the first Ethiopian minister to the United States, and in February 1945 on his way home from the Crimean conference the President met Haile Selassie. Ethiopia, appropriately as one of the first victims of fascism, won further international leverage as a founder member of the United Nations. Shortly after the end of the war it commissioned an American public relations consultant, J. C. Cairns, who enlisted the help of prominent personalities, including Mrs Roosevelt, to ensure popular goodwill was translated into effective diplomatic support.[17] There was no Somali lobby to counter the support of African-American organizations and such celebrities as Paul Robeson for Ethiopia in what they believed to be a British attempt to bully a small black state with which they personally identified.

Pre-war geological surveys by the Italians indicated that oil might be found in the Ogaden. In 1944 the American-owned Sinclair Oil Company, backed by the State Department, began secret negotiations with the Ethiopian government for sole prospecting rights. Should oil be found in commercial quantities such a monopolistic agreement would give the United States greater power to fix world oil prices. In 1945 when the news broke that Sinclair had succeeded in secretly negotiating such a deal during wartime in a British area of operations there was anger in London and disquiet elsewhere.[18]

An amalgam of sentiment, suspicion and hard-headed commercial interest worked against the presumed 'special relationship' in the Horn. Here was a fine opportunity for the United States to demonstrate anti-colonial credentials while protecting the interests of an American oil company. Henceforth the three-way relationship between Britain, Ethiopia and the United States provides an intricate study in the diplomacy of dependency, with the Emperor attaching himself firmly to the United States just when the British were being forced to come to terms with American dominance.[19]

This was the situation when Bevin took up the cause of Greater Somalia by proposing the reunification of all the Somalilands, including the Ogaden, as a United Nations Trust Territory. In Bevin's eyes this amounted to simple justice. He read the treaties of partition, which underwrote colonial and Ethiopian boundaries, glossed by the Somali experts in the British Military Administration, and agreed that the Europeans and Menelik had reached their agreements at the expense of the peripheral peoples. Indeed, some of the treaties which were regarded as giving a legal basis for incorporating the Somali within alien political structures seemed to have been wilfully misinterpreted. But Bevin's proposal to reunite the Somali nation met stiff international opposition, not just from influential sections of American opinion, but also from Molotov in the 1946 Paris meeting of the Council of Foreign Ministers. Britain generally took the same line in the immediate postwar discussions between the 'Big Three' as it had in the war, 'that nineteenth century imperialism was dead in England, which was no longer an expansionist country'; in this particular case Bevin 'was merely trying to right nineteenth century wrongs.'

Molotov, intent on forcing recognition for the pro-Soviet Bulgarian and Rumanian governments, pounced: 'England has troops and military bases in Greece, Denmark, Egypt, Iraq, Indonesia, and elsewhere. The Soviet Union has no bases beyond its borders, and this shows the difference between expansion and security.' He also, mischievously, suggested that the Soviet Union be granted an African colony, such as Tripolitania; should none of Italy's be available then the Belgian Congo would do nicely. (The location, as he did not need to remind his Anglo-American audience, of their strategically vital supplies of uranium.) Pierson Dixon, Bevin's Private Secretary thought the Soviet attack on 'Greater Somalia' was designed to impress the Americans: 'The Russians . . . know the American phobia about the British Empire'.[20] Bevin decided to cut his losses and withdraw the Greater Somalia plan, at least for the time being, much to the surprise and chagrin of many of his officials. (There is an obvious parallel between Bevin's clash and American support for Zionism to the neglect of Palestinian rights, which was developing at the same time.) Instead of a Greater Somalia under joint trusteeship, with the threat of Soviet participation, the Western allies now proposed a brief revival of Italian colonialism to be devoted to guiding Italian Somaliland to independence under a United Nations' mandate.

What made this particularly attractive to Bevin was that it fitted into the context of British foreign policy by corresponding with British and Italian efforts to revive their traditional friendship after the Axis interlude. With the largest support for Communism in Western Europe but an apparent anti-Communist majority, post-Fascist Italy was courted by both sides as the Cold War developed. The head of the East African Department of the Colonial Office, Andrew Cohen, realistically acknowledged that African questions must be kept subordinate to grand strategy because Italy had to be kept 'on the right side of the iron curtain'.[21] The approach of the April 1948 Italian general election intensified this ideological competition. With the future of Italy's colonies still undecided but now in the hands of the General Assembly, the issue of allowing Italy to administer them in trust for the United Nations became important as signifying that post-Fascist Italy under the Christian Democratic leader, Alcide de Gasperi, had worked its way back to international respectability. Just before the election the United States, under intense pressure from the Italian–American lobby, signified its support for Italian trusteeship. So also did France despite its long-standing dispute over the boundaries of Libya and Chad. The way seemed clear for Britain, with its strategic interests and current administrative responsibilities, to reach an accommodation with Italy and the United Nations. Bevin, hard-pressed by the Egyptians over Suez, was intent on securing Cyrenaica as a strategic alternative.

British officials were reluctant to accept their government's abandonment of Greater Somalia. Officers in all ranks of the Military Administration, drawn from the army which had defeated Mussolini's forces, still believed they had the right to redraft boundaries unilaterally and promised the Somali there would be no return to Italian rule whatever the safeguards. They established a close working relationship with the nascent political party, the Somali Youth League, founded in 1943, which was similarly committed to Greater Somalia. But Somali nationalism was always liable to disintegrate into clan rivalry. When, under the terms of the Italian Peace Treaty, the Four Power Commission of Investigation visited Mogadishu in January 1948 to determine the inhabitants' wishes, rival factions clashed in bloody riot. Several senior officials who had worked closely with the nationalists were replaced and Bevin, goaded by Attlee's wish not to be saddled with further 'deficit areas',[22] determined to withdraw as quickly as possible from both the Ogaden and Somalia.[23]

The Ogaden was, therefore, relinquished to Ethiopia. What had been Italian Somaliland was made into a United Nations trusteeship, much smaller than that projected by Bevin, under Italian administration, to last for 10 years. In 1952 the General Assembly decided that Eritrea be federated with Ethiopia as a locally autonomous state, despite evidence of considerable opposition from the large Muslim population. (The highly centralized Ethiopian regime regarded such autonomy as dangerous and from the outset sought to reduce Eritrea to central control. In 1962 the Eritrean parliament was suborned to dissolve itself and Eritrea reduced to an ordinary Ethiopian province.)

Undoubtedly Haile Selassie profited from this four-way play involving Ethiopia, the United States, Britain and Italy. So did the United States. With Italy originally sidelined, then readmitted as a badge of rehabilitation, the main losers in European colonialism's end-game at the Horn were not the British – who, in any case, even if they did not get all they wanted in this instance cashed in on the Anglo-American relationship elsewhere, notably in Cyrenaica. Just as at the start of colonialism at the 'scramble', it was the uncentralized, egalitarian peoples of the periphery, notably the Somali, who lost out in Ethiopia's transactions with the West. When the United Nations General Assembly eventually disposed of the Italian colonies in 1949, its President, General Romulo of the Philippines declared, with unconscious irony, that the decisions taken constituted a triumph for the principle of self-determination.[24] In the very process of decolonization, the centralized Ethiopian state thus triumphed over the peoples of the periphery.

On 24 December 1951 the ex-Italian colony of Libya joined Egypt, Ethiopia, Liberia and South Africa to become the fifth independent state on the continent, under King Sayyid Muhammad Idris, the head of the powerful Sanusi order of Cyrenaica. The new state, conventionally regarded as the creation of the United Nations, can equally be seen as a client state fabricated to meet the needs of Britain and the United States. Britain's prime aim, determinedly pursued by Bevin, was to ensure its command of the eastern Mediterranean by creating forceful military backup in Cyrenaica for its Suez base. In furtherance of that aim it adapted its policies to the changing international situation.

At the outset the British preferred to see Libya broken into three parts with themselves responsible only for Cyrenaica, while Tripolitania, with its large body of Italian settlers, would be the responsibility of Italy, and the French would take over the Fezzan which adjoined their territory to the south. Britain had established good wartime relations with the Sanusi of Cyrenaica, in the struggle against Italy, and expected to capitalize on these in its search for a strategic base to reinforce Suez. It gave Idris, leader of the Sanusi religious brotherhood, the religio-political title of Emir, prior to devolving power to him.

Such a transition from religious to political leadership accorded with the research of E. E. Evans-Pritchard who had served as political officer in the British Military Administration of Cyrenaica. Evans-Pritchard's *The Sanusi of Cyrenaica*, published in 1949, made an immediate impact on both scholars and administrators. He argued that the Sanusi brotherhood of the Beduin of Cyrenaica had been transformed in the face of Italian attack into a proto-state; thus primary resistance to colonial invasion evolved into a nationalist movement for independence.

That same year, 1949, the General Assembly rejected the plan for a three-way Libyan split, under assorted European tutelage, in favour of independence as a single state in the next two years. Both Adrian Pelt, the Libyan High Commissioner of the United Nations charged with guiding Libya to independence, and British policy-makers, who quickly switched to supporting the Assembly's plan, found inspiration and practical guidance in Evans-Pritchard's book as a manual for nation-building. But, as so often during decolonization, the findings of social science were transformed by enthusiastic men of action. Evans-Pritchard had been careful to confine his analysis to the Sanusi, pointing out that Cyrenaica and Libya had quite different cultural orientations. The distortion of his findings is easily explained. European colonialism had denied the capacity of those it ruled to organize satisfactory political communities. And it was taken for granted that it was a mark of civilization to live in states rather than tribes. Notions of social evolution therefore combined with racism to suggest that stateless people were inferior. Hence men of goodwill in the West tended to inflate any social-science finding which might undermine the enormous residual condescension blocking progress to independence.[25]

Britain, therefore, settled for second-best in Cyrenaica: Libya unified under 'friendly' King Idris who obligingly granted the strategic facilities Bevin and the Chiefs of Staff requested. Here was the pay-off for deference to the United States over Greater Somalia. Even Attlee was quieted when he understood that by 1948 the Americans had been persuaded to redevelop and expand their gigantic wartime air-base at Wheelus Field, simultaneously subsidizing the new state and relieving Britain from the expense of garrisoning Tripolitania.

The implications of the General Assembly's decisions and the manœuvres of the great powers, over the future of the ex-Italian colonies were profound. Libya, by the standards of both the United Nations and enlightened colonialism considered to be one of the poorest and least prepared of all African countries for independent statehood, was admitted to the comity of nations in 1951. The rest of the Mahgreb, Islam – indeed all of Africa and the remainder of the colonial world – inevitably made invidious comparisons.

Somalia, the former Italian Somaliland, even less developed by such standards, was scheduled for independence within 10 years. This was the United States model of timetabled preparation for self-government on the pattern of the Philippines expedited by the political pressures of the General Assembly. Given a bare decade to prepare this 'backward' territory for self-government, with little in the way of trained local personnel or basic political and administrative infrastructure to work with, the Italian trustees set about their task with vigour and imagination. Within six years they held country-wide elections to the first Somali parliament and granted a large measure of internal self-government in 1956.

British colonial officials, on the other hand, were disheartened by their government's abandonment of Greater Somalia and believed the despised Italians had accepted an impossible task. There was indeed a basic difference of approach within the ranks of British policy-makers between Foreign Office *realpolitik*, which prided itself on its ability to adapt rapidly to changing international circumstances, and Colonial Office paternalism, even when transmuted and updated as 'trusteeship', 'partnership' or 'developmentalism'. Walter Bowring, seconded by the Colonial Office to the British Military Administration in Somalia from 1947 to 1950, expressed the traditional corporate ethos of the Colonial Service when he reported that the majority of his colleagues 'felt that they had been let down badly. A number of them in senior posts had held appointments in the pre-war colonial service and were conditioned to believe that *the first claim on their loyalty was to the people they administered*: they fully grasped the implications of handing back Ogaden to Ethiopia.'[26] This was the colonial service stereotype of arrogant, wilfully ignorant, Foreign Office officials meddling in African affairs in pursuit of their own superpower version of the higher diplomacy. With friends like these, might have been the burden of complaint, who needs the Americans and the General Assembly!

If this caricature bears some relation to the realities of the diplomacy of decolonization, so, equally, does the complementary stereotype of a Colonial Service blinded by nostalgia for an idealized pre-war world to the practicalities of the contemporary international situation. The corporate ethos of the Colonial Service had developed within the sealed borders of empire. The imperial pax was intended to guarantee stability, with the archetypal relationship the affinity between the administrator and 'his people'. (Under Indirect Rule that between the district commissioner and the Chief.) Quite suddenly, the colonial service was expected to adapt to a volatile postwar world. The cosy arrangements of district commissioners and chiefs were imperilled by the flight to the cities and invasion by the new nationalist organizations and a host of itinerant experts such as soil conservationists and labour inspectors. Worse, the destabilizing threat of express timetables for decolonization emanating from the United States and the General Assembly, mingled with the menacing ideologies of Soviet-sponsored international socialism, Pan-Africanism, Pan-Arabism and Pan-Islamicism, to create a permanent atmosphere of crisis. In response, the Foreign Office was suspected of cutting corners, the Colonial Office of dragging its heels. Key individuals certainly contradicted the stereotypes: Bevin was hardly the traditional diplomat and Andrew Cohen prided himself on his grasp of the broader international context. And it is significant that Bowring identified entrants to the pre-war Colonial Service as being most affronted. Generational, as well as departmental, differences marked the arguments over accelerated decolonization.

Twin ironies crown this history of great-power manipulation of the first round of African decolonization. There was to be no oil bonanza for the Americans in the Ogaden. Sinclair drilled 17 wells without success.[27] Nor did Bevin get his Cyrenaican base. Bowring was present when senior army officers and Foreign Office officials examined an especially bleak patch of desert, selected after months of negotiation: 'After ten minutes the senior officer present exclaimed "It won't do" – and the meeting broke up.'[28]

FRENCH NORTH AFRICA

The Fourth Republic pursued contradictory policies in North Africa: repression in Algeria, reform in Morocco and Tunisia. In a series of rapidly changing premierships that of the Radical Socialist Pierre Mendes-France (June 1954 to February 1955) was most important. Before taking office Mendes had hammered home certain linked themes, the need for economic modernization through giving industrial investment priority over military expenditure and the disastrous impact of the Indo-China war on both the economy and French foreign policy. The war cost France more than it received in Marshall Aid, consuming annually 10 per cent of the national budget and destroying the yearly output of officers from the crack St Cyr academy inside three years. To govern, said Mendes, was to choose, hence he was only prepared to take office on his own terms. Such stress on policies, rather than the mere pursuit of office, contrasted with the immobilism characteristic of French parliamentary politics and cost him the premiership in 1953. But on 7 May 1954 at Dien Bien Phu the French suffered the most devastating defeat ever inflicted on a Western regular army by a colonial resistance movement. French public opinion had remained apathetic because the war was fought so far away largely by colonial troops and the French Foreign Legion. But the only way the fight could now be continued was to send French conscripts and this was deemed politically impossible. The government of Joseph Laniel – France's twentieth premier since the Liberation – fell and Mendes assumed power because he seemed the only politician capable of extricating France from the Indo-China morass. To an astounded Chamber he kept his promise to pull France out of Indo-China within 30 days, negotiating the Geneva agreements which divided the country into North and South Vietnam.

The governments preceding that of Mendes-France had sought to repress movements for independence in the protectorates of Tunisia and Morocco just at the time when the example of Libyan independence galvanized nationalist politics in the Mahgreb. In December 1951 France ended cooperation with the Tunisian Neo-Destour and arrested its leader, Habib Bourguiba, in January 1952. A guerrilla movement gathered strength in response to French repression and the Bey of Tunis found it almost impossible to get anyone to assume ministerial office.

In a speech made on the neutral ground of Tangiers in 1947 the Sultan of Morocco, Mohammed ben Yusuf, had emphasized that his country must be considered part of the Arab world. The Independence (Istiqlal) Party, formed in 1944, was rapidly gaining support, especially in the towns. Alarmed at the threat from a populist monarchy, the French stirred up a revolt of privileged Berber aristocrats against the Sultan. Istiqlal supporters were arrested and the Sultan was forced to abdicate. He was deported on 20 August 1953.

Mendes-France travelled to Tunis on 31 July 1954 directly after the Geneva conference on Vietnamese independence. He settled the conflict between the French and Neo-Destour by agreeing to self-government. The Tunisian guerrillas handed in their arms and left as free men. The political settlement had pre-empted an armed struggle, to the relief of moderate leaders on both sides. He also opened talks on the future of Morocco. Edgar Faure, Mendes-France's successor, continued these policies. Bourguiba returned in triumph to Tunis on 1 June and France again recognized the legitimacy of Sultan Mohammed at the end of October. Full independence was now negotiated for Morocco on 2 March 1958, followed by independence for Tunisia on 20 March.

The scope of this achievement in skilful and determined decolonization during 1954–6 becomes apparent when compared with Britain's dealings with its settler colonies at the same time. There were 239,000 Europeans resident in Tunisia in 1946 and 325,271 in Morocco in 1951 as against 207,000 in Southern Rhodesia in 1958, 72,000 in Northern Rhodesia in 1958 and 67,700 in Kenya in 1960. The ratios of non-European to European populations were: Tunisia 14:1; Morocco 22:1; Southern Rhodesia 13:1; Northern Rhodesia 31:1; and Kenya 93:1. Both Morocco and Tunisia experienced a steady postwar increase in their European populations. And the North African settlers were effectively organized within the political system of the Fourth Republic through their ability to influence – indeed, frequently to control – the North African policy of the Radical Party. By contrast in 1959, half a decade after Mendes-France and Edgar Faure had outwitted the formidable settler lobby over Tunisia and Morocco, the British Colonial Secretary Lennox-Boyd and his East African governors were proposing 1975 as a suitable date for Kenyan independence.[29]

In line with the new realism of *Mendesisme* the French had withdrawn from two-thirds of their North African possessions. But the future of the final third, Algeria, by far the largest, with the most difficult political problems, was still uncertain. (There were close to 1 million Europeans in Algeria and the ratio of the non-European to the European population was a mere 9 : 1.) For Mendes-France colonial reform was always intended to be the necessary preliminary to decisive action over domestic and European affairs. Eager to get to grips with the problems of the nascent European Economic Community and European defence, Mendes dispensed with a deeper analysis of the political situation in the French Mahgreb, accepting instead the traditional French constitutional distinction between Algeria as part of France and Tunisia and Morocco as protectorates with their own statehood. When faced by heightened militancy in Algeria he instituted a policy of repression there while accelerating decolonization in Tunisia and Morocco. (Ironically, although he had appeased the immobilist conservatism of the Fourth Republic over Algeria, it was an unholy coalition over North African policy which brought Mendes down after seven hectic months.)

A mere three months intervened between the end of the Geneva conference on Vietnam and the outbreak of the fight for Algerian independence on 1 November 1954. By 1954 the Algerian nationalist movement had come under the control of a faction which believed force was the only way independence could be achieved. Encouraged by the success of Ho Chi Minh in old Indo-China the National Liberation Front (FLN) opened guerrilla war. To the French, however, this new war of liberation seemed to have far less chance of success than its Vietnamese predecessor. Ho Chi Minh had ruled over a firmly established national Communist power apparatus as early as 1946. By contrast the Algerian revolutionaries had a mere 3,000 men with military training to pit against almost 50,000 French soldiers, reinforced to 80,000 by February 1955.

The French army craved success to boost its morale after the Vietnamese débâcle. General Lionel-Max Chassin sought to develop a new theory of counter-revolutionary warfare out of the writings of Mao Tse-tung. Henceforth, he argued, wars would be fought for the control of the masses by a blend of organizational and psychological techniques. Mao's writings supplied the organizational procedures. The psychological strategies were derived from Serge Chakotin's *The Rape of the Masses* (1940), written before the outbreak of the Second World War to instruct European democrats on how they could defeat Hitler by 'violent propaganda' based on the techniques of Pavlovian conditioning. Algeria, like Indo-China, was deemed a suitable social laboratory for these experiments in the technology of violence. General Andre Beaufre brilliantly deployed these ideas to develop his concept of 'total strategy' which proved highly influential not only in Algeria but also with the Americans in Vietnam and in Portuguese and South African counter-insurgency.[30]

Francois Mitterand, minister of the interior in Mendes-France's government, declared on 5 November: 'Algeria is France; from Flanders to the Congo there is only one law, one nation, one parliament, the Constitution wills it so, we will it so. . . . *La seule negotiation, C'est la guerre*' ('War is the only negotiation'). On 26 January 1955 Mendes-France appointed the Gaullist assembly representative Jacques Soustelle as the new Governor-General of Algeria. Soustelle declared a month later before the Algerian Assembly: 'France will no more evacuate from Algeria than it will from Provence or Brittany. France has made her choice. She has chosen integration.' 'Integration', as developed by Soustelle, involved a new agency, the Special Administrative Service (SAS), formed from highly trained French officers who would serve in the Algerian countryside as technicians and consultants to the local Muslim population.

The Algerian revolutionaries responded in kind to French military escalation. They too had their theorist of insurgency to codify and develop the practice of Mao and Ho. Ramdane Abane was 30 years old when he was jailed for five years for revolutionary activities in 1950. He embarked on the longest hunger strike yet seen in a French jail, inflicting acute stomach ulcers on himself and a consequent ferocious temper. He also read voraciously on revolution, including *Mein Kampf* as well as the Marxist-Leninist classics. He was released in 1955 and proved as innovative, pragmatic and ruthless a technocrat and theoretician of violence as even the most brilliant of St Cyr's graduates. The FLN set him in charge of reorganizing its Algiers networks which had been badly disrupted by French counter-intelligence the previous winter. He accomplished this quickly and efficiently.[31]

The French became aware they were dealing with a newly formidable revolutionary machine when Abane issued the call to insurrection on 1 April 1955 in response to the French declaration of a state of emergency. In contrast to the original verbose FLN manifesto of the previous November, Abane's proclamation was a compact masterpiece of propaganda. It also signalled that the

FLN intended to take the fight to the civilian population threatening that its 'tribunal . . . will be pitiless towards traitors and enemies of the country.' This was basic to Abane's strategy. 'One corpse in a jacket is worth more than twenty in uniform' became a favourite dictum.[32] The standard FLN initiation ritual required that the recruit kill a designated 'traitor', *mouchard* (police spy or informer), French gendarme or *colon*. He embarked on his mission accompanied by a 'shadow' who executed the recruit summarily should he show any sign of flinching. The FLN combined ridicule with terror. A Muslim loyalist would be found tied to a stake, his throat cut, and right arm fixed in grim parody of a French army salute. French soldiers responded with gallows humour, dubbing the widespread Algerian predilection for throat-slitting *le grand sourire* ('the broad smile').

In the stifling heat of 20 August at Philipville the FLN slaughtered 123 people, of whom 71 were Europeans. The modes of execution were often sickening. Limbs were hacked off, heads kicked in. European mothers – some pregnant – and their children were found with bellies ripped open and throats cut. Among the Algerians killed was Messali Hajj's nephew, a warning that the FLN would brook no competition or criticism even from revolutionary allies. Inevitably there were discrepancies in the statistics of slaughter. Soustelle states that 1,273 'insurgents' died, admitting that many innocent Muslims were killed in the backlash. (Only a few months earlier he had expressly forbidden the *colons* to arm 'in self-defence', but the administration hastily reversed this in the aftermath of Philipville.) A French newsreel showed a young para shooting an unarmed Algerian then casually reloading as the man, still writhing, clutched his belly. The FLN, giving names and addresses, claimed 12,000 Algerians died at the hands of the French.

The Algerian War, most brutal of all colonial struggles, had begun. The spiral of violence now determined policy. Half a million soldiers, including raw French conscripts, were sent to Algeria, wrecking Mendes-France's original aim to divert resources from colonial war to domestic modernization.

The shift from non-violent nationalism to national liberation through armed struggle was completed when Ferhat Abbas, once the eloquent advocate of assimilation by the extension of citizenship, was finally persuaded to join the FLN in 1956, commenting, retrospectively, 'the era of broken promises has gone forever.'[33] Abbas was promptly elected to the National Council of the Algerian Revolution (CNRA) and in 1958 he became premier of the provisional government of the Republic of Algeria.

CONCLUSION

The triumph of the Jewish state of Israel in 1948 was simultaneously a defeat for Pan-Arab arms and for British diplomacy. The humiliation worsened for successive Egyptian governments. The economic situation, after the heavy cost of the war, deteriorated as Egypt became increasingly indebted. The swelling tide of unrest led to the growth of extremist politics: the Communists and the Muslim Brotherhood, an Islamic fundamentalist movement which by mid-century had become the most powerful mass organization in the Middle East.

These drastic political changes exacerbated already deteriorating Anglo-Egyptian relations. At the end of the Second World War, with the threat from the Axis powers removed, Egypt sought to renegotiate the 1936 Anglo-Egyptian defence treaty. Negotiations broke down, as so often in the past, over British insistence that the Sudan's international status as an Anglo-Egyptian condominium be maintained. (In practice Britain would retain control, while encouraging anti-Egyptian Sudanese nationalism, thus dividing and dominating the Nile valley.) After the breakdown of negotiations Egypt brought the treaty before the United Nations but, despite considerably embarrassing Britain, the issue was not resolved.

In 1950 the two sides tried once more. Although there were fresh ideas to be discussed, especially US proposals for new defence arrangements, the problem of the Sudan again frustrated agreement. With no indication of likely voluntary withdrawal by the British, the Egyptian government unilaterally abrogated the treaty in October 1951.

The British stayed on, but the costs of confrontation mounted. Traditionally the British had been able to capitalize on Egyptian politics being dominated by a struggle between the king on the one hand and a combination of large landholders and middle-class interests on the other: a conflict which often gave scope for British arbitration. Increasingly Egyptian politics became a patriotic struggle to remove the occupying power with the king and politicians competing in anti-British attitudes. Such hostility led to the almost complete withdrawal of local labour from the Suez base. British property and personnel were attacked by terrorists undeterred by the Egyptian police. The British reacted to the spiralling violence with increasing severity. In January 1952 their tanks attacked an Egyptian police barracks killing 41 Egyptians. Anti-foreign riots swept Cairo in which much property was torched and 11 Britons were killed. For the monarchy and the old political class the breakdown of order and sequence of humiliations proved fatal. In July 1952 a conspiracy of junior officers, average age 33, swept away the old regime. The coup by the 'Free Officers' was masterminded by Colonel Gamal Abd al-Nasser but General Mohamed Neguib – a bluff popular 50-year old, half-Sudanese hero of the Palestine war – was invited to lead the Arab revolution.

The new revolutionary regime was both a threat and an opportunity to the British. It is possible that they were privy to Nasser's conspiracy through the Americans and were warned not to intervene, though in reality there was little that they could do to stop a well-planned coup.[34] There was no doubting the radical nationalism of the 'free officers'. In 1954 Nasser squeezed out Neguib signalling that there would be no restoration of parliamentary government. On the other hand the 'free officers' seemed finally to be an Egyptian regime with which the British could strike an agreement and one which had the power to enforce it. In 1953 and 1954 reconciliation seemed close. In 1953 the British agreed to end their rule over the Sudan, a former Egyptian colony but a British-dominated condominium since 1898. In 1954 the problem of the Canal Zone was settled between Nasser and the British Foreign Secretary Sir Anthony Eden: British troops were to be withdrawn over 20 months, leaving behind vast stockpiles of arms and ammunition for the base was to be available in the event of a threat to any Arab state in the Middle East or to Britain's NATO ally Turkey. Egypt's 'temporary occupation', begun in 1882, was to be ended after 74 years.

As a result of the Anglo-Egyptian Agreement of 12 February 1953 the Sudan obtained independence on 1 January 1956. Compared to subsequent ceremonies this was a low-key affair. Indeed some suspected that the actual date was influenced by the Governor's wish to get home for Christmas. The Sudanese encouraged their British and Egyptian masters to settle their affairs with minimum fuss. On the British side there was strong resentment on the part of the Sudan Political Service, and such sympathizers as Margery Perham, that Foreign Office *realpolitik* rather than concern for Sudanese welfare had dictated the pace of events.[35] The Colonial Office was concerned that apparent precipitateness in the Sudan might encourage 'the more advanced colonial territories' to expect similar acceleration.[36]

France, meanwhile, increasingly focused on Egypt and Nasser as the source of all its troubles in North Africa. Without Egyptian ideological and logistical support the French believed the Algerian revolution would easily be defeated. In his search for a Pan-Arab movement Nasser made a populist appeal over the heads of existing Arab governments to mobilize mass nationalism as a protest movement against Western dominance. Suddenly mid-century transistor technology made Pan-Arabism feasible through Cairo radio's *Voice of the Arabs*. Eden succeeded Churchill as Prime Minister in 1955, taunted by the Tory right with being an appeaser for the very success of his negotiations with Nasser. Diverse chains of events were moving towards a confluence which culminated in the Suez crisis of 1956.

NOTES

1 Cited in W. R. Louis, 'Libyan Independence, 1951: The Creation of a Client State', in William R. Louis and P. Gifford, eds., *Decolonization and African Independence: The Transfers of Power, 1960–1980* (New Haven, Yale University Press, 1988), p. 162.

2 William R. Louis, *The British Empire in the Middle East, 1945–1951* (Oxford, Clarendon Press, 1984), p. 303.

3 Hugh Dalton, *Diary*, 5 October 1946, 9 March 1947, III (London, Muller, 1962), p. 10.

4 Louis, *British Empire*, pp. 15–20, 108–10.

5 *Op. cit.*, pp. 272–3.

6 Javier G. Alcade, *The Idea of Third World Development: Emerging Perspectives in the United States and Britain, 1900–1950* (Lanham, Va., University of Virginia, 1987), especially pp. 191–7, for the background to Euro-Africa.

7 John Kent, *The Internationalization of Colonialism: Britain, France, and Black Africa, 1939–1956* (Oxford, Clarendon Press, 1992), p. 169.

8 David Reynolds, *Britannia Overruled: British Policy and World Power in the Twentieth Century* (Longman, London, 1991), p. 168.

9 J. Kent, 'Bevin's Imperialism and the Idea of Euro-Africa, 1945–49', in Michael Dockrill and John W. Young, eds., *British Foreign Policy, 1945–56* (Houndmills, Macmillan, 1989), pp. 47, 71.

10 Louis, 'Libyan Independence', p. 171.

11 The pronouncements on British policy cited in notes 1, 2, 5 and 10 were all in response to the issues involved in disposing of the Italian Empire. Bevin's preference for peasants rather than pashas is referred to in F. Roberts, 'Ernest Bevin as Foreign Secretary', in Ritchie Ovendale, ed., *The Foreign Policy of the British Labour Governments* (Leicester, Leicester University Press, 1984), p. 29.

12 Louis, *British Empire*, especially pp. 6, 24, 87, 107–8, 274–5, 277.

13 W. Bowring, 'Great Britain, the United States, and the Disposition of Italian East Africa', *Journal of Imperial and Commonwealth History* XX (1992), p. 90.

14 *Op. cit.*, p. 98.

15 *Op. cit.*, p. 91.

16 The best introduction to the complex interplay of the precolonial, colonial, and postcolonial history of the Horn is I. M. Lewis, ed., *Nationalism and Self-Determination in the Horn of Africa* (London, Ithaca Press, 1983).

17 Bowring, 'Italian East Africa', pp. 99, 106.

18 *Op. cit.*, pp. 99–100.

19 Harold Marcus, *Ethiopia, Great Britain and the United States, 1941–1974: The Politics of Empire* (Berkeley, University of California Press, 1983) is especially illuminating on why Britain failed to resolve the Somali problem.

20 Louis, *British Empire*, p. 281; Alan Bullock, *Ernest Bevin: Foreign Secretary, 1945–1951*, (London, Heinemann, 1983), p. 133; Louis, *British Empire*, p. 281; Bowring, 'Italian East Africa', pp. 99, 105.

21 Louis, 'Libyan Independence', p. 161.

22 Louis, *British Empire*, pp. 274–5.

23 Bowring, 'Italian East Africa', p. 97.

24 *Op. cit.*, pp. 103, 107.

25 E. E. Evans-Pritchard, *The Sanusi of Cyrenaica* (Oxford, Clarendon Press, 1949); Adrian Pelt, *Libyan Independence and the United Nations* (New Haven, Yale University Press, 1970) p. 6, n. 3; J. Lonsdale, 'States and Social Processes in Africa: A Historiographical Survey', *African Studies Review* XXIV (1981), p. 139, points out that neither Africans nor Africanists have been immune from this condescension towards stateless societies.

26 Bowring, 'Italian East Africa', p. 96, emphasis added.

27 *Op. cit.*, p. 107.

28 *Op. cit.*, pp. 96, 105.

29 See Miles Kahler, *Decolonization in Britain and France* (Princeton NJ, Princeton University Press, 1984), especially pp. 316–25 for the political background to decolonization. There is a useful, compact account of this period in K. Panter-Brick,

'Independence – French Style', in Prosser Gifford and William R. Louis, eds., *Decolonization and African Independence: The Transfers of Power, 1960–1980* (New Haven, Yale University Press, 1988), pp. 73–104.

30 For the developing theories of revolutionary warfare see Eric R. Wolf, *Peasant Wars of the Twentieth Century* (London, Faber, 1971). Andre Beaufre's ideas on 'total strategy' are handily summarized in A. Beaufre, *Strategy for Tomorrow* (London, Macdonald and James, 1974). For their impact on southern Africa see M. Swilling and M. Phillips, 'State Power in the 1980s: From "total strategy" to "counter-revolutionary warfare" ', in Jackylin Cock and Laurie Nathan, eds., *War and Society: The Militarisation of South Africa* (Cape Town, David Philip, 1989), pp. 134–48.

31 For the transformation of Franco-Algerian relations in this period see Alistair Horne, *A Savage War of Peace* (London, Macmillan, 1977).

32 *Op. cit.*, p. 132.

33 Ferhat Abbas, *La Nuit Coloniale* (Paris, Juillard, 1962), p. 232.

34 Miles Copeland, *The Game of Nations* (London, Weidenfeld and Nicholson, 1970), pp. 53–70.

35 Margery Perham, *Colonial Sequence, 1949–1969* (London, Methuen, 1970), pp. 9–12, 40–2, 45–67, 72–84, 90–2; and William R. Louis, 'The Coming of Independence in the Sudan', *Journal of Imperial and Commonwealth History* XIX (1991), pp. 142–58.

36 Sir John Martin, minute, 16 December 1953, cited in M. W. Daly, 'The Transfer of Power in the Sudan', in Prosser Gifford and William R. Louis, eds., *Decolonization and African Independence: The Transfers of Power, 1960–1980* (New Haven, Yale University Press, 1988), p. 197.

9

Imperial Recalculations

By 1948 the British Colonial Office had devised the broad outlines of an overall policy for its African colonies: all governors were to have as their goal the preparation of their colonies for self-government, not at some vague and unspecified date, but within the foreseeable future. This amounted to a revolutionary change in policy, even if its principal architects, the postwar Labour Colonial Secretary, Arthur Creech Jones, and Andrew Cohen in the Colonial Office, like the good Fabians they were, intended it to be a revolution guided from above. Fabian belief in 'the inevitability of gradualness' was also tactically appropriate given the tension between some Colonial Service officers in Africa and the civil servants in Whitehall. The Colonial Service, with its powerful mystique of 'the man on the spot', naturally resented bureaucratic interference whether at district or colonial level. Such powerful opposition had to be circumvented or, to use the classic Fabian term, 'permeated'. At least the Colonial Service was not monolithic: there was a significant shift towards approval of African advancement among the younger officers.[1] Perhaps this was why Cohen and Creech Jones eventually formulated their timetable for the transfer of power using the somewhat elastic phrase 'within a generation'.[2] (Conventionally a generation meant 12–20 years to those thinking of education and the professions; though to others it meant the 25 or even 30 years between the generations of a family.)

From the outset Creech Jones and Cohen were careful to cloak their policies in as uncontroversial, and therefore as traditional, a guise as possible. Yet just how revolutionary a change they were recommending can be gauged from the fact that even such a liberal Governor as Sir Alan Burns, who presided over the Gold Coast from 1941 to 1947, did not believe that it would gain independence within his lifetime. (He died in 1983.)

The new policy was embodied in two instruments: the Local Government Despatch of 25 February 1947 and the report of a committee set up early in 1947, chaired by Sidney Caine, to chart a 'new approach' to African policy. The despatch finally abandoned the view, exemplified by Indirect Rule, that Africans could only be ruled effectively through their traditional institutions. Instead, these institutions should yield to organs of local government more closely modelled on those in Britain.

For members of the British Labour movement – particularly perhaps if, like Creech Jones, they were drawn from the working class – the momentous electoral triumph of 1945 signalled a new regime, rather than a simple change of government. African self-government involved a somewhat similar transfer of power. The analogies were close enough to suggest that some of the hard-won lessons derived from the struggle for socialism and working-class emancipation in Britain could be applied to decolonization. The Labour Party believed that local government constituted an ideal training school for national political responsibility. Indeed 56 per cent of Labour MPs, including Creech Jones, had graduated from local government.[3] He believed that it should fulfil the same function in Africa. Africans, drawn from the educated minority, were every-where increasingly focusing on the politics of central government and were in danger of becoming so absorbed by events at colonial capitals, like Lagos and Freetown, that they were in danger of losing touch with the people in the localities. He believed that government must provide the people with opportun-ities to develop expertise in the art of popular control, meanwhile avoiding the premature transfer of power to small and unrepresentative groups.[4]

This was an approach calculated to appeal to conservative colonial officials by presenting local government reform as a measure designed to slow the pace of political advance. To some extent the appeal worked. Even such a formidable opponent of the general trend of the new policy as Sir Philip Mitchell, the governor of Kenya, was induced to support the proposed local government reform on the grounds that: 'Democratic institutions improperly understood and badly handled may become perverted. Time is needed to inculcate a sense of responsibility and obligations involved, and for this purpose the devices of local government offer the best approach.'[5] The despatch announced only the broad aims of the policy. The means of implementation were not revealed but would be discussed with administrative officers, with an average of six of varying seniority from each African colony, at the July 1947 Summer School at Queens' College, Cambridge.

Meanwhile, Caine's committee on the whole range of British African policies reported on 22 May 1947, with Cohen responsible for its constitutional proposals. Its basic premise was an expectation of the rise of African nationalism on the strength of which it concluded that 'Britain must assume that perhaps within a generation many of the principal territories of the Colonial Empire will have attained or be within sight of the goal of full responsibility for local affairs.'[6] The burden of the report was that Britain must consciously plan the political, economic, educational and social developments necessary if the transfer of power was to be smooth and effective. It would be necessary to transfer power to an educated élite of Africans, hence, although all levels of education must be expanded, priority would be given to higher education. There would be no attempt to hang on to power. At the same time every effort should be made to attain the maximum amount of development before ending colonial rule in order to provide the basic requirements of the new states. The cooperation of the educated élite would be needed for this to be successful, and constitutional advance was the best way to secure this.

There was the danger, though, that their very Westernization and focus on 'national' politics would alienate the educated élite from the concerns of the illiterate rural majority. The 1947 plan, therefore, sought to use Provincial Councils as electoral colleges to link local issues with central politics in such a way as to exclude 'ballot box' politicians. Power would only be devolved to the nationalists when they had achieved the popular support necessary to insist on its transfer. It was a policy of deliberate ambiguity: read one way power was to be transferred at the earliest possible date, while read with only a slight change of emphasis, at the latest. Within the divided ranks of the Colonial Service it could be presented so as to appeal to either progressive or conservative audiences. Indeed the report as a whole stuck to generalities to avoid giving the impression that it was dictating to the individual colonial governments or to African opinion.

The Summer School was adroitly stage-managed by Cohen. Mitchell, the only governor present, supported local government reform from a conservative standpoint. A close friend of Creech Jones, Carol Johnson, Secretary of the Parliamentary Labour Party and an Alderman of Lambeth Borough Council, argued that the principles of English local government were clearly applicable in the colonies. Officers reported on the hierarchy of democratically elected councils in the Eastern Province of Uganda and the provincial councils in the Gold Coast. The officers split up into six working parties, each of which elaborated one aspect of local government policy, such as finance, land usage and race relations. But the most significant was that concerned with political aspects. Here Cohen wrote the initial paper, chaired the discussions and supervised the preparation of the final report endorsing most of his original proposals. Indeed Cohen's magnetism gave the conference proceedings intellectual coherence.[7] His genius lay in his ability 'to appeal to both radicals and conservatives and to present what he considered desirable as what was expedient and necessary.'[8] Substantial agreement on policy was reinforced by collegiate goodwill. One officer present commented that Cambridge 1947 'was to mark the beginning of a new era . . . relationships between us and our opposite numbers in the Colonial office were to undergo an almost complete transformation. Their visits to us would become more frequent and more welcome, for now they would often come as personal friends.'[9]

The original Colonial Office strategy, following a recommendation from the Fabian Colonial Bureau, was to present the new policy to a conference of unofficial members of Legislative Councils in 1948. Before that though it was discussed at the Governors' Conference held in London in November 1947.

Here the Colonial Office policy met serious opposition. Mitchell, the most outspoken critic, confessed himself bewildered by the new policy.

We conferred all day largely on dry theoretical ideas of Colonial selfgovernment totally divorced from the realities of the present day. The C.O. has got itself into a sort of mystic enchantment & sees visions of grateful, independent utopias beaming at them from all round the world, as if there was – yet – any reason to suppose that [an] African can be cashier of a village council for 3 weeks without stealing the cash. . . . There is really no understanding whatever of contemporary realities in the C.O. – Creech blathered a good deal.[10]

The East African Governors as a group resisted the Colonial Office proposal for a single conference of non-officials, calling for two separate meetings for East and West Africa. They did not get this but the Colonial Office compromised by allowing certain subjects to be discussed separately.

Mitchell was dismayed, however, that the West African Governors were 'a silent lot', save Lord Milverton, the retiring Governor of Nigeria. Milverton, as Sir Arthur Richards, had resisted the wartime trend, exemplified by his predecessor Sir Bernard Bourdillon, to give a greater role to the educated élite. He was responsible for the 1946 Richards Constitution, based on indirect election from the native authorities. Indeed, only on the insistence of Creech Jones did he retain from the old constitution four directly elected members from Lagos and Calabar. At the conference he similarly demanded that nothing should be done to derogate from the authority of the chiefs. But Milverton was on his way out and his chosen successor, Sir John Macpherson, was sympathetic to the new strategy. In fact, as the Colonial Office was well aware, all three senior West African governors were due to retire.

The African Conference opened in London on 29 September 1948. By then, though, much had happened to change the context of decision-making. The Cold War worsened with the Communist coup in Czechoslovakia on 25 February, leading even Western left-wingers and liberals to consider the possibility of a world-wide Communist conspiracy. June brought both the Berlin blockade and the beginnings of the Malayan Emergency which threatened the sterling area's biggest dollar earner with Communist insurrection. Britain's Middle Eastern policy was jeopardized by the creation of Israel and the First Arab-Israeli War in May. In Africa General Smuts was narrowly defeated by the leader of the Purified Nationalist Party, Dr Malan, in the May general election. (Even so, the Chief of the Imperial General Staff, Field Marshal Montgomery, lectured African Legislative Councillors in October on the need for a 'Master Plan' to contain Communism by a union of African territories led by 'the great dominion' in the south.)[11] And already in February, three days after the Prague coup, there were riots in Accra, capital of the Gold Coast, considered 'the model African colony', and second only to Malaya as a dollar earner.

POLITICAL CHANGE IN THE GOLD COAST

The riots in Accra on Saturday 28 February 1948 are deemed to have changed the course of African history. They did. But the outcome, accelerating the process of decolonization so that the Gold Coast Colony became the independent state of Ghana within a decade, was also the result of careful planning by the Colonial Office before the riots in order to take advantage of just such events. And these carefully laid plans to maintain Britain's tactical initiative, were, in their turn, subverted by radical political developments in the Gold Coast.

A procession of some 2,000 ex-servicemen, angry that their war bonus had not been paid, marched on the Governor's residence, the old Danish slave fort at Christiansborg Castle. The veterans had diverted from the agreed route of their march, which was supposed to culminate with the presentation of a petition to the secretariat office, in order to complain to the Governor in person. Circumventing the secretariat in order to present a petition for redress of grievances directly to the sovereign's representative was the action of exasperated loyalists, hardly dangerous insurrectionists. Unfortunately the civil security forces reacted disastrously. The Police Commissioner had personally sanctioned the ex-servicemen's march, being 'satisfied that untoward incidents arising from this large assemblage of men were improbable.' Not so the local commander of the Royal West African Frontier Force who had put his troops on stand-by from dawn on the day of the march.[12]

A small police detachment of two white officers and 12 African constables was rushed to the scene. Superintendent Colin Imray's force, ill-equipped, far too small and very frightened, confronted the marchers at Christiansborg crossroads. Imray ordered the veterans to halt. After confused threats and stone-throwing, they moved forward again. Imray ordered his men to open fire. He recalled:'. . . [N]othing happened at all. We were obviously going to be overrun at any moment. I retreated back onto the firing party and tore a rifle out of the hands of one of the men, and I myself fired at the man in front, who was urging the crowd forward within a sort of wooden bugle which he was blowing. And I killed him. I think I fired a total of another five shots. And the crowd turned and made off.'[13] The bugler, Sergeant Adjetey, died instantly. Another man died in hospital. Four were wounded.

The angry crowd retreated but did not disperse. One of their complaints was that the European firms, which dominated trade through import licences granted in wartime, were exploiting postwar shortages to make excessive profits. These firms were already subject to an effective boycott organized by an Accra chief and businessman, Nii Bonne, with 'a messianic sense of civic duty' and a long record of public campaigning.[14] Local youths were rampaging through the trading quarter of Accra when the ex-servicemen arrived. The shops and offices of the United Africa Company (part of Anglo-Dutch Unilever and the biggest trading company in West Africa) were set on fire and other European and Lebanese firms were looted and burned. Many ex-servicemen had used their gratuities and savings to become the owner-drivers of lorries, often buying on credit from Lebanese businessmen. But by 1947–8 high interest rates and the rising cost of spares frequently led to bankruptcy with the Lebanese repossessing the drivers' means of livelihood.

Next day rioters battered down the gates of Usher fort prison, releasing some of the prisoners. By Monday riots were breaking out in other towns, including Kumasi, the capital of Ashanti. There was unrest in the countryside over government measures to control 'swollen shoot', a cocoa disease, over unemployment among literate school-leavers as well as discharged soldiers, and general distress over shortages and rising prices. When order was finally restored on 16 March 29 people had been killed, 237 injured and the trading quarter of Accra lay in ruins.

Governor Sir Gerald Creasy had already broadcast to the people on the morrow of the first riots promising a 'prompt, thorough and impartial investigation into the disturbances and underlying causes.' Creasy had only arrived from a Colonial Office desk job in January, with a theoretical rather than a practical understanding of African administration and was still learning his way when the riots erupted. But the same day he telegraphed Creech Jones, the Colonial Secretary, that he could find no other explanation for the violence than that it had been 'thoroughly planned' by the United Gold Coast Convention (UGCC). This body had been set up in 1947 by a respectable group of lawyers, businessmen, chiefs and intellectuals, headed by Dr J. B. Danquah, to press for full self-government. They engaged Kwame Nkrumah as General Secretary on the strength of his reputation as an able and energetic organizer. He arrived in the Gold Coast from London in December 1947.

Communists had seized power in Czechoslovakia a few days before the riots and Creasy's senior officials soon convinced him that he, too, was dealing with an international Communist conspiracy directed by the Convention's working committee, the 'Big Six' which included Nkrumah. (The release of prisoners was held to be a characteristic Communist technique when launching a coup.) Suspicion centred on the recently arrived Nkrumah, whose activities in London were well-known to the Colonial Office through police surveillance. The 'Big Six' were arrested and the Colonial Office view that Nkrumah was a 'thoroughgoing Communist' was confirmed when his British Communist Party membership card was found. He protested that it signified so little that he had not bothered to sign it and that he had associated with all parties when abroad, whether of the left or the right, in studying party organization with a view to setting up his own nationalist party 'on the best possible lines' when he returned home.[15]

A governor with more experience beyond Whitehall might have found explanations outside conspiracy theory and restored order at less cost. No convincing evidence was produced to link the Convention with the original riots.

It seems clear at this safe distance that a few key players in the Gold Coast crisis, from top officials to 'insurrectionists, were in the grip of psychosis: many more simply indulged in highly imaginative elaborations of conspiracy theory, enlivened by entertaining gossip. Acute and sympathetic commentators remarked on histrionic role-playing by both sides: intelligence reports by the security services which occasionally transcend mere malicious gossip to be pure John Buchan and, on the nationalist side, 'comic opera politics' by African politicians who telegraphed their highly coloured version of events to the wider world.[16] Nor did this stop once the immediate crisis of the riots was resolved and Britain had stiffened security. The vastly extended Special Branch found fresh scope with the multiplication of political activists as the 1951 general election approached, working overtime to supply dossiers of character analysis, mixing crude stereotypes with objective information, on the aspiring African political class.[17]

Certainly after the event the Convention sought to turn the situation to its advantage, cabling the Secretary of State and the world's press to publicize their demands for self-government. Danquah's thousand-word rambling telegram claimed 'Civil Government . . . broken down . . . disorder and lawlessness . . . unprovoked massacre of civilians and unarmed ex-servicemen.' He warned of worse violence unless a new government was installed, declared the Convention ready to form an interim government and ended: 'God Save the King and Floreat United Gold Coast.'

Nkrumah sent a much shorter telegram to the United Nations and to a rather idiosyncratic selection of journals, the *Pan Africa* magazine in Manchester, the *New York Times*, the London *Daily Worker* and the Moscow *New Times*, claiming the civil authorities had lost control, asking for the governor's recall and stating 'People demand Self-Government immediately'.[18] (Presumably his very varied choice of recipients, as well as reflecting his personal predilections, was intended to ensure that events in the Gold Coast were somewhere – even if only in an ephemeral publication like *Pan Africa* – a matter of international record.)

It was George Padmore who dismissed this telegraphic bid for international significance on the part of his protégé as mere 'comic opera politics'. As a veteran of the 1930s struggles surrounding the Comintern, he had developed a sharp eye for revolutionary play-acting and – in that sardonic socialist tradition of Marx, Engels and Trotsky – an even sharper pen to record such follies. On this occasion, though, 'comic opera politics' brought remarkable results. The café manifestos and gesture politics of exile student groups and minute left-wing sects in London and Manchester suddenly acquired national, indeed international, significance to a state apparatus caught up in a 'red scare' in the aftermath of the Czechoslovak take-over.

When Nkrumah was arrested he had in his possession a plan for a secret lodge known as 'the Circle', which he had drawn up for use by West African students in London. It blended traditions of ritual and organization deriving from his membership of a student fraternity in America, with left-wing ideas of a vanguard revolutionary party. Nkrumah's proposal outlined a clandestine organization composed of a small band of devoted followers, complete with secret signs, monthly days of fasting and meditation, and threats of reprisal against traitors, who should 'except as a last resort avoid the use of violence'. Members would swear an unbreakable oath of loyalty to each other and accept the unconditional leadership of Nkrumah. Cells were to meet monthly and the Grand Council annually. The first objective of the Circle was a United States of West Africa, its ultimate aim a union of African socialist republics.[19] Nkrumah himself protested at the way the sinister term 'Soviet' tended to slide into the official reports of his political aims. Now he was accused of promoting a 'Union of West African Soviet Socialist Republics'.[20]

Creasy's government took this all very seriously, citing it as significant evidence of Nkrumah's complicity in planning the riots. It was on evidence such as this that the six top Convention leaders were detained and removed, first to Kumasi. Immediately Nkrumah and the rest of the 'Big Six' were transformed into heroes and martyrs. When it seemed likely that sympathizers would attack the gaol in hopes of freeing them, they were sent to individual prisons in the Northern Territories. There was a strong element of self-fulfilling prophecy in colonial conspiracy theory. The authorities realized their response to the riots was counter-productive after a few weeks and the prisoners were released to be acclaimed as national heroes.

Policy-makers in Whitehall chose to respond both to Creasy's original promise of a 'thorough and impartial investigation' and his fears of a *coup d'état*. Whatever the shock to Creasy when he left Whitehall to cope with African actualities on the ground, policy-makers back in the Colonial Office had their response ready. In the long sequence of colonial insurrection and bloody repression, the Accra riots hardly rank with Amritsar or, in Africa, with the thousands of Muslim victims after the victory riots at Setif in Algeria or the massacre by the South African police at Sharpeville in 1960 which killed 67 Africans and wounded 186. Most were shot in the back. But these few casualties were enough. They gave the Colonial Office the signal it needed to put into operation the 'new approach' to African policy outlined by Sydney Caine's committee in 1947. Far from the riots shaking the Colonial Office out of any complacency, its very anticipation of nationalism led it to read much more political significance into them than was justified by the facts. 'Creech Jones was not slow to recognise the force of nationalism: he saw it even before it existed',[21] commented R. D. Pearce, the historian of the transformation of British policy at this time.

Creech Jones, Cohen and Caine were quite deliberately seeking to anticipate the development of African nationalism in order, in Cohen's words, 'to channel this emotion and concept towards constructive courses.'[22] This was the non-paranoid corollary of Special Branch conspiracy theory: if Communists could manipulate nascent nationalism in pursuit of the Cold War so, too, could Fabian Socialists intent on creating a social democratic Commonwealth. They had seized on one of nationalism's most significant attributes: its protean character, evident in the bewildering variety of adjectives attached to nationalist movements. Emergent African nationalism, to their way of thinking, was both powerful and malleable. Their Fabian 'civilizing mission' was to ensure that whatever ideologies African nationalists originally embraced – conservative, liberal, populist, fascist or communist – they were converted into good parliamentary social democrats during the preparations for decolonization.

Nationalism was the continuation of imperialism by other and more efficient means claimed Ronald Robinson, the historian of empire and biographer of Cohen. Britain expected to find cooperative politicians in the newly decolonized territories with whom it could work as effectively as it had done with those in the old white dominions. It was ominous that Smuts, the arch-collaborator, had recently been humbled by an Afrikaner nationalist party that contained Nazi-sympathizers in its upper echelons. But the defeat was so narrow, with more votes actually going to Smuts's United Party despite its lacklustre campaign, that it seemed quite sensible to hope the reverse was only temporary. And even if the worst-case scenario prevailed and Malan's men were there to stay, the period 1910–48, spanning two World Wars, represented a lasting achievement for Britain's previous round of African decolonization.

In any case the Colonial Office was engaged in crisis management as well as long-term planning. Certainly Creech Jones and Cohen were working against a background of continual metropolitan economic crisis and ever aware of the importance of the Gold Coast as a major dollar earner in sustaining sterling. The attraction of decolonization, which would force Gold Coast nationalist politicians to discipline the cocoa farmers over swollen shoot, was that it appeared to combine an expedient reaction to immediate crisis with a comforting sense of continuity through the working out of the Commonwealth project in a black African setting.

Pearce was writing nearly three and a half decades after the fatal shots at Christiansborg crossroads. He can deconstruct Creech Jones's understanding of African nationalism because the original concept, elastic enough to attract both Creech Jones and Nkrumah, Cohen and Kenyatta, had already destructed. He writes with similar critical hindsight to that which crystallized theoretically in the remarkable trio of books on nationalism by B. Anderson, J. Breuilly and E. Gellner published at virtually the same time. Creech Jones, Danquah and Nkrumah were part of overlapping generations caught up in the rising excitement of the 'springtime of the nations'. They both shaped the original nationalist paradigm and were shaped by it. At the time it appeared to have great explanatory power, certainly much more than the imperial paradigm which it superseded.[23]

The Colonial Office appointed the Watson Commission to investigate the causes of the Gold Coast crisis. It greatly exceeded its terms of reference in recommending the institution of a ministerial system of government with several African ministers responsible to a partly elected and partly nominated Legislative Council. It endorsed local government along English lines, rather than chiefs and native authorities.

On the other hand there should be no early transfer of power. A new constitution drafted on the lines of the report should be in force for 10 years. The Commission pointed out that barely a tenth of the population was literate:

> We have no reason to suppose that power in the hands of a small literate minority would not tend to exploit the illiterate majority in accordance with the universal pattern of what has happened elsewhere in the world. His Majesty's Government . . . has a moral duty to remain until
>
> (a) the literate population has by experience reached a stage when selfish exploitation is no longer the dominant motive of political power, or
>
> (b) the bulk of the population has advanced to such a stage of literacy and political experience as will enable it to protect itself against gross exploitation, and
>
> (c) some corresponding degree of cultural, political and economic achievement has been attained by all three areas, now part of the Gold Coast.[24]

Such conditions appeared more exacting than those proposed in the Caine report. Something more urgent was needed. In 1949 Creasy, prompted by Creech Jones, appointed an all-African 38-member commission under Mr Justice (later Sir) Henley Coussey to consider the question of constitutional change. These included eight members arrested after the riots, but considering that the security forces in their panic had detained some highly respectable men of education and property this was hardly a radical move. Danquah was a member, but not Nkrumah – as it eventually turned out to Nkrumah's advantage. Immediately, though, the old nationalist élite was happy to be back with the old politics of lobbying and negotiation with the colonial authorities; the dangerous and demeaning business of populist politics could be left to their hired minion. Danquah proved to be one of the most percipient and cooperative participants, from Creech Jones's standpoint, in the African Conference which began in late September.[25] The Colonial Office strategy seemed to be working successfully.

The Coussey Commission reported in August broadly endorsing the Colonial Office plan for advance towards internal self-government by recommending a form of 'semi-responsible' government, with a nationally elected assembly and eight African ministers in the Executive Council. Henceforth it was clear that the colony was accelerating towards self-government.

At the same time London prepared to improve security. In immediate response to the Accra riots a British battalion was made available to fly out from Gibraltar in support of the four 'native battalions' of the Gold Coast garrison, and two ships from the Cape squadron were ready to sail north in support. Creech Jones visited West Africa six months later pressing all four Governors, as a matter of utmost urgency, 'to deal with internal security and strengthening the police and intelligence arrangements, and to discuss how information services could be improved and communist and other subversive tendencies checked'. A start had already been made before the riots. A Police Mobile Force had been set up in 1947 and was used some 200 times in the next four years. Twenty-four police officers were quickly drafted in; 21 had served in Palestine, so brought up-to-date experience of dealing with riots and terrorism. Special Branch was doubled between the end of 1947 and 1952.[26]

It was decided to replace Creasy with Sir Charles Arden-Clarke from Sarawak who was familiar with the security system in South-East Asia. Creech Jones told him, 'I want you to go to the Gold Coast. The country is on the edge of revolution. We are in danger of losing it.'[27] Before an orderly transfer of power could begin, 'the thin blue line' of security had to be strengthened. Patrol cars and walkie-talkie radios, tear gas and barbed wire, as well as ballot boxes would be needed to effect an orderly transition to self-government. Arriving in August 1949, Arden-Clarke spent his first months tightening security. Even before he had completed his preparations he showed his mettle in January 1950 by dealing easily with a much more difficult situation than that which defeated Creasy, when Nkrumah having broken with the UGCC, called on his followers to resist the Coussey plan with his own plan of 'positive action', a form of vigorous civil disobedience adapted from that of Ghandi in India.

Nkrumah appeared to have been sidelined by the new constitution, the joint production of the British and the old nationalist élite. He denounced it as just that, a fraudulent attempt by the British to delay self-government as they gradually handed over to the men of property and education rather than the 'people'. But he found that he could both work within the constitution and denounce it as a fake. He gained massive support from a multiplicity of aggrieved factions whom he addressed as the 'people'; first in a 'people's assembly' which he called to test opinion on the new constitution and finally, when sure of his support, by the Convention People's Party (CPP) he launched in June 1949, with the simple uncompromising slogan: 'Self-Government NOW'.

Nkrumah's 'positive action' took the form of a call for a general strike in January 1950 but against the now incomparably better-organized police this quickly collapsed. He was again imprisoned. His lieutenants in the CPP through their speeches and the new party paper, the *Evening News*, based in Accra, now succeeded in focusing the diverse grievances of the electorate on the martyrdom of their jailed leader. The CPP was extremely well organized providing indispensable assistance to officials coping for the first time with the difficult task of registering a mass African electorate. In February 1951 the CPP won 34 out of 38 elective seats fought under the Coussey constitution which it had denounced as fraudulent (even so the number of nominated members denied it an overall majority). Nevertheless, assuming approval from that other – albeit First World War – prison graduate, Creech Jones, Governor Arden-Clarke immediately summoned Nkrumah from prison and invited him, as Leader of Government Business, to nominate colleagues as ministers.

Elections, disciplined parties and cabinet government, these were the political institutions by which the colonies of British West Africa were expected to proceed to self-government. The models and precedents for the phased devolution of power from the Governor, representing the Crown, to the leader of the majority party were pivotal to the British view of their own constitutional history and to the standard Commonwealth vision of its piecemeal evolution, colony by colony, out of the Empire. This powerful Whig myth of British and imperial history, with its focus on compromise and co-option rather than conflict, permeated the thinking of the central core of the postwar British political establishment from Fabians like Creech Jones to liberal Conservatives.[28] Once Nkrumah was accepted as the likely inheritor of the colonial state by Arden-Clarke and the Colonial Office, it was no longer necessary to demonstrate the CPP's revolutionary strength through 'Positive Action', hence radical Gold Coast nationalism was enfolded within this consensus Commonwealth constitutionalism. (Ironically, just when Nkrumah was winning his election in 1951, the parliamentary career of Creech Jones, who had done so much to make this transformation of Gold Coast – and African politics in general – possible, was drawing to a close as he lost his seat in the British general election which brought the Conservatives back to power.)

The six years intervening between Nkrumah becoming Leader of Government Business in February 1951 and full Ghanaian independence in March 1957 were boom years induced by rapidly rising cocoa prices stimulated by the Korean War. Government revenues rose by 50 per cent. At the same time United States economic expansionist policies, adopted a short while before Korea, were reinforced by the wartime boom. This eased the pressure on sterling and offset, to some extent, the effects of devaluation, contributing to more genial relations between British officials and Gold Coast nationalists. Money was available for development projects and naturally ministers saw that it was mainly channelled to areas of strong CPP support.

Neither the industrialist and former Guards officer Oliver Lyttleton who became Colonial Secretary in 1951, nor Alan Lennox-Boyd who succeeded him in October 1954, came from the liberal wing of the Conservative Party. Nor, of course, did Churchill have any relish for imperial devolution. When Lyttleton secured Cabinet agreement for Nkrumah to take the title 'Prime Minister' in February 1952, Churchill drafted a cable to Dr Malan, the South African Prime Minister, hoping that 'you recognize that the decisions taken about the Gold Coast are the consequences of what was done before we became responsible.'[29]

Yet Conservative cynicism about the more idealistic aspects of the Commonwealth, verging into racism about what might properly be expected from peoples of non-British stock, meant that once colonies were in the fast lane to independence politicians like Lyttleton adopted a brisk, no nonsense, good-riddance approach to decolonization. (More like Attlee and Dalton rather than Creech Jones and Bevin.) In February 1954 Lyttleton reported that although the Minister of Works admitted receiving £2,000 from a contractor towards election expenses there was no other evidence of corruption among senior ministers. Better still, Nkrumah's government had agreed on new anti-Communist policies, undertaking to ban Communist literature and exclude Communist sympathizers from key posts in the administration, police and education while curtailing travel behind the Iron Curtain. After Nkrumah won another election in 1954, Lyttleton's successor Lennox-Boyd accepted December 1956 as target date for 'full self-government within the Commonwealth.'

The most serious opposition to Nkrumah was now internal. A fixed price for cocoa, with the profits of the commodity boom going into the general exchequer, antagonized farmers, especially in Ashanti, the centre of the National Liberation Movement (NLM) which sought a federal future. Growing violence from the NLM led the British to force another election on Nkrumah before they would concede independence. Thus in mid-July 1956 the Gold Coast went to the polls once more. The issue was really independence under CPP rule or delay and federation. The voters gave the party a slightly higher vote, 57 per cent of the total. On 6 March 1957 the Gold Coast Colony became the independent sovereign state of Ghana and the first black dominion in the Commonwealth of Nations.

Afrique Noire, French West and Equatorial Africa

The immediate postwar years, 1945–51, witnessed a great political restructuring of French-controlled *Afrique noire* (Black Africa). Africans gained rights to electoral politics, trade unions, and made progress towards citizenship, all within the French political community. A French Constituent Assembly was elected in October 1945 with 64 out of 586 delegates from the colonies, 24 of whom were elected by subjects as against citizens. The composition of the Chamber differed significantly from its predecessors. The Radicals, so long dominant, now comprised a mere 10 per cent, while the Right amounted to only another 16 per cent. Three large, roughly equal, parties constituted three-quarters of this postwar Assembly. The biggest were the Communists, second came the Socialists and third a completely new party, the MRP (*Mouvement Republicaine Populaire*) a Christian Democrat – or progressive Catholic – party. Although this simplified the multiplicity of parties in the Third Republic, it was still a multiparty system in which each of the main metropolitan parties was forced into tactical cooperation with politicians from France Overseas. Both Socialists and Communists sought allies among the new colonial representatives, while the MRP looked to the settler lobby.

That lobby was largely based in the Mahgreb but even in *Afrique Occidentale Française* (AOF) and *Afrique Equatoriale Française* (AEF) there were proportionately significantly more colons and petits blancs than in British West Africa. The European settlers in the Cameroon mandate took the lead in organizing a settler lobby within *Afrique noire* by inviting other French settlers to a grandly titled *Etats-Generaux de la Colonisation Française* in September 1945. They called on the Assembly for assisted European immigration and greater control over African labour in French settler colonies on the pattern of Kenya and Mozambique.

This Assembly drew up the Constitution of April 1946 which established a French Union with all colonial inhabitants included in its citizens. But this proposed constitution was narrowly rejected by the electorate – French and those holding citizenship in 'France Overseas' – and the whole process of constitution-drafting had to be gone through a second time. Some laws, though, had been carried by the Constituent Assembly which were allowed to stand, including the critically important law abolishing forced labour in the colonies, proposed by Felix Houphouët-Boigny of the Ivory Coast and the equally significant law ending the legal distinction between subjects and citizens introduced by the Senegalese Socialist Lamine Gueye.

In June 1946 a second Constituent Assembly was elected. It was more conservative with the MRP strengthened at the expense of the Socialists and Communists. This new Assembly adopted a constitution which was much less liberal towards the colonies. Distinctions between citizens and subjects were maintained, as well as distinctive levels of privilege among the subjects and a complex voting system involving two electoral lists. Most overseas voters opposed it as a reactionary affirmation of colonial status in place of assimilation to citizenship.

All 22 elected African deputies signed a protest manifesto in September 1946, calling for a congress of African deputies and parties at Bamako, inviting the metropolitan parties to attend. The Socialist Minister of Overseas Territories, Marius Moutet, at first supported the idea. But as the date for the congress drew near new divisions over domestic and international issues complicated metropolitan politics. The upshot was that only the Communist Party supported the colonial demand for full citizenship. Moutet and the Socialists cooled towards the Congress. Hence those African leaders closest to the Socialists – including Lamine Gueye and Leopold Senghor of Senegal – kept away. Of the metropolitan parties only the Communist Party attended Bamako in October 1946. Thus began the great divide in the postwar politics of French Africa.

The Bamako Congress, with delegations present from most of the French African colonies, set up the African Democratic Assembly (*Rassemblement democratique africain* or RDA), an interterritorial alliance of parties formed earlier in each of the colonies. Gabriel d'Arboussier of Senegal became Secretary-General and Felix Houphouët-Boigny its leading parliamentary figure. The RDA dominated the politics of French West Africa and, to a lesser extent, Equatorial Africa for the next decade.

In terms of the sheer number of elections and changes of electoral regime it was to be an intensely political decade, for the French expected the inhabitants of their African colonies to register their opinions much more frequently than did the other colonial powers.[30] Voters elected delegates to the National Assembly, to the Assembly of the French Union, to the Grand Councils in Dakar and Brazzaville and to the territorial assemblies. From 1945 to 1948 they voted on four referenda, two constitutions, three national assemblies and three territorial assemblies. The territorial councillors elected members to the Assembly of the French Union twice, to the Federal Grand Council three times, and to the French Senate three times. In some cities mayors and councillors were elected. Sometimes the same politician would run for several offices at different levels simplifying the voters' choice but making governing more difficult; the Grand Council of French West Africa, for example, often had no quorum because several members were in Paris at the National Assembly.

Voting qualifications were the more complicated because there were two electoral colleges. Only full French citizens qualified for the first college, but the second, far from being a residual category of all non-citizens, was composed of select groups drawn from those not granted full citizenship. Indeed the concept of citizenship as a privileged status for which one gradually qualified as an *évolué*, rather than a democratic right, permeated the whole system producing a bewildering array of 'fancy franchises'. In 1946 the second college included ex-soldiers, civil servants, registered property holders, and holders of hunting and driving licences. In 1947 all persons literate in French or Arabic were added while in 1951 the vote was extended to tax-paying heads of households, mothers of two ex-soldiers, and pensioners. Such widening of the franchise was welcomed – in Cameroon, for example, 40,000 voters in 1946 mushroomed to 592,000 by 1953! – but it was a bewilderingly complex, frequently changing system.[31]

Finally, on 23 June 1956 the '*Loi Cadre*' for the French overseas territories came into effect. It granted the African colonies semi-autonomy with parliaments based on a general franchise. In AOF in 1945 only 54,888 voters had been enrolled in the first electoral class and 117,700 in the second electoral class, whereas now over 10 million people were enfranchised. Elected representatives were given a certain amount of governmental responsibility, although important powers were retained by France. Potential states thus emerged from what had hitherto been essentially administrative districts.

DEVELOPMENT: DILEMMAS AND DÉBÂCLES

Development became the watchword for colonial empires in the postwar world. The gathering momentum of Afro-Asian anti-colonial nationalism, as well as criticism from the Soviet Union and the United States, meant that the traditional notion of the Western civilizing mission needed updating. Gradually 'colonial development' emerged as the appropriate transformation of the traditional 'civilizing mission', pledging state-directed economic and social change, reinforced by policies designed to ensure the advance of the subject population. In 1929 and 1940 Britain enacted Colonial Development Acts which, in Lord Hailey's authoritative elucidation, marked:

> the translation into the Colonial sphere of . . . a new concept which had come to be increasingly accepted in domestic politics, the doctrine, namely, that active State intervention was a necessary lever to the amelioration of social conditions. . . . The aim of good Colonial administration thus came to be defined positively as the promotion of economic and social advance to provide the essential basis for political self-rule.[32]

After the war other colonial powers hastened to publicize similar commitment to 'development'. In 1946 France, following up development ideas canvassed at the 1944 Brazzaville Conference, established FIDES, an attractive acronym that compressed the long title 'The Fund for Investment and Social and Economic Development of the Overseas Territories'. In 1950 Belgium followed with a 10-year plan for public investment, boasting a strong welfare content. Indeed, France which had invested $542.5 million through FIDES by 1957, achieved much higher levels of public investment in per-capita terms in its relatively sparsely populated West African dependencies than Britain.[33] Until the late 1950s, however, 'development' – which would bind colonies and metropole together by webs of economic and cultural interdependence – was candidly recommended by France and Belgium as providing a superior route to African advancement than the nationalist path to political independence.

Yet, however generous the rhetoric of new-fangled developmentalism, the postwar economic circumstances of all the European metropoles meant that actual colonial practice was akin to old-fashioned imperial exploitation. Such was certainly the case with Socialist Britain. Colonial investment and development projects were shamelessly manipulated to suit British rather than African needs, though some of the most spendthrift examples of socialist planning also succeeded in squandering metropolitan resources on a colossal scale.[33]

The Tanganyikan groundnut scheme was seized on by right-wing critics in order to discredit large-scale socialist planning generally. Its origins lie in the postwar scarcity of oils and fats with less than two-thirds of the pre-war supply available on the international market in 1947 and shortages predicted to continue for a further 20 years. In British domestic politics this translated itself into short rations of margarine and cooking fat. The scheme grew out of proposals to increase groundnut production in northern Nigeria but was eventually concentrated in tsetse-infested western Tanganyika. Implementation was entrusted to the Ministry of Food. (The Colonial Office being considered all too likely to use its expertise to follow up its initial criticism of the scheme's feasibility with foot-dragging caution.) Minister of Food John Strachey, a noted socialist theorist, was considered sufficiently dynamic to administer such an imaginative scheme. The locale was chosen partly for its low population density which facilitated negotiations over land use. The consequent labour shortage was not envisaged as serious for the whole operation was predicated on utilizing labour-saving technology. A veritable mystique of the bulldozer, which would sweep away the obstacles hitherto blocking African development, permeated the entire enterprise. The scheme was staffed by men and women, chiefly from Britain but including many from the Commonwealth, seeking to recapture the camaraderie and 'can do' spirit of 'the people's war' while demonstrating that the socialist middle way was superior to both capitalism and communism.

Unfortunately there was a world shortage of tractors and bulldozers. US war-surplus Sherman tanks were imported from the Philippines as makeshift substitutes but their engines tended to seize up and when they did work they ripped up the tree stumps from the cleared land leaving it pitted as if by bomb craters. The Colonial Office caveats turned out to be well founded and when the harvest wilted the organizers in the field realized that the reason African Tanganyikans shunned the area was that it was ecologically low-grade and prone to drought. In face of overwhelming evidence Strachey insisted the scheme would work. Good money was thrown after bad. The European field staff, most of whom were ex-service men and women, adapted *Lily Marlene* once more, the great German war song which had sustained them through the Western Desert and the Italian campaign, with gently satirical lyrics about the misadventures of 'Mr Strachey's army'. More groundnuts were bought as seed than ever were harvested. The scheme was finally halted, without a single groundnut being sold, after £36 million had been wasted, equal to the Tanganyika government's total expenditure between 1946 and 1950.[34]

A scheme to turn the Gambia into an egg-producing country was also botched. Not a single egg was sold and £5 million was lost, part of a general write-off of ill-judged loans to Britain's tropical colonies at this time. The fallacies of state-induced development were witheringly analysed in Peter Bauer's seminal *West African Trade: A Study of Competition, Oligopoly, and Monopoly*, which appeared in 1954. And the official stamp of disapproval on all such late 1940s ventures in neo-mercantilist imperialism came in a confidential study commissioned by Harold Macmillan's government in 1957 which determined that no serious losses would be incurred through liquidating the Empire via decolonization.

If the groundnut scheme became a music-hall joke and a byword for cack-handed, crackbrained socialist incompetence in Britain, then aid fiascos also added a new term '*cartierisme*' to French political discourse when *Paris-Match* published a series of widely discussed articles by the journalist Raymond Cartier in 1956 which exposed aid scandals. Henceforth *cartierisme* became shorthand for the view that public investment and aid in Africa merely squandered vital metropolitan resources while usually doing more harm than good to its recipients.[35]

Cartierism was but the popular face of a profound transformation and massive reappraisal. Its origins must be sought in the radical plans for modernization proposed by the 'technocrats' of the Vichy regime. The *Ecole Nationale d'Administration* (ENA) was founded in 1946 to ensure that postwar France was well supplied with a dynamic corps of highly trained administrators. Jean Monnet and his team drew up the first Five Year Plan, implemented between 1947 and 1953, designed to renovate the infrastructure and key industries through a close partnership between the state and private enterprise along with some selective nationalization. Planners and technocrats ensured that American aid, chiefly through the Marshall plan, was channelled into modernization. There was tremendous economic progress and a spread of prosperity throughout the 1950s, with France enjoying the highest rate of economic growth of all the countries which entered the Common Market (the European Economic Community, EEC) in 1957. The tenfold multiplication of tractors between 1946 and 1958 signified the transformation of agriculture while industrial production surged by 85 per cent between 1950 and 1958. Such was the 'French Economic Miracle' of the 1950s and on into the 1960s. Its achievement was largely credited to the ascendancy in both state and economy of the new breed of modernizing technocrats.

When these modernizers turned their attention to the Empire their calculations convinced them that colonial rule was no longer cost-effective. France, which had been so slow to comprehend the price of colonial commitments in the immediate postwar period, was now much quicker to appreciate the alternatives to colonialism than Britain. As part of the process of becoming a founder-member of the EEC, France required its top policy-makers to carry out a searching reappraisal of the country's economic prospects. They decided that the first priority must be to transfer resources into high-tech industries which could compete in the postwar world of increasingly multinational capitalism. It seemed clear that too much concern for privileged colonial economic interests could only frustrate general modernization. Some army officers were making parallel reappraisals: colonial wars were wasting lives and diverting resources that should go into making France an effective nuclear power. Ironically the writings of General Beaufre which inspired South African and Portuguese counterinsurgency had exactly the opposite effect in North Africa, focusing French military thought on the deterrent effect of the *force de frappe*.

The flip side of *Cartieriste* disillusion with public investment in the African colonies was recognition of greater potential for economic growth through closer ties with other industrial powers. The modernizers brought the argument full circle when they pointed out that increased profits generated by switching public investment from the colonies to the metropolis gave greater potential for private investment in Africa.

There were political corollaries to these economic arguments which influenced the way the Common Market was implemented. During the early stages of the negotiations over the Treaty of Rome, formally establishing the EEC, both France and Belgium sought to protect their colonial vested interests against pressures from the other powers to open them up to competition from fellow EEC members. But by 1956 both France and Belgium were urging other EEC participants to share responsibility for aid to Africa in return for access to these colonial markets. (The culmination of this trend was the negotiation of trade privileges within the EEC for the former French and Belgian dependencies – plus Somalia, courtesy of the Italian connection – through the 1963 Yaoundé Convention.)

The disasters of British and French efforts at state-induced colonial development during the late 1940s and early 1950s forced them to reassess their policies. Their prestige as imperial rulers was damaged in the eyes of their own metropolitan publics and their colonial officials, as well as international opinion and, not least, their African subjects for whom the myth of the white man's wisdom was weakened by such crass ineptitude. The idea of development persisted beyond such fiascos but only by presenting itself as nation-building and shedding much of the imperialistic ideology which hitherto encrusted it. Further, it was increasingly understood that only by loosening the ties which bound the colonies to them could the metropoles gain the freedom to pursue their own modernization.

NOTES

1 R. D. Pearce, *The Turning Point in Africa* (London, Cass, 1982), p. 177.
2 *Op. cit.*, p. 167.
3 'Local Government as a Training-Ground for Parliamentary Government', n.d. Cited from the Creech Jones Papers in Pearce, *Turning Point*, p. 151.
4 Pearce, *Turning Point*, pp. 148–9.
5 *Op. cit.*, pp. 150–1.
6 *Op. cit.*, p. 167.
7 Sir B. Sharwood Smith, *But Always as Friends* (London, Allen and Unwin, 1969), p. 170.
8 Pearce, *Turning Point*, p. 163.
9 Smith, *Always as Friends*, pp. 171–2.
10 Pearce, *Turning Point*, p. 179.
11 John D. Hargreaves, *The End of Colonial Rule in West Africa* (London, Macmillan, 1979), p. 127.
12 R. Rathbone, 'Political Intelligence and Policing in Ghana', in David M. Anderson and David Killingray, eds., *Policing and Decolonisation* (Manchester, Manchester University Press, 1992), p. 84.
13 Brian Lapping, *The End of Empire* (London, Paladin, 1985), p. 437.
14 The phrase is from Dennis Austin, *Politics in Ghana* (London, Oxford University Press, 1970), p. 71; pp. 70–7 deal with Nii Bonne and his boycott committee.
15 Kwame Nkrumah, *Ghana: The Autobiography of Kwame Nkrumah* (Edinburgh, Nelson, 1957), p. 65.

16 Rathbone relished Special Branch's 'delicious Buchanish description: "one of the three most dangerous men in Bekwai". ' Rathbone, 'Political Intelligence', p. 89. George Padmore commented 'a piece of comic-opera politics' on the episode of the telegrams. George Padmore, *The Gold Coast Revolution* (London, Dobson, 1953), pp. 62–4.

17 Rathbone, 'Political Intelligence', pp. 89–90.

18 Austin, *Politics*, p. 75.

19 Nkrumah, *Autobiography*, Appendix B.

20 *Op. cit.*, p. 71.

21 Pearce, *Turning Point*, p. 190.

22 *Op. cit.*, p. 173.

23 See Chapter 7, this volume, for a general discussion of nationalism. For Robinson's views on continuity between imperialism and nationalism see R. Robinson, 'Non-European Foundations of European Imperialism: Sketch for a Theory of Collaboration', in Roger Owen and Bob Sutcliffe, eds., *Studies in the Theory of Imperialism* (London, 1972), pp. 117–42; and R. Robinson, 'Imperial Theory and the Question of Imperialism after Empire', in R. F. Holland and G. Rivzi. eds., *Perspectives on Imperialism and Decolonization* (London, Cass, 1984), pp. 42–54. For an illuminating discussion of the relationship between imperialist and nationalist discourse see M. Crawford Young, 'Nationalism, Ethnicity and Class', *Cahiers d'Etudes Africaines* XXVI (1986), pp. 421–95.

24 G. E. Metcalfe, *Great Britain and Ghana: Documents of Ghana History* (Legon, University of Ghana, 1964), p. 685.

25 Pearce, *Turning Point*, pp. 181–2.

26 Rathbone, 'Political Intelligence', p. 84.

27 R. Rathbone, 'The Government of the Gold Coast after the Second World War', *African Affairs* LXVII (1968), p. 217.

28 For the political theory of the Commonwealth see W. David McIntyre, *The Commonwealth of Nations* (Minneapolis, University of Minnesota Press, 1977), pp. 3–16.

29 D. Goldsworthy, 'Aspects of Colonial Policy during the Churchill and Eden Governments', *The Journal of Commonwealth and Imperial History* XVIII (1990), pp. 83–4.

30 Ruth B. Collier, *Regimes in Tropical Africa: Changing Forms of Supremacy* (Berkeley, niversity of California Press, 1982), a careful statistical comparative study brings this out well.

31 Ruth Schacter Morgenthau, *Political Parties in French-Speaking Africa* (Oxford, Clarendon Press, 1964), pp. 55–6.

32 Lord Hailey, *An African Survey: Revised 1956* (London, Oxford University Press, 1957), p. 203.

33 V. Thompson, 'French Economic Policy in Tropical Africa,' in Peter Duignan and L. H. Gann, eds., *Colonialism in Africa, 1870–1960. The Economics of Colonialism* (Cambridge, Cambridge University Press, 1975).

34 Alan Wood, *The Groundnut Affair* (London, Bodley Head, 1950), especially pp. 202–3. See also John Iliffe, *A Modern History of Tanganyika* (Cambridge, Cambridge University Press, 1979), pp. 440–2.

35 Jacques Marseille, *Empire coloniale et capitalisme française: Histoire d'un divorce* (Paris, Albin Michel, 1984), pp. 357–65.

10

Suez 1956: The Turning Point?

Anthony Eden, Foreign Secretary and Deputy Prime Minister in the Churchill government, and Churchill's successor from April 1955, frequently differed from his old leader on foreign affairs in general and the preservation of British interests in the Middle East in particular. Whereas for Churchill the keystone of British policy was the special relationship with the United States, Eden resented America's increasing predominance within the Atlantic alliance. Churchill, though reluctantly accepting that his old hopes for maintaining British power and prestige through the imperial connection were now doomed, shared the doubts of many members of his party about accepting new Commonwealth members as leading actors in world politics. Eden, by contrast, prided himself on his good relations with Pandit Nehru, Prime Minister of India and senior statesman of the non-aligned movement, and, not yet being prepared to commit Britain to the movement towards European unity, envisaged a world role as patron of the developing nations inside and outside the Commonwealth. Eden was less inclined to sympathize with South African hesitation over a multiracial Commonwealth and found the evasively antagonistic attitude of the South African Prime Minister Johannes Strijdom to Gold Coast membership particularly irritating.[1] With his long experience of Anglo-Egyptian relations – he had been involved in negotiating the 1936 treaty, as he reminded Nasser after greeting him in Arabic on first acquaintance – and his academic background in Oriental studies, he regarded himself, and impressed many well-informed observers, as exceptionally well equipped to promote Anglo-Arab understanding.[2] Like all his predecessors, Eden believed in a strong military presence in the Middle East to protect oil supplies and sustain Britain's imperial strategy; but, like Bevin he hoped to achieve this by cooperation with friendly Arab governments, for 'In the second half of the twentieth century we cannot hope to maintain our position in the Middle East by the methods of the last century.'[3]

Nasser's obvious popular support made it easier to conclude the Anglo-Egyptian Treaty which had eluded Bevin. The arrangements were complex: a phased withdrawal of British troops was to be completed by June 1956, but the base was to be maintained ready for use in the event of war: Egypt was to join a Middle East defence organization and to receive military and economic aid. To many contemporary observers the negotiation of this complicated agreement seemed further confirmation of the considerable diplomatic skills of Eden – manifest in the succession of diplomatic triumphs from 1951 to 1954, including his handling of the Geneva peace talks on Indo-China – and of the pragmatic reasonableness of Nasser.

The new Egyptian regime smoothed the path to agreement by waiving its claim to sovereignty over the Sudan, a sticking point for King Farouk who had considered himself sovereign ruler of both countries. With General Neguib, half-Sudanese and educated at Khartoum, as nominal head of state, self-determination for the Sudan seemed likely to operate in favour of Egypt. In any case, the 'free officers' were making a Pan-Arab appeal, transcending colonial frontiers.

In 1954 Nasser published his political testament *Egypt's Liberation: Philosophy of the Revolution*, proclaiming Egypt's anti-imperial destiny through its unique command of the strategic space where the three circles of Islam, the Arabs and Africa overlapped.[4] Those who actually read the work discovered some quite paternalistic ideas about Egypt's 'civilizing mission', especially within the 'second circle', Africa.[5] Indeed, initially, British officials in Cairo responded favourably, though – predictably – patronizingly, finding that the book 'has a certain breadth of vision, humanity and idealism which one might be excused for not expecting from a man of his background'.[6] At the same time a suitably bland summary of Nasser's ideas was packaged for the American foreign policy élite, projecting him as a moderate leader bent on a constructive policy of economic development through cooperation with the West.[7] (Interestingly, that other great mid-twentieth-century patriot, Churchill, claiming, like Nasser, a major world role for his country despite its relatively limited resources, popularized the same geopolitical conceit of three interlinked circles.)[8]

Eden, hoping Nasser would prove the reforming leader the Arabs needed, had persuaded Churchill to accept the risk of phased, conditional withdrawal from the Suez base. With King Idris still cooperative, British forces were withdrawn to Cyrenaica and to Cyprus. Eden expected Nasser to collaborate with the West in organizing regional defence.

Eden's policy of cooperation with Arab nationalism, despite his suspicion of the United States, was closer to the strategy devised by the new President, Dwight D. Eisenhower, and his Secretary of State, John Foster Dulles, to cope with the threat of disorder subsequent to decolonization than Churchill's had been. No other postwar American president demonstrated such determination to slash military budgets as the famous wartime commander. He had no wish to fight conventional wars in Asia or Africa. Korea had vividly demonstrated the danger of such involvement. Instead, Eisenhower devised a fourfold strategy. First, he made extremely skilful use of the Central Intelligence Agency (CIA) both to ensure that American policy-making was relatively well-informed and for covert intervention in areas which threatened to become unstable and therefore liable to left-wing take-over. Second, he sent United States military advisers to train native troops and encouraged their officers to come to America for advanced instruction. Third, they – for this was Dulles's main contribution, dubbed 'pactomania' by his critics – encouraged the development of a series of military alliances uniting friendly rulers in a common fight against the Soviets outside, and left-wing subversion inside, their various regions. Like Eden, they were on the look out for an Arab strongman and thought Nasser might fill the bill. Finally, Eisenhower predicated his general military policy on powerful hydrogen bombs as well as small tactical nuclear weapons, threatening to deploy them should Soviet or Chinese forces launch an invasion or become heavily involved with revolutionaries. This last was familiarly characterized as getting 'more bang for your buck' but the whole package was designed to curb military spending which had reached $50 billion annually under Truman. Eisenhower was convinced that the continuation of such profligacy would induce runaway inflation, crippling the American economy and threatening the very fabric of Western capitalism. Within two years he succeeded in shearing nearly a third from Truman's military budget bringing it down to about $34 billion.

Eisenhower and Dulles took over shortly after the July 1952 Free Officers' coup but local American agents had already laid the foundations for such a policy. Arriving in January Kermit Roosevelt of the CIA quickly established close contact with at least two of the Free Officers involved in the coup, six of whom had been to American military schools.[9] Whereas the British embassy was completely surprised by the coup, the Americans knew what to expect. Indeed, to add insult to injury to the one-time paramount power, the plotters chose to transmit their warning to the British not to interfere through a member of the United States embassy.[10]

The contrast, though galling to the British, is not difficult to explain. The Free Officers had spent years intriguing against the British presence so their whole security system was designed to keep them ignorant. Certainly the British had plenty of Egyptian friends but by 1952 they were the wrong sort in the wrong places. Bevin's admonition that he wanted cooperation 'with peasants not pashas', ran counter to the actual social and cultural configuration of the Anglo-Egyptian connection as it had evolved since 1882. 'British' in Cairo meant something different from its meaning in the United Kingdom; it also included the polyglot and cosmopolitan community of Greeks, Cypriots, Maltese and others, the *habitués* of Shepheard's Hotel, certain chic nightclubs and department stores, principally distinguished by their wealthy lifestyle. Wealthy Egyptians, too, were involved in the Anglo-Egyptian connection: favourites of the exiled king and pashas – especially those pashas who profited from cotton exports to Britain. These were precisely the Egyptians the Free Officers were determined to be rid of as corrupt collaborators in foreign domination. The ardent Anglophile Egyptian ambassador 'Amir Pasha, who had dispatched his 'secret' reports from London in the Foreign Office diplomatic bag, was recalled and the journalist Mohammed al-Kebir, a confidential British embassy contact of long standing, was arrested.[11] After July 1952 Britain's friends from the *ancien régime* were marginalized and apprehensive.

The South-East Asia Treaty Organization (SEATO) and the Baghdad Pact in the Middle East became the best-known examples of Western 'pactomania'. For his part Nasser was vividly aware of the economic plight of Egypt's rapidly rising population and hoped for Anglo-American support for the Aswan High Dam. This was a huge project to harness the lower Nile for irrigation and hydroelectric power, symbolizing the way Nasser's regime would triumphantly bring Egypt into the twentieth century.

The problem for Western strategy was that Arab nationalism, anti-imperialist since the end of the First World War, had become 'revolutionary' after 1948. The defeat in Palestine revealed that the Arabs, despite their formal independence, were politically disunited, militarily weak and economically backward. Their impotence was still blamed on imperialism. Arab nationalists discerned a global conspiracy in which Israel was intruded into their heartland to ensure continued Western domination. But intellectuals also began to identify chronic weaknesses within Arab society and culture, arguing that these had eased the way for Zionist penetration. The new nationalist leaders, stern young officers, promised a social revolution which would eradicate weakness, delivering unity, power and prosperity to Arab civilization. They usually defined this revolution as socialism – but a specifically Arab socialism, lest they be charged that their revolution was not authentically Arab in inspiration. Arab nationalism was now much more than cultural revival and opposition to European imperialism. It involved land reform, extensive nationalization, and five-year plans, all in the name of 'the revolution'. And if, in this new radical discourse, the Free Officers considered themselves 'revolutionaries', then their opponents, by definition, must be 'reactionaries'.

Eisenhower and Dulles understood and sympathized with much of the new anti-colonial nationalism. Their own people, after all, had begun the first modern anti-colonial struggle in 1776. But from the start Americans disliked revolutions which ranged beyond the political, social, and economic boundaries of their own, which they believed superior to revolutions of the 'Right' (as John Quincy Adams viewed the Latin American revolts) or of the 'Left', like the French Revolution. In 1917, when Lenin joined violent insurrection to a doctrine with worldwide ambitions which was repugnant to most Americans, 'revolution' became the mark of a society in desperate crisis.

This was the significant ideological legacy inherited by the new administration. Eisenhower and Dulles both realized, moreover, that the British and French Empires were close to collapse. They wanted their European allies to get rid of their remaining imperial commitments because the longer the Europeans stayed the more the nationalist opposition veered leftwards towards revolution. And they had no wish to become involved in the costly business of propping up such rickety structures. Better all round for the Europeans to decolonize quickly so that the new states could take on their own defence in alliances like SEATO and the Baghdad Pact.

Arab nationalism, though, constituted a problem for the Americans. There was, of course, the constraint of Israel and the Zionist lobby, although Eisenhower was less inclined to reflex obedience to that pressure than Truman or subsequent presidents. And then Arab nationalism claimed to be both revolutionary and socialist – but at least it was 'Arab Socialism' and not 'Scientific Socialism' or 'Marxist-Leninism', oriented to Moscow. And the Egyptian brand of socialism, Nasserism, was notably more pragmatic than its rigorously ideological rival, Ba'thism, which had been founded by Sorbonne-trained Syrians and drew its most influential support from junior officers in Syria and Iraq.[12] Nasserism, as its name implies, blended revolutionary nationalism with a personality cult. In 1955, with the appearance of G. A. Nasser's *Philosophy of the Revolution*, it began to take on its characteristically flexible shape, combining socialist policies for the transformation of Egyptian society with the notion that Nasser's charismatic leadership would inspire Arab unity.

Three events that same year – the Israeli raid on 28 February across the 1948 armistice line to attack an Egyptian camp (allegedly in response to *fedayeen* guerrilla raids); the Baghdad Pact, finalized in April; and the Bandung Conference of non-aligned states, also in April 1955 – combined to radicalize Nasserism. In 1955 David Ben-Gurion, the legendary founder of Israel, returned as Prime Minister and Minister of Defence, signalling a hard-line policy towards the Arabs. Before the Israelis withdrew they had killed 38 Egyptians and wounded 31 more, revealing Egypt's vulnerability and thereby provoking the hectic Middle Eastern arms race of the 1950s and 1960s. In theory the Western powers – the United States, Britain and France – had placed an arms embargo on the Middle East but it was well-known that France was supplying Israel with modern weapons, because of Egyptian support for Arab nationalism in the Mahgreb.

The Baghdad Pact was mooted in January when Turkey, a recent member of NATO, and Iraq announced they were to form a defensive alliance, with the blessing of Britain and the United States. Until then Nasser had cooperated with the West, as evident from his 1954 defence agreements with Eden. As well as hoping to entice Egypt into the Baghdad Pact through supplying Western funding for the Aswan Dam, Britain also made strenuous, but ultimately unsuccessful, secret efforts to resolve the Arab–Israeli dispute through Israeli concessions.

But Nasser refused to join. Indeed he campaigned forcefully against the new pact on the grounds that it undermined Arab unity. The United States sensed that the West might alienate Arab opinion generally and backed off. In any case, concerned about Israel's reaction, and the Zionist lobby at home, America had promised its support conditional on an Arab–Israeli *rapprochement*. Not so

Britain which made the Pact the cornerstone of its policy in the region. Britain joined in April, followed by Pakistan and Iran. But Egypt was successful in evoking refusal from Syria, Saudi Arabia, Yemen, Lebanon and Jordan, in an impressive display of Pan-Arab solidarity. (Oil-rich Iraq, which Nasser feared the West was promoting as his rival for Arab leadership, was thus isolated as the only Arab member.)

The Baghdad Pact was concluded on the eve of the Bandung Conference of non-aligned states. Nasser travelled to Bandung, Indonesia – his first visit outside the Middle East – to join other leaders equally intent on establishing the postcolonial states of Asia and Africa as a force to be counted in world affairs. osBorn in 1919, he was by far the youngest of the major figures present. (Jawaharial Nehru, the Indian Prime Minister, was in his mid-sixties; Achmed Sukarno, the host, was in his mid-fifties; even Nkrumah, about to become leader of independent Ghana – who was absent at Bandung but very much present in spirit through his emissary – was 10 years older.) He carried weight at such a global conference because of his country's geopolitical importance, 'the geographical crossroads of the world',[13] as he proclaimed, bridging Asia, the Middle East and Africa, with strong links to the Mediterranean basin. Bandung gave him a world platform from which to proclaim his ideas on international relations. Impressed by the size of the conference – 29 states from Asia and Africa were present – and its support for Arab causes, he considered that the days of the bipolar world order were numbered as more and more states struggled free from imperial domination or, if nominally independent, became truly so by detaching themselves from the East–West blocs. (Marshal Tito of Yugoslavia was present, and profoundly influential, at Bandung.) But so long as the bipolar system persisted then non-aligned states should use it to play the powers off against each other in a game Nasser called 'positive neutralism'. (The term 'Third World' was coined in France in the early 1950s to identify this powerful trend in international politics. It was described as a 'third' world precisely because it insisted on its separation from the antagonistic blocs dominated by the United States and the Soviet Union.)[14]

The death of Stalin in 1953 saw the beginnings of a more flexible Soviet policy towards the Afro-Asian world, opening the way for Nasser's adventures in 'positive neutralism'. In July 1953 the Soviet Union promised to give 4 million roubles – approximately £500,000 – to the United Nations programme of technical assistance to underdeveloped nations, reversing a long period of opposition to that fund. Trade and aid to India followed. Plainly Soviet policy to those still dubbed 'national bourgeois' leaders had altered. By the time Khruschev codified the change, during his wholesale onslaught on Stalinism at the twentieth Communist Party Congress in February 1956, Nasser had become its most spectacular beneficiary.

Both Nasser and the West played a rough game of international politics. Radio Cairo's *Voice of the Arabs*, the first international programme by a Middle Eastern

country, urged the masses to oppose 'the stooges of imperialism' and warned
pro-Western regimes to stay away from 'imperialist devices' (meaning the
Baghdad Pact). Nasser's propaganda against the Pact and his emphasis on Arab
solidarity worked. Arab public opinion dissuaded other rulers from joining. Nor
was the 'African Circle' neglected. Broadcasts to East Africa angered the
colonial governments; during the Mau Mau emergency Cairo's *Sauti ya Uhuru*
(Voice of Freedom) purported to originate from a mobile transmitter in the
Mount Kenya forests.[15]

Nasser responded to the successful Israeli raid by negotiating with both the
Western and Communist sides for modern weapons. Declaring that American
prices were not competitive, he concluded an arms agreement with Czechoslovakia in late September 1955. Dulles now became very interested in helping
Egypt finance the Aswan Dam. As the United States realized, Nasser would have
trouble paying for both the arms deal and the dam. Britain and the United States,
along with the World Bank, accordingly agreed to help. But Dulles became
trapped in Washington politics with pro-Israeli congressmen slowing down,
indeed virtually vetoing, his initiative. Nasser reached agreement with Eugene
Black, President of the World Bank, on the latter's visit to Cairo. In February
1956 he wrote to Washington to discuss implementation. Five months later he
was still waiting for a reply. In April Egypt, Saudi Arabia, Syria, and Yemen
formed a joint military alliance obviously aimed at Israel. In May Nasser further
irritated the Americans by switching recognition from Chiang Kai-Shek to
Communist China.

The hard men on the British side were all for making Egypt pay for such
intransigence. Macmillan, most hawkish member of the British Cabinet next to
Eden himself, summed up their response, 'So it comes to a mild squeeze on
Egypt, and benefits to the loyal Arabs. . . . Let unpleasant things happen to
Nasser, and pleasant things to the others.'[16] Macmillan's 'mild squeeze'
amounted to threatening to withdraw support from the Aswan Dam; the
'pleasant things' referred chiefly to supplying arms, especially British Centurion
tanks, to participants in the Baghdad Pact, notably to Nasser's rival Iraq. Dulles
satisfied such hard-liners with a cold dismissal of the Egyptian request on
19 July.

Nasser retaliated by nationalizing the Suez Canal Company on 26 July 1956.
At a stroke he regained his prestige and also the Company's $25 million annual
profit to finance building the dam. He also threatened the European economy;
67 million tons of oil had moved to Europe through Suez in 1955. As long as he
compensated the Company's shareholders, he was legally justified in seizing the
canal. He promised, further, to keep the waterway open to all former users of the
canal. The British and French then withdrew their pilots and engineers. Old
racist stereotypes died hard. There was much talk from the descendants of
Ferdinand de Lesseps and George Stephenson that the 'gyppos' were far too
stupid and cack-handed to run anything as complex as the canal, left to them it

would simply silt up. In fact, the overworked Egyptian pilots did a magnificent job of keeping the traffic flowing.

The pathology of British decision-making during the crisis was affected by the pent-up frustrations of a decade of retreat. Already in March, Eden's Private Secretary, Sir Evelyn Shuckburgh, observed 'Ministers – led by PM mad keen to land British troops somewhere to show we are still alive and kicking.'[17] They resented their reduced Middle Eastern role and suspected the Americans, Soviets and Egyptians of supplanting them. Since the superpowers were too big to lash out at, Nasser became a convenient scapegoat. (Or, as the wits put it, Nasser was the camel that broke the straw's back.)

The mood in the Cabinet was increasingly febrile. Eden, living on his nerves, suffering from recurrent worsening bouts of mistreated illness, punctuated by occasional spells of heavy drinking, constantly interfered on matters of detail. Within the Conservative Party the 'Suez group' of MPs had opposed the 1954 agreement on withdrawal believing it would undermine Britain's standing in the Middle East. Some 27 voted against the government. When future events appeared to prove them right – though their own stand-pat policy was hardly realistic – Eden was under considerable pressure. The dread words 'Munich' and 'appeasement' were bandied about. The right-wing press taunted the government about the need for 'the smack of firm government'.[18] Churchill, a late-convert to phased withdrawal, started grumbling. Eden, determined that the charges against him should not stick, began demonizing Nasser as a latter-day Mussolini if not Hitler. In his memoirs Eden regretted that Western readers had been slower to read *Philosophy of the Revolution* than *Mein Kampf* with the implication that had they done so there would have been no danger of appeasement. He also feared in Africa reactions, specifying the case of a Nigerian Muslim chief, 'if Nasser were allowed by the world to seize his spoil and keep it'.[19]

When the US government worked for a compromise, the French Socialist Prime Minister Guy Mollet and Eden entered into an elaborate conspiracy with Israel. (Growing personal animosity between Eden and Dulles weakened Western coordination. In the fortnight before Suez Britain did its best to keep Washington ignorant.) The French, British and Israeli conspirators met at Sèvres, at French instigation, to discuss the ingenious plan of a French General, Maurice Challe. Israel was to launch a blitzkreig on Egypt, using the pretext of *fedayeen* attacks across the armistice line. Then Britain and France would act.

The French took the initiative in organizing the so-called 'Challe scenario' because they were the most eager to attack Nasser and not at all worried how the war was launched, as long as it actually broke out. Their anger over Radio Cairo's support for the FLN increased with the nationalization of de Lesseps's canal. But behind this anger were clear enough aims. France thought that a defeat for Nasser might pave the way to a favourable settlement in Algeria and hoped to reassert its presence in the Middle East. The French had least to lose and therefore had the least incentive to caution. All three French ministers at Sèvres, moreover, had been active in the Resistance and relished the return to 'cloak and dagger' diplomacy.

Of the three conspiratorial states Israel had most to lose, but correspondingly most to gain. It wished to end Anglo-American plans for a compromise in the Arab–Israeli conflict which would involve sacrificing 'land for peace' and it was acutely aware of the danger posed by any strong Arab – but particularly Egyptian – ruler. Israeli policy-makers had given much thought, and a semi-public airing, to the implications of a preventive war against Egypt. In a strict military sense 1956 was too early. A stream of new weapons from France, such as the Mystère IV aircraft, which would redress the military balance upset by the Czech arms deal, was just beginning to arrive when the canal was nationalized. On the other hand the Israelis needed to keep the arms flowing so were very susceptible to French pressure. Their main worries were over Britain. They were afraid that their cities would be bombed and felt that only British air power operating from Britain's Middle Eastern bases could save them. Above all they were concerned that having committed themselves they would be left in the lurch, when Britain – subject to international pressure, especially from the United States and the Commonwealth – drew back from fulfilling its role in the plot. At Sèvres, therefore, they were intent on locking the British into the conspiracy. Given the war psychosis in the British Cabinet they need not have worried.

On 29 October the Israelis attacked Egypt. Britain and France delivered simultaneous ultimatums to Egypt and Israel, warning both sides to keep their forces away from the canal. Everything was carefully drafted to provoke Nasser into rejection so that the British and French could seize the canal area. Whether Nasser resisted or caved in his prestige with the Arab masses would be fatally damaged and the conspirators rewarded with a more tractable Egyptian government.

International fury aborted the conspiracy to reoccupy Suez. Britain and France used their vetos, for the first time, in the UN Security Council to prevent condemnation of the Anglo-French invasion on a resolution proposed by Henry Cabot Lodge, the American representative. The USSR under Khruschev, happy to see world attention diverted from its simultaneous invasion of Hungary, threatened the aggressors but also offered to mediate. The State Department hurried to counter these Soviet moves. It forced a resolution through the UN General Assembly urging a truce and openly doubted whether the French in Algeria and the British in Cyprus were pursuing a justifiable policy. Only Australia and New Zealand of the Commonwealth states gave Britain their reluctant support, almost all the rest joined in the general condemnation. South Africa kept discreetly quiet, while Canada was especially critical. In Britain itself the crisis was ultimately more divisive than any other postwar foreign-policy issue.

The United States kept up the pressure. It organized the withholding of Latin American oil supplies to Europe so that Britain and France could not obtain alternative supplies to replace the oil which could not get through the clogged canal. The British and French agreed to a cease-fire hours before they would have seized the canal. Throughout November Washington carefully rationed the oil flow to Europe. Not until the United Nations resolution was obeyed and the troops withdrawn was the oil allowed to flow freely. Washington also conveyed to Chancellor of the Exchequer Harold Macmillan, originally a strong supporter of the operation, that American willingness to sustain the sterling area as a basis for British power was conditional upon acceptable international behaviour.

French opinion was much less divided over Suez. France also had more to lose in Algeria and less to lose in the Arab world as a whole. It was, therefore, the British government which buckled first before international opinion. Britain had most to lose merely by being involved in the conspiracy, whatever its outcome. Two of the 'three circles' through joint membership of which British policy-makers believed their superior international standing derived – the Commonwealth and the Anglo-American connection – had been badly deceived. Eden went off to recuperate in the West Indies and Macmillan, half-American as some commentators pointed out, took over the premiership in January 1957. Eisenhower moved quickly to restore Anglo-American relations. France felt it was being left in the lurch once more, with echoes of the British retreat from Dunkirk and 'perfidious Albion'. Strong antipathy to *les Anglo-Saxons* coloured French policy in the aftermath of the Suez débâcle.

The speed and completeness of Nasser's diplomatic triumph was matched by the humbling of British power throughout the whole of the Middle East. Collusion with Israel, coupled with the stark revelation of economic weakness, swept away British pretentions to run a world system on the cheap. The politically astute young King Hussein, Hashemite monarch of Jordan, had already responded to riots in Amman in January 1956 by dismissing General Glubb as British Commander-in-Chief of the Jordanian Arab Legion. In July 1958 the Hashemite regime in Iraq, Britain's last bastion, was overthrown and its leaders murdered.

Nasser's humiliation of Britain and France entranced an Arab world fixed to its radios throughout the crisis. Suez transformed Nasser from a little-known colonel behind the 1952 coup into a colossus bestriding both non-aligned and anti-colonialist movements. The Ba'th in Syria sought to participate in his triumph and pushed Nasser towards unity. In 1958 the birth of the United Arab Republic – a union of Egypt and Syria – was presented to the Arab world as the first stage in the march towards general Arab unity. Wildly enthusiastic crowds greeted Nasser on his first visit to Damascus. All over the Arab world, while their rulers cowered, 'Nasserists' thronged the streets to praise the long-awaited Arab strongman. In a gesture that endorsed his standing alongside Nasser as joint leader of the anti-imperial forces in Africa, Nkrumah married an Egyptian

Christian woman from Nasser's circle. Cairo gave salaries, normally £100 a month, to refugee African nationalists. They also had access to Radio Cairo's 'Voice of Africa from Cairo calling East, Central and South Africa', broadcasting for four hours daily in Amharic, Swahili, Lingala, Sesotho, Nyanja, Somali and English, while 'Voice of Africa Calling West Africa' broadcast in French, English, Fulani and Hausa. And in Algeria FLN morale soared. In 1958, two years after Suez, the provisional government of the Algerian Revolution was established – in Cairo.[20]

What foiled the British and French effort to remake the Middle East in 1956 was a double change in the structure of world power. Most obvious was the bipolar world order dominated by the United States and the Soviet Union. Threats and sanctions by the superpowers, especially economic warfare by America, brought them to heel. But they also failed to evolve policies adapted to an emerging multipolar order based on the multiplication of new states since the Second World War. Their strategy seemed sensible enough. After all it amounted to the traditional British recipe for running a world system on the cheap through informal imperialism: identify an effective regional power which would shoulder the burden of maintaining order in return for diplomatic and economic support and a share in the profits of development.[21] In the postwar period locally dominant states, of the type classified by political scientists as regional superpowers, emerged at either end of Africa: South Africa at the continent's southern tip and, eventually, Israel to the north-east. (Regional superpowers being states which are so predominant over their neighbours that they can function locally as superpowers.)

The emergence of local superpowers promised political stability to areas otherwise afflicted with postimperial turbulence. Some regional powers offered very much more. By coordinating communications, finance, commerce and industry they served as gatekeepers to the hinterland in much the same way as their imperial predecessors had done – indeed they represented the old colonial networks updated. South Africa, through the Rand goldfields and their offshoots in secondary industry, commerce and finance, provided such comprehensive coordination.

In neither the South African or the Israeli case, though, was their hegemony uncontested. South Africa and Israel were quickly lumped together by the majority of new states in the United Nations as enemies of African and Arab self-determination; hence, however successfully they practised *realpolitik*, they could never be effective ideological surrogates for the Western imperial connection. That Israel remained a liberal cause in the West long after it had been linked with South Africa in Third World demonology complicated things somewhat. Hugh Gaitskell, the Labour leader, was the first to compare Nasser's actions with those of Hitler and Mussolini, while some of his more irreverent backbenchers joked about their own 'settler lobby' with reference to the number of committed Zionists among their leadership. The Democratic leader in the

Senate also wanted Eisenhower to back Eden.[22] Neither South Africa nor Israel was therefore simply confronted by states wishing to supersede them as the predominant regional power. The challenge to both was much more radical, involving their right to exist as presently constituted. African nationalism disputed the legitimacy of an expansionist South African state increasingly dominated by Afrikaner nationalism. More immediately and seriously, the legitimacy – indeed the very existence – of Israel was challenged by Arab nationalism, marshalled by Egypt, in strong competition for the role of local superpower. Hence Israel, lacking the economic attractions and coercions available to South Africa, pursued military hegemony to survive.

Britain was aware of the dangers of backing Israel, especially when Ben-Gurion regarded preventive war as a feasible policy option deserving cool, pragmatic consideration. Once the dispute over the Suez base was settled, Britain recognized 'it is in our interest to maintain the present Egyptian Government in power' and serious attention was given to providing effective economic aid towards Egyptian development and 'modernisation of her armaments'.[23] As late as the end of 1955 the British believed it would be necessary to go to war against Israel in defence of Jordan in order to maintain its credibility as a great power in the region by honouring its treaty obligations.[24] But if Britain turned to the Arabs rather than the Israelis then it was caught in the crossfire between its old ally Nuri es-Said of Iraq and Nasser, the new Arab strongman. In the end it was Egypt not Israel that Britain invaded. And, of course, that was the way the search for a strong local power to back in pursuit of imperialism on the cheap had usually ended in the 1880s and 1890s. Impatience gave way to exasperation when chosen collaborators showed a stubborn disposition to pursue their own interests and the diplomacy of informal imperialism collapsed into invasion and occupation. But this was the mid-twentieth century not the late nineteenth. Nasser and Ben-Gurion were the rulers of internationally recognized sovereign states not tribal potentates. Both, moreover, were incorruptible patriots with a clear sense of their countries' interests and sharp strategic intelligence, backed by diplomatic skills of an unconventional sort, which tended to nonplus more orthodox negotiators – poor material for manipulation in the service of informal imperialism. Indeed, as had often happened in the preliminaries to the scramble for Africa 70 years earlier, the Europeans were sucked into the vortex of regional politics at the behest of their local collaborator. Britain eventually shrank back from the price Nasser put on his collaboration only to stumble into the trap sprung by Ben-Gurion and the French.

The recent opening of the relevant British archives, under the 30-year rule, has generated a flurry of controversy about the significance of the Suez crisis in precipitating decolonization – hence the question mark after the title. Hitherto the 'conventional wisdom' of historians had endorsed the contemporary evaluation by politicians, journalists and the general public that the Suez crisis suddenly revealed the true costs of a mid-twentieth century empire. Consequently, so the argument goes, the European imperial powers were forced to recognize that the game was up and hastened to adjust their policies to their reduced circumstances through rapid decolonization. That point of view was put forcibly by Brian Lapping in the book which accompanied his Granada television *End of Empire* series where he claimed that 'The Suez operation wrote "finis" not only to the British empire but to all the empires of western Europe.'[25] Hitherto, Lapping argued, despite the decolonization of Asia and some movement in North and West Africa, the European imperial powers showed no disposition to quit their remaining African colonies, believing them to be many decades short of readiness for independence. After the 'imperial cataclysm' of Suez, though, they swiftly loosened their grip so that by the end of 1960 decolonization accelerated leaving only what he termed 'the citadels of settler domination' – in the Portuguese territories, Algeria, the Rhodesias and the Union – and those dangerously isolated.

This 'conventional wisdom' about decolonization, Lapping's phrase, had hitherto been challenged from the periphery. Historians of African nationalism had argued that it arose and developed powerfully chiefly for reasons rooted in the internal histories of individual African countries. Hence, although an external crisis, like Suez, might provide some encouragement, the prime causes of decolonization were to be sought in the development of anti-colonial nationalist movements within each individual colony. Now the opening of the archives has exposed the conventional wisdom to a new line of attack, originating from the centre rather than the periphery, with imperial historians finding marked continuities of policy before and after November 1956. All that sound and fury with massive crowds harangued by A. J. P. Taylor in Trafalgar Square, rebukes from both the USA and the USSR as well as the UN, the Commonwealth buckling and Prime Minister Eden collapsing under the strain – what in the end did it all signify? Not a lot, argue the revisionists, because, so far as the actual implementation of a policy of decolonization was concerned, British politicians and officials continued much as before. (The two revisionist arguments can of course be neatly combined. If Suez was not the 'imperial climateric' hitherto assumed then a new factor or factors must have entered the situation to produce rapid decolonization around 1960. The emergence of strong nationalist movements in individual European colonies would constitute such a transformation of the situation.)

As this is a controversy about what happened before November 1956, and even more about what followed, the narrative analysis of the actual unfolding of the crisis has not resolved it. In particular, the elucidation of the controversy must be sought in the subsequent section on the changing nature of the colonial metropoles and the effect of this on decolonization.

Nevertheless, it is worth pointing out that different interpretations derive from differences of perspective and scale. And this is inevitable for Suez was a critical event, for example, in international history – indeed world history – and the history of the Commonwealth, as well as in the unfolding of a policy of decolonization. It looms larger than almost any other event taking place on the African continent in the postwar period. Thus, in the field of international history Walter le Feber in a capsule account of the end of empire in Africa states flatly that 'the Suez crisis and the termination of British control in Ghana in 1957 . . . set off a chain reaction.'[26]

Undoubtedly it was, as Nasser intended it to be, a landmark in the non-aligned movement's involvement in international relations. The 'Czech arms deal' marked the Soviet bloc's first overt arms agreement with a Third World state. Russian military and economic advisers moved in. The Soviet Union certainly was not decisive in ending European empire in Africa, and Nasser had no more intention of surrendering Egypt's hard-won independence to the Soviets than to the West, so Soviet–Egyptian relations were often tense. Nevertheless Suez did give the Soviet bloc its first foothold in Africa. Henceforth its efforts to strengthen anti-colonial nationalism were extensive, involving, for example, help in the fight against Portuguese rule in Angola and Mozambique and support for Joshua Nkomo in Rhodesia.

United States policy was also transformed. Until 1956, Americans treated Africa as primarily a Western European responsibility. Backing the Europeans might conflict with America's self-image as the original anti-imperial great power. In Africa, though, the colonial powers, particularly Britain, convinced the Americans of their expertise and were left to get on with it. After Suez, and the arrival of the Russians, this was patently not so. Africa was suddenly too serious to be left to such bunglers. Vice-President Nixon in a speech at the time of Suez put forward the new United States line, 'For the first time in history we have shown independence of Anglo-French policies towards Africa and Asia which seemed to us to reflect the colonial tradition. This declaration of independence has had an electrifying effect throughout the world.'[27] In 1957 the State Department institutionalized its changed priorities by creating a separate Bureau of African Affairs.

J. D. B. Miller, in his definitive survey of Commonwealth relations, similarly had no doubt, writing in 1974, that Suez was even more significant 'though more complex and indirect' than it seemed at the time.[28] That international history *tout court* and Commonwealth history both impinge on the history of decolonization in Africa is an added complication. But it is possible to avoid a good deal of argument once the particular genre of historical writing has been identified.

The revisionists have concentrated on the impact of Suez on *policies* of decolonization. Indeed, their argument focuses closely on the activities of Harold Macmillan, both before and after he became Prime Minister. It is appropriate, therefore, to consider it in the general context of metropolitan change, which will also give scope for comparison with France, Britain's co-conspirator.

CHANGING METROPOLES

In Britain the immediate political consequence of the Suez crisis was the resignation of Anthony Eden on 9 January 1957 and the appointment of Harold Macmillan to the premiership the following day. In France the chain of events leading from the North African débâcle to Charles de Gaulle's return as premier on 1 June 1958 was longer but correspondingly more significant. De Gaulle had made it clear that he was only prepared to take power on his own terms, which were nothing less than the demise of the Fourth Republic. On 28 September the French people approved the constitution of the Fifth Republic drafted under de Gaulle's direction. He became first president of the new Republic in January 1959 and ruled for over 10 years. And in April 1962 he achieved, what many of his original supporters had put him in power expressly to prevent: French recognition of Algerian independence to take place that July.

De Gaulle's criticisms of the Fourth Republic predated its foundation when he resigned as head of the provisional government at the beginning of 1946. Ostensibly he left office over a question of military credits, but his general criticism was that, like its predecessor the Third Republic, the executive of the new Republic would prove much too weak for effective government. From the time the new constitution came into force in 1947 to de Gaulle's return in June 1958 France had 19 cabinets. (The comparable figure for Britain was five and that discounts the continuity between the first and second Attlee administrations and that the fifth ministry, Macmillan's, would continue until 1963.) Ironically, de Gaulle contributed to the instability and immobilism when he withdrew his RPF (Rally of the French People) from direct participation in party politics and retired to write his memoirs in 1953, whereupon his following splintered into factions forming new political groups. With the Communists marginalized on the other political flank, this left the Fourth Republic back in the hands of those Radicals and assorted conservatives who had presided over the collapse of its predecessor – and who were supposed to have been swept away in the liberation of 1944–6. *Immobilisme*, the traditional parliamentary 'gamesmanship' of the Third Republic, where decisiveness was to be avoided in order to retain friends and jobs, became once more the hallmark of French politics.[29]

Government was steadier of purpose than the rapid turnover of ministries suggests, due to the bureaucracy which maintained day-to-day activities and stability of performance in many areas. Indeed, French technocrats proved highly effective in modernizing the economy as well as planning and implementing a whole series of innovative international economic agreements, such as the Marshall Plan, the European Coal and Steel Community, and the Common Market.

The most serious consequence of immobilism was that it left the Fourth Republic unable to cope with imperial problems. In the end this is what destroyed the regime. Mendes-France made a determined attempt to institute dynamic government when in 1954, like de Gaulle four years later, he insisted on taking power on his own terms. But after seven hectic months of dynamism he had accumulated an array of enemies. An unholy coalition including Communist, MRP, and Rightist deputies, combined to bring down his government in the course of a debate on North Africa in February 1955. The defeat of *Mendesisme* created further disillusion with the Fourth Republic.

Suez aggravated the constitutional crisis although its immediate political consequences appear slight compared with those in Britain. Not only did Guy Mollet, the Prime Minister, remain in power – unlike Eden who was forced to resign – his position was even strengthened. On 20 December 1956 the government won a vote of confidence by 325 to 210. Public opinion polls in November 1956 and March 1957 confirmed that military intervention in Egypt was popular. The French gamble had seemed close to success. There was an obvious decrease in FLN activity, and the Muslim population was more docile in the wake of French military deployment. But when France was forced to withdraw from Egypt its prestige among the Muslim masses plummeted. The Egyptian victory was exploited by the most militant faction of the FLN. Mollet, too, capitalized on French popular support. The phrase 'national-Molletism' was coined to characterize a resentful nationalism that involved the country more deeply in the Algerian War.

'National-Molletism', essentially a transitional phenomenon, was symptomatic of the aggravated political crisis. The Fourth Republic had suffered another defeat. Expensive oil imports increased the budget deficit. Inflation rose and the franc weakened. Mollet's Socialist Party began to fragment. The MRP was disunited and the Communists were discredited after Hungary. More than ever, de Gaulle seemed the answer. He was thought to have discreetly approved intervention, but let it be known that he condemned its being carried out under British command.

The increasingly militant FLN resorted to terrorist bombs both in Algeria and mainland France. The French army, especially General Massu's paratroops, did not scruple to use torture, notably in the Battle of Algiers in January 1957 and forcibly resettled the Muslim population in fortified villages, in effect concentration camps. Altogether, it has been estimated that perhaps 1 million Algerians died in the struggle.

The French army had convinced itself that it was defending Western civilization against Communism. But by 1958, French public opinion was uneasy both about the cost and the conduct of the war. Despite censorship, disturbing allegations of torture leaked out, notably in the book, *La Question* (1958), by Henri Alleg, an Algerian journalist, himself a victim of army torture. The bombing of Sakhiet, a Tunisian village, by the French air force, in defiance of civilian orders, created furore both at home and in the international arena, and led to the downfall of the government. At the end of yet another ministerial crisis Pierre Pflimlin formed a cabinet which was due to seek parliamentary approval on 13 May 1958.

On that very day rumours that the prime-minister-designate was about to negotiate with the Algerian nationalists provoked a revolt among the 'Ultras' in Algeria. They seized control in Algiers and the army chiefs refused to act against them. General Salan called for the withdrawal of Pflimlin and on 24 May paratroops invaded Corsica and seemed poised to stage a coup on the mainland. The crisis of the Republic, long forecast by de Gaulle, was finally at hand.

In the event only the General himself seemed able to offer a way out. Whether he had encouraged his supporters to plot against the regime remains a moot point, but what is not in doubt is that among the conspirators were a number of Gaullist agents. With consummate political skill, de Gaulle made himself master of the situation, manœuvring adroitly between the army and the National Assembly. He refused to put himself at the head of a military coup, so as not to be the prisoner of the army. Most intellectual of soldiers, he had thought long and hard about the relationship between military and political leadership. *Le fil de l'épée* (The Sword's Cutting Edge), published as long ago as 1931, set out his basic ideas. He regarded prestige as a vital, but scarce, attribute in modern society. Traditional sources of authority, particularly birth, no longer commanded respect. Unlike Max Weber, however, de Gaulle did not believe the future lay with the bureaucratic and technocratic élites; rather he accepted the traditional French maxim, '*L'intendance suivra*' – the view that bureaucrats were essentially followers, not leaders (provided that real leadership existed.) Given this vacuum, the military should be a crucial source of political leadership in modern society: first, because it trains for the *use* of leadership and power (and not merely the appearances) and, second, it is dedicated to some conception of national interest and solidarity. (Bureaucrats, by contrast were preoccupied with formalities and procedures, the crux of Weber's argument, and the business or trade union élites were concerned with sectional ends rather than the national interest.)[30] With immense prestige, the backing of the army, and a clear theory of political power, de Gaulle negotiated with the demoralized parliamentarians. Although invested legally by the National Assembly, he obtained the right to draw up a new constitution. By voting for de Gaulle on 1 June 1958, the Fourth Republic effectively voted itself out of existence.

De Gaulle's first priority was the elaboration of a new constitution, strengthening the powers of the presidency and of the executive at the expense of the legislature. After the referendum of October 1962, the president became electable by universal suffrage, immensely reinforcing the idea that the head of state was especially entrusted by the people to exercise power on their behalf. Cabinet ministers were no longer to be MPs responsible to parliament; indeed, if appointed to the government, a deputy had to resign and his seat would then be taken by a reserve who had been elected at the same time as himself. Parliament's power to make and unmake governments, so characteristic a feature of the Third and Fourth Republics was also radically curtailed, along with the legislature's right to initiate legislation. In the end, though, the government still had to seek parliamentary support.

Conflict was avoided in practice because both prime minister and parliament accepted de Gaulle's pre-eminence. While the Algerian problem remained at the top of the political agenda, the Assembly, too, recognized the lack of any viable alternative. Indeed, the Algerian crisis was in some respects an immense asset to de Gaulle in the consolidation of his rule, as he seized every opportunity to make presidential predominance the fundamental reality of French political life.

Once he had elaborated the new constitution, Algeria had served de Gaulle's purpose. His next priority became to end the Algerian War. '*L'Algerie bloque tout*', he was wont to say: in other words, the war was an immense strain on French resources and prevented France from embarking on the politics of grandeur which he had taken office to pursue. In fact, de Gaulle had gradually modified his views on Algeria and the rest of the empire in his years out of office, 1946–58, though few heeded his veiled comments. He apparently believed the long years of colonial warfare in Indo-China and Algeria had slowed modernization of French military power in terms of atomic weapons and weakened France's influence in Europe.

A strong nationalist himself, he had to substitute a new sense of pride in the glory of France for the still lingering but outmoded pride in empire. Unlike many European nationalists, moreover, he had genuine sympathy with Third World nationalism – not least, because by breaking up the bipolar United States–Soviet Union divide it offered opportunities for French initiatives. De Gaulle's nationalism thus clearly helped him in the transition from the 'old' France to a newer France, focusing on its role in Europe and world politics in place of the old obsession with empire. He stressed that decolonization should be a crucial part of the economic modernization of France in order to exploit the opportunities arising from the Treaty of Rome (Common Market) of 25 March 1957. It is significant that de Gaulle's strongest financial supporters in the drive to decolonization came from the most dynamic sectors of banking and industry, especially from manufacturers of aircraft and chemicals, the flagship industries of the new economies of the major powers.[31]

Macmillan also sought to restore Britain's prestige in the aftermath of Suez. As Churchill's protégé he sought to restore 'the special relationship' with the United States and was rewarded in October 1957 with 'the great prize',[32] the restoration of full Anglo-American cooperation in the development of nuclear weapons, suspended since 1946, and essential if the updating of Britain's nuclear armoury was to be affordable. He also sought to mend relations with the

Commonwealth by his 1958 tour. He returned impressed with the independent approach of the new Commonwealth states to international affairs, but also with the fragility of the new ruling élites with their Western sympathies and enormous social and economic difficulties. The lessons he drew were that the West must assist their economic development and that for the Commonwealth to provide a counter to the growth of worldwide Communism, friction between Britain and the new Afro-Asian states – above all over the issue of colonial self-government – must be minimized. Consequently he pressed forward with decolonization while overseas aid was doubled between 1957 and 1960.

This policy was underwritten by the Radcliffe Report in 1959 which insisted that it was still in Britain's interest to maintain the sterling area: 'We do not think it is possible to dissociate these arrangements either from the longstanding trading arrangements that lie behind them or from the political and other links by which most members of the area are joined in the Commonwealth. What is decisive . . . is the general harmony of interest between the United Kingdom economy and the rest of the Sterling Area.'[33] Britain, the Report concluded, must continue to strengthen the links between its economy and those of the 'great primary producing countries of the world'; the government was committed, for political reasons, to the rapid development of the Commonwealth countries; moreover, severe reductions in the supply of capital would make serious difficulties for British exports.[34]

Britain, therefore, must substantially increase its export earnings to strengthen its reserves as sterling-area banker and to provide funds for heavier investment overseas. Decolonization, according to the Radcliffe Report, pivoted on a developing global economy which would bring mutual prosperity to metropole and periphery.

Behind this reasoning was the assumption that the agricultural and mineral-based economies of the Commonwealth sterling area would experience rapid growth through rising commodity prices. But such optimistic forecasts proved badly wrong. The terms of trade of developing countries deteriorated by some 16 per cent between 1955 and 1965, which made them less valuable as markets. The most buoyant sector of world trade in the period was between industrialized countries: it was the United States and the rapidly growing economies of Western Europe which offered British exporters their best prospects. By neglecting European markets for Commonwealth outlets, where preferences reinforced the advantages of exchange control, Britain's exports grew less rapidly than those of its main competitors. Britain's share of world markets declined from 29 per cent in 1948 to 20 per cent in 1954 and 13.7 per cent in 1964. By the late 1950s it was doubtful whether the overseas sterling area was more of a liability than an asset, although official economic policy still held that Britain's leadership of the Commonwealth and sterling area was fundamental to its international position in both diplomacy and commerce.

DÉBÂCLE IN THE BELGIAN CONGO

Belgian preparation for decolonization was minimal. The first call to action came from a little-known Belgian academic, A. J. van Bilsen who published a plan for gradual 'emancipation' over a 30-year period in 1955, provoking furious protest from the colonial establishment. But Belgian policy, influenced by events in other European empires, as well as at home and in the Congo itself, changed abruptly.[35]

The tradition that issues in the Congo should be removed from Belgian party politics was breached when in 1956 anti-clericalism was one of the few tenets that the Liberal–Socialist coalition had in common. When the government attacked the mission-dominated educational system in the Congo, the Catholic bishops responded with a strong statement in favour of the 'emancipation' of the Congo. In view of the impending decolonization of neighbouring French Africa, Bakongo living in the French Congo enjoyed local self-government by 1958; it would have been impossible to deny similar autonomy to the majority of the Bakongo under Belgian rule without resorting to force. Riots in Leopoldville on 4 January 1959 following the banning of a political meeting and widespread unrest in the countryside underlined the message. And the Belgians knew from the wars fought by their European neighbours – the Dutch in Indonesia and France in Algeria – how costly this could prove. Accordingly they devised a plan for rapid decolonization, quickly fabricating a constitutional superstructure of electoral politics on the solid base of an authoritarian colonial state.

Dubbed at the time the *pari congolais* (Congolese wager) this was a bold – indeed, as it turned out, a reckless – gamble that the period of transition normally involved in constitutional decolonization would largely occur *after* independence. The 'steel frame' of colonial administration, the army and bureaucracy, would continue to be directed and staffed by Europeans but operate under the formal authority of elected assemblies and African ministers. While the new African political class was gaining experience by holding the trappings of power, pending the methodical training of a Congolese officer corps and managerial bureaucrats, firm control would be maintained by experienced Belgian administrators. (In 1960, the year of independence, only three out of 4,600 top civil servants, and no commissioned officers – indeed, only three sergeant majors – were African, in marked contrast to the situation in the British and French colonies.) In practice, this meant that the elected politicians enjoyed, in comparison with all other Africans, very high salaries.

On 5 July 1960 the *Force Publique* mutinied. The immediate occasion was the provocative policies of its last European commander, General E. Janssens. By early 1960 there was growing dissatisfaction that his plans for gradual Africanization would prevent the force from enjoying their proper share of the benefits of independence. The elected politicians feared that Janssens would use their own divisions as pretext to turn the soldiers on them. They therefore cultivated soldiers from their own ethnic groups who would apprise them of any such danger; thus they themselves became involved in the politicization of the army.

As independence approached the politicians backed the soldiers' demand for Africanization. Janssens countered by summoning the non-commissioned officers of the Leopoldville garrison to a meeting on 5 July, following the first acts of indiscipline the day before. He wrote on a blackboard, 'After Independence = Before Independence' and stated flatly, 'the Force Publique continues as before'.[36] That night soldiers ordered to march on Leopoldville to curb the insubordination refused to go. Overnight the expatriate officer corps disappeared and discipline crumbled. The mutiny had begun.

In response, Prime Minister Patrice Lumumba promoted all soldiers one grade and dismissed Janssens. But still the mutiny spread. As panic spread among the European Community, the Belgian government decided to use metropolitan troops to protect European lives and property. When Belgian naval vessels bombarded Matardi the *Force Publique* transmitted the news of a general massacre of civilians – although only 19 deaths were finally attributed to this shelling – worsening race relations throughout the country. The Congo crisis now became an international crisis. With French decolonization, involving the failure of plans for a French Union or French Community, suddenly there were not three or four but 13 new independent states within the United Nations. Indeed the African bloc became the largest grouping there. There seemed a real danger of the Congo breaking apart, with mineral-rich Katanga bidding for 'independence' under Moise Tshombe and Belgian forces intervening on his side by threatening to expel all central government troops. United Nations intervention froze the situation setting limits to disorder and further foreign intervention.

The image of the Congo, compounded of disintegration and bloodshed, dominated much Western thinking about decolonization. By the time effective central government had been restored, Patrice Lumumba had been captured, taken to Katanga and executed. In his memory the membership cards of his party henceforth carried a red spot symbolic of the blood of the martyr. 'Lumumbism' became the creed of rebels condemning the mundane realities of the post-colonial regime in contrast with the Utopian expectations engendered in the heady electioneering of 1959–60.[37]

NOTES

1 D. Goldsworthy, 'Keeping Change Within Bounds: Aspects of Colonial Policy during the Churchill and Eden Governments, 1951–57', *Journal of Imperial and Commonwealth History* XVIII (1990), pp. 94–6.

2 Was it quite such a good idea of Eden to remind Nasser of his role in fashioning the 1936 Agreement, the occasion of so much Egyptian bitterness against British imperialism?

3 Memorandum by Eden, 'Egypt the Alternatives', 16 February 1953, cited in W. Roger Louis, 'The Anglo-Egyptian Settlement of 1954', in W. Roger Louis and Roger Owen, eds., *Suez, 1956: The Crisis and its Consequences* (Oxford, Clarendon Press, 1989), p. 53.

4 Gamal Nasser, *Egypt's Liberation: The Philosophy of the Revolution* (Washington, DC, Public Affairs Press, 1955). Some thought that the book was largely written by Mohammed Heikel, the well-known Egyptian journalist, who had done other ghost-writing for Nasser.

5 Nasser, *Liberation*, pp. 111–12.

6 Sir Ralph Stevenson to Eden, 'Confidential', 14 September 1954, FO 371/108317, cited in W. R. Louis, 'The Tragedy of the Anglo-Egyptian Settlement of 1954', in W. Roger Louis and Roger Owen, eds., *Suez, 1956: The Crisis and its Consequences* (Oxford, Clarendon Press, 1989), p. 50, along with much more in like vein.

7 G. A. Nasser, 'The Egyptian Revolution', *Foreign Affairs* XXXIII (1955), pp. 199–211.

8 Britain, Churchill maintained, was unique among 'the free nations and democracies' in playing a major part in all three interlinked circles through its 'special relationship' with the United States, leadership of the Commonwealth and close 'association' with the institutions of European security and prosperity. And, just like Nasser, he claimed his country's influence in each was reinforced by its role in the other two. David Reynolds, *Britannia Overruled* (London, Longman, 1991), p. 202.

9 M. Mason, ' "The Decisive Volley": the Battle of Ismailia and the Decline of British Influence in Egypt', *Journal of Imperial and Commonwealth History* 19 (1991), p. 53.

10 Mason, 'Decline', p. 57.

11 *Op. cit.*, pp. 58–9.

12 *Ba'th* literally meaning 'resurrection'.

13 Nasser, *Liberation*, p. 61.

14 P. Lyon, 'The Emergence of the Third World', in Hedley Bull and Adam Watson, eds., *The Expansion of International Society* (Oxford, Clarendon Press, 1984), pp. 229–37.

15 Donald A. Low, *Eclipse of Empire* (Cambridge, Cambridge University Press, 1991), p. 211.

16 Alistair Horne, *Macmillan, 1894–1956* (London, Macmillan, 1988), p. 369.

17 A. Adamthwaite, 'Suez Revisited', in M. Dockrill and J. W. Young, eds., *British Foreign Policy, Nineteen Forty-five to Fifty-six* (New York, St. Martin, 1989), p. 229.

18 The phrase which became notorious was coined by Donald McLachlan in the *Daily Telegraph*, 3 January 1956.

19 Low, *Eclipse*, p. 211.

20 Alistair Horne, *A Savage War for Peace* (London, Macmillan, 1977), pp. 315–16.

21 The classic account of collaboration is R. Robinson, 'Non-European Foundations of European Imperialism: Sketch for a Theory of Collaboration', in Roger Owen and Bob Sutcliffe, eds., *Studies in the Theory of Imperialism* (London, Longman, 1972), pp. 117–42.

22 Philip Williams, ed., *The Diary of Hugh Gaitskell* (London, Cape, 1983), p. 566. For Eisenhower's relations with the Democrats and the Zionist lobby see Stephen E. Ambrose, *Eisenhower: the President* (London, Allen and Unwin, 1984).

23 'UK Economic Aid to Egypt', December 1954 with a minute by G. E. Millard, 23 August 1954, FO 371/108411 in A. N. Porter and A. J. Stockwell, eds., *British Imperial Policy and Decolonization, Volume 2, 1951–64* (Houndmills, Macmillan, 1989), pp. 363–6.

24 K. Kyle, 'Britain and the Crisis', in W. R. Louis and R. Owen, eds., *Suez, 1956*, p. 107.

25 Brian Lapping, *End of Empire* (London, Paladin, 1985), p. 334.

26 Walter LaFeber, *America, Russia and the Cold War, 1945–1992* (New York, McGraw-Hill, 1993), p. 243.

27 Cited in Christopher Hitchens, *Blood, Class and Nostalgia: Anglo-American Ironies* (London, Chatto and Windus, 1990), p. 275.

28 J. D. B. Miller, *Survey of Commonwealth Affairs: Problems of Attrition and Expansion, 1953–1969* (London, Oxford University Press, 1974), p. 44.

29 James F. Macmillan. *Dreyfus to de Gaulle: Politics and Society in France, 1898–1969* (London, Edward Arnold, 1985), pp. 152–7.

30 Philip G. Cerny, *The Politics of Grandeur: Ideological Aspects of de Gaulle's Foreign Policy* (Cambridge, Cambridge University Press, 1980), pp. 63–6.

31 Miles Kahler, *Decolonization in Britain and France: The Domestic Consequences of International Relations* (Princeton, Princeton University Press, 1984), pp. 372–3.

32 Harold Macmillan, *Riding the Storm* (London, Macmillan, 1971), p. 323.

33 *Radcliffe Report*, para. 657.

34 *Radcliffe Report*, para. 739.

35 Crawford Young, *Politics in the Congo* (Princeton, Princeton University Press, 1965) is still the most illuminating account.

36 Young, *Politics*, p. 316.

37 Crawford Young, 'Rebellion in the Congo,' in Robert I. Rotberg, ed., *Rebellion in Black Africa* (London, Oxford University Press, 1971), pp. 244–5.

11

Delayed Decolonization

In the early 1960s the pace of decolonization changed. Until then it had rapidly accelerated, reaching a climax in 1960, 'the Year of Africa', when 16 new African states, including such heavyweights as Nigeria and Zaire, entered the United Nations. Pundits, confidently speculating along the lines of Harold Macmillan's 'wind of change' speech of February 1960, expected the trend to continue. In 1962 the Marxist historian and theoretician Perry Anderson proclaimed, 'The end of the epoch is imminent, it is now clear that the Portuguese Empire is coming to an end.'[1] In the same year the South African editor of the Penguin series on the 'New Africa', Ronald Segal, in a foreword to James Duffy's *Portugal in Africa* drew bold comparisons – complete with precise periodization – between the trend of events in the Portuguese territories and what had happened earlier elsewhere. The race riots in Leopoldville in January 1959 were the 'moment of awakening' for Belgium: a similar moment had already arrived for Portugal on 15 March 1961 with the outbreak of revolution in northern Angola. Segal commented that 'The delusions of centuries were the first victims of the ferocity with which Portugal's rule was assailed by Portugal's African subjects . . . [The Portuguese] are placing their faith in force.' But, he predicted, they will be driven from Angola, Mozambique and Guinea, just as they had been from Goa by India in December 1961: 'Only the number of months left to them allows speculation.'[2] In fact it was to take 13 years, and the 25 April 1974 'Revolution of the Flowers', before Portugal's African territories were free. White minority rule persisted in Southern Rhodesia through UDI (Unilateral Declaration of Independence) in November 1965 for 15 years to a second independence, this time under majority rule, in April 1980. White-ruled South Africa gave up South-West Africa which became independent under United Nations auspices as Namibia in March 1990. South Africa also formally renounced apartheid and came under majority rule in 1994.

TAKING STOCK

The rush to independence was followed by an expansion of African studies at similar breakneck speed. Ironically, therefore, the mass production of African experts coincided with the great slow-down in African political progress after 1962. Just as the earlier phase of quickening decolonization had contradicted the conventional wisdom so also did delayed decolonization thereafter. Why were the experts wrong-footed once more? Was it simply that Africanist expertise, having been too cautious in the 1940s and 1950s, overreacted in the early 1960s? That was certainly part of it. Africanists had identified – and identified with – what they took to be the critical factor shaping modern African history, namely African nationalism. Henceforth predicting the future was simply a matter of extrapolating current trends. Partly, too, it was wishful thinking: most Africanists were committed supporters of African freedom who wanted, as well as expected, decolonization to sweep aside all opposition.[3]

They also thought that national liberation following prolonged guerrilla wars and the overthrow of existing political and social structures would lead to a more authentic independence than decolonization by constitutional procedures where the incoming African government inherited the framework of the colonial state. These ideas were strongly influenced by disappointment with the poverty and political instability of many of the new states whose leaders were forced to beg for help from their former colonial masters and the capitalist West generally.

This reading of contemporary history was stimulated by the conjuncture of events outside Africa with developments within African studies. The victory of the Chinese Communists in 1949 enlarged the contemporary meaning of 'revolution' – hitherto possessing an urban bias from its association with France and Russia, and orthodox Marxist-Leninist theory's focus on the industrial proletariat[4] – by including both guerrilla warfare and the revolutionary potential of the peasant within its scope. Further revolutionary success in Vietnam, Cuba and, within Africa itself, in Algeria, strengthened this emphasis on peasant guerrillas.

The dominant theme of resistance in contemporary African historiography reinforced this viewpoint. It traced the development of nationalist opposition to foreign incursion, beginning with patriotic resistance to imperial annexation, through the hut-tax wars and other modes of opposing the consolidation of colonial rule, culminating in either constitutional decolonization or the emergence of people's revolutions guided by Marxist principles and fought by guerrilla armies.[5]

In much of the liberation literature the significance of achieving independence y such contrasting strategies was exaggerated. As recently as 1983 *The History of Central Africa*, edited by Birmingham and Martin, dismissed the constitutional route as achieving nothing more than 'flag independence', the country concerned negotiating neo-colonial relationships with Britain and power being transferred to compliant businessmen and collaborative bureaucracies. However, the 'revolutionary processes' in Mozambique and Angola and, more ambiguously, in Zimbabwe were assumed to have generated political and economic structures attuned to the needs of the peasant masses and to have set the agenda for socialism.[6] But this view of African insurrection was over simple. Also, it badly underestimated the strength and determination of the opposition which now confronted African nationalism through the sheer speed of its advance. Portugal, Southern Rhodesia and, above all, South Africa, along with their international allies, were altogether more formidable citadels of white resistance than any that insurgent nationalism had encountered earlier.

The possible exception was French Algeria, at the other end of the continent - and the Algerian Revolution quickly acquired exemplary force. Both Eric Wolf, in 1971, and John Dunn, in 1972, in their comparative analyses of successful modern revolutions included chapters on Algeria as their sole African example. And practitioners of revolution – Regis Debray, Ben Bella himself, and, above all, Frantz Fanon – propounded both theoretical and practical lessons.[7] After all, if the might of France had been humbled by Arab nationalism in the north, surely Africans of proud warrior stock could do the same to the much less powerful white polities to the south? But there were special reasons why the nationalists might, and did, draw overly optimistic lessons from the Algerian case.

In applying the lessons of world history to contemporary events in Africa it would, in retrospect, have been more realistic to balance the study of successful twentieth-century revolutions and peasant guerrilla movements with equal attention to case studies of failure. Despite the triumphalist litany – Russia, China, Vietnam, Cuba, Algeria – there were many more failures than successes as the enemies of the guerrillas knew from their manuals of counter-insurgency. (Indeed the post-revolutionary history of most of these successful revolutions, such as Russia or China, is littered with the ruthlessly effective suppression of peasant insurrection.) Nor were guerrilla movements always left-wing as Ian Smith knew from his dealings with RENAMO (Mozambique National Resistance) in Mozambique and Ronald Reagan in his support for UNITA (*União Nacional de Independência Total de Angola*) in Angola.

THE PORTUGUESE TERRITORIES

The Algerian War was primarily an urban war – 'the Battle for Algiers', the title of Pontecorvo's film classic, accurately describes the decisive engagement. But in Portuguese Africa, by contrast, there was almost no fighting in built-up areas. Hence, whereas journalists and academics, especially if they were sympathetic to the cause of African revolution, frequently drew comforting comparisons with Algeria – and the nationalist organizations sent their guerrillas for training there – the Portuguese military themselves found the American experience in Vietnam more relevant. Like the Portuguese in Africa, the Americans in Vietnam were trying to seal off a long border while they sought to seek out and destroy small bands of insurgents in dense jungle, who had infiltrated from bases outside the country to which they could retreat. (Similarly in Southern Rhodesia and South Africa white farmers still dominated much of the rural areas so the insurrection could never be primarily urban, unlike Algeria where the *colons* had deserted the countryside.)

There were, however, critical differences between the Americans in Vietnam and the Portuguese in Africa. Although there were a mere 7 million Portuguese, as against some 200 million Americans, and though the Americans were incomparably better armed, not all the advantages lay with the bigger battalions – as the Portuguese well understood. As one Portuguese officer observed, 'The Americans can never win in Vietnam, because everyone knows that sooner or later they will be leaving. Here we will win because everybody knows we are staying.'[8] Conscription for Americans in Vietnam, as for the French in Algeria, was relatively short and, especially in the American case, far from universal. By contrast, the average Portuguese conscript spent four years in Africa. Portuguese conscripts were both accustomed to a tougher civilian life than their comparatively affluent French and American equivalents and more likely to be battle-hardened. There was surprisingly little actual desertion once conscripts were inducted, though, as the wars dragged on, and casualties increased, morale suffered.[9]

The degree of commitment by the Portuguese dictatorship to retaining all three African colonies was qualitatively different from that displayed by the other European powers in the age of decolonization. Precisely when Britain, France and Belgium sharply reduced their colonial commitments in the late 1950s, Portugal strengthened its presence so that by 1974 a quarter of adult Portuguese males were in the armed forces. Simultaneously, despite the pull from more developed areas of Europe and the United States, the government increased the export of white settlers until there were about 335,000 in Angola and 200,000 in Mozambique. (Given the small size of Portugal, this number – along with their kinsmen in the metropole – amounted to a considerable settler lobby.) Portuguese industry relied on the colonies for raw materials although it became increasingly obvious that some of these could be obtained more cheaply on the world market. Also, during the 1940s and 1950s deficits in the Portuguese balance of payments were compensated by surpluses in the overseas territories.

The commitment, however, was more political than economic. In 1951 the Portuguese constitution was revised and the term 'colony' dropped as Portuguese Guinea, Angola and Mozambique were formally proclaimed overseas provinces of Greater Portugal to parry international pressure for decolonization. That Portugal was no ordinary small power became central to the propaganda of the regime. A Ministry of Education poster, much used in schools during Salazar's time, depicted a map of Europe with Portugal's overseas empire superimposed, boldly declaring, 'Portugal is not a small power'. This map graphically drove home the twin messages that the colonies were 22 times the size of the metropole and that both together now comprised a single political entity, Portugal.[10] The dictatorship became a prisoner of its own propaganda, relying so heavily on an ideology of imperial greatness that it was difficult to survive without it.

The dictatorship had been thrown very much on the defensive in the postwar period. Internal and external pressure to democratize its political institutions and conform to the Western European norm – as against the authoritarian politics of Eastern Europe – increased and many observers believed Salazar would fall from power in the late 1950s. Nor, under Salazar, did the dictatorship have any constructive ideas for dealing with nationalist stirrings in the colonies. In 1957 branches of the secret police, PIDE (*Policia Internacional de Defesa do Estado*, International Police for the Defence of the State), were set up in the colonies to crush organized opposition, with many suspects interned or simply disappearing. Nationalist leaders were driven into exile at a time when Britain, France, and even Belgium were engaged in dialogue with their equivalents. Portugal found itself increasingly criticized, along with South Africa, and not just by the growing Afro-Asian bloc at the United Nations, for its repressive policies were also seen as the negation of the civilizing mission when judged by mid-twentieth-century Western standards.[11] In 1960 a United Nations resolution called on Portugal to accept self-determination for its colonies but the regime stubbornly reasserted that within the colonies there was no serious opposition to Portuguese rule.

In the 1958 election General Delgado, standing against the Salazarist candidate for president, received nearly a quarter of the votes although the ballot was largely restricted to the better-off and there was massive vote rigging. In April 1961 high-ranking officers made a bid to oust Salazar. It was unsuccessful but Salazarism seemed to be cracking apart. It was ironic, therefore that the Angolan War which had erupted in February, and even more Nehru's seizure of Goa in December, produced a surge of nationalism which Salazar manipulated to save himself and his regime.

At the same time, though, long-term fundamental economic and demographic changes, comparable to those which had transformed France, weakened the colonial connection. The economy boomed in the 1960s and early 1970s, making Portugal 'a kind of Taiwan of southern Europe',[12] which attracted investment because of its low wage levels. Textiles and wine, the leading exports to the colonies, also did well in wealthy north-western Europe to which trade was increasingly oriented because of Portugal's membership of EFTA (the European Free Trade Association) from 1960. In 1960 Portugal adhered to the General Agreement on Tariffs and Trade (GATT), thereby agreeing to foreswear the cruder methods of restricting foreign competition and investment. When the Angolan administration brought in draconian restrictions on importing wines from the metropole in 1971 in order to encourage the making of fruit wines locally, Portuguese manufacturers concentrated on producing high-quality table wines, such as Dão and Vinho Verde, for north-western Europe. In 1972, for the first time in decades wine exports to foreign destinations surpassed those to the Empire.[13] The textile industry, hoping to repeat its success in EFTA, found its colonial connections a major impediment to negotiating an agreement with the EEC, which was eventually achieved in 1972.

The figures for emigration to the colonies, nearly doubling in both Angola and Mozambique, were deceptive. Few were settlers of the South African or Rhodesian type. Three out of four went out to the colonies to make some money then returned to Portugal as quickly as possible. Most Portuguese preferred a town job to farming and guerrilla war made them even more reluctant to venture into the countryside. Moreover, the preponderance of colonial emigration in the 1950s proved atypical. The Americas and the more prosperous areas of Europe quickly reasserted their superior attractions, especially for men evading conscription.[14] At the downfall of the dictatorship in 1974 there were roughly 1 million Portuguese working in the Americas and a further million in Europe, chiefly France, as against 500,000 in Angola and Mozambique. And their remittances were proportionately more important to the Portuguese economy than those from the colonies. The postwar development of the Algarve tourist industry, attracting relatively affluent Europeans and Americans, further oriented the Portuguese economy away from empire.

In September 1968 Salazar collapsed with a blood clot on the brain. He was succeeded by Marcelo Caetano who seemed for a time to offer the prospect of liberalizing the regime in ways that would harmonize with these forces of economic and social modernization. But on Africa Caetano was firmly traditionalist: 'Africa is for us a moral justification and a *raison d'être* as a power. Without it we would be a small nation, with it we are a great power.'[15] By 1971 moderate reformers lost hope that through Caetano the regime could be liberalized from within.[16]

The revolt which began in the north of Angola in 1961 was essentially a Bakongo movement inspired by the independence of the Belgian Congo some nine months earlier. Its leader, Holden Roberto, at one time dreamed of restoring the old Kongo kingdom, though he now proclaimed a more orthodox nationalist message as the leader of the Union of Peoples of Angola, known later as the FNLA (*Frente Nacional de Libertacao de Angola*). There were also bitter grievances from the loss of African land to Portuguese farmers for their coffee plantations. When the revolt began in mid-March there were no colonial troops in the area. But by August the Portuguese had 17,000 men in the field and the revolt was easily suppressed. There were atrocities on both sides during the six months of fighting in which probably some 20,000 Africans and about 700 whites died. Tens of thousands of refugees fled to the Congo, giving a foretaste of what was to be one of independent Africa's most desperate problems. As the first to mount an armed rising, Roberto won support in several African states. He also gained American backing because he seemed less radical than the group of

Marxist ideologues centring on Luanda known as the MPLA (*Movimento Popular de Libertacao de Angola*).

Throughout the 1960s several competing liberation movements emerged in the Portuguese colonies, sponsored by various newly independent African states and by non-African powers engaged in the Cold War. Eventually three revolutionary parties emerged which, applying Marxist doctrine somewhat pragmatically to their own countries, grasped control of the state apparatus when the Portuguese left.

In the West African mini-colony of Portuguese Guinea the PAIGC (*Partido Africano de Independencia da Guine e Capo Verde*) was formed in 1956 by a small group of civil servants, teachers and clerks. Many were from Cape Verde whose independence they also demanded. Late in 1962 they began their insurrection in Guinea. It was led by Amilcar Cabral, probably the most important theorist of African revolution, who was equipped with a close knowledge of rural society by his experience as an agronomist.[17] The nationalists made rapid gains, capturing two-thirds of the countryside despite well-armed and substantial Portuguese forces. But the war drifted towards stalemate with the Portuguese holding the cities and a number of fortified camps. Cabral, committed to revolutionary democracy and agrarian socialism, held elections in the liberated countryside in 1972. The voting rubber-stamped the election of the single candidate nominated by each constituency but, on the whole, the PAIGC left the choice of representative to the localities.

Cabral's attempt to make Guinea's revolutionary vanguard party accountable to the people was unique; there is no other example of a revolutionary nationalist movement holding elections before independence and setting up structures to maintain accountability. He was determined to learn from the mistakes and disappointments of his predecessors. Cabral saw decolonization as a process rather than an event. He did not live to see independence for Guinea-Bissau, but – based on his knowledge of botched decolonization elsewhere – insisted that formal independence must be followed by social and economic liberation. *A luta continua*: The struggle goes on. Hence also his notion of delayed liberation: the speed of military advance must never outstrip the capability of the party and the people behind it. Several times, but especially in 1972, some colleagues challenged his insistence on a balance between political and military activity which would allow sufficient time for dialogue between party and people. His opponents contended that the PAIGC should throw everything into the battle and finish off the Portuguese; he insisted, on the contrary, that the human and political costs of such single-mindedness would outweigh the military gains.

There were also arguments on the Portuguese side. General Antonio de Spinola reported on Portuguese political and military weaknesses in Guinea and was sent back in 1968 with what he took to be a free hand to improve the situation prior to negotiating an honourable settlement with the guerrillas. He succeeded in raising Portuguese morale and set about winning 'hearts and minds' with his programme 'to build a better Guinea' with schools and clinics and a system of 'People's Congresses' designed to create a dialogue between the people and government.[18] Such policies, intended to compete with the pragmatic Marxism of the nationalist guerrillas, raised the political consciousness of the Portuguese military who saw that they had metropolitan as well as colonial relevance. In 1972 Spinola reported to Caetano, who was rumoured to favour limited decolonization, that the moment was ripe for negotiation, especially as neighbouring Senegal, which had previously backed the PAIGC, was now willing to broker an agreement. He was rebuffed. For the first three years of his rule many reformers cherished the hope that Caetano would liberalize the regime from within. Now, as well as being lukewarm about domestic reform, he intimated to Spinola that he would rather see the army suffer an honourable defeat than negotiate. Caught between hard-liners like Arriaga, the generalissimo of Mozambique – and possible leader of a right-wing coup – and reformers like Spinola and Costa Gomes, the left-wing Chief of Staff, Caetano offered no clear lead.

Cabral was assassinated in January 1973. Immediately thereafter the PAIGC military effort drastically increased. In September 1973 the PAIGC declared the independence of Guinea and within a few weeks it was recognized by over 60 governments. By the time of the Portuguese Revolution in 1974 the PAIGC believed that it was on the point of defeating the Portuguese. Perhaps it was.[19] Certainly Guinea was the first Portuguese African colony to which Portugal granted formal independence in September 1974.

In Mozambique three exiled organizations united in 1962 in a common front named FRELIMO (*Frente de Libertacao de Mozambique*) based in Tanzania and led by Eduardo Mondlane with Nyerere's backing. War began in 1964. Crossing the border from Tanzania, FRELIMO's initial successes were gained in the Makonde areas of northern Mozambique. FRELIMO scored a considerable propaganda success by holding its Second Congress within the country in 1968. This witnessed a bitter struggle between rival élites, with the 'revolutionaries', young men who had returned from military training in Algeria, winning out over the chiefs, who were accused in Marxist parlance of 'bourgeois tendencies' and 'tribalism'. At issue was the position of the Makonde chiefs and elders who regarded themselves as the guardians of tradition in the liberated zone. FRELIMO activists with their own ideas about access to land, disposal of produce and the role of women, clashed with these neo-traditionalists. (That there were a great variety of customary systems of land use in this area both incited FRELIMO to draconian standardization in the interests of 'nation-building' and made it difficult to mount concerted traditionalist opposition.)

Mozambique was also a very difficult national community to imagine, and identify with, for those whose mentalities were moulded by African oral culture. Strung out along the coast of the Indian Ocean, it was the eastern remnant of Portugal's vast territorial claims after stronger European powers had seized those parts of the interior which promised most in the way of mineral riches during the late-nineteenth-century scramble. The trade and labour migration routes ran east to west into other countries, rather than north to south within Mozambique. Indeed, until the Portuguese constructed strategic highways to cope with FRELIMO, long-distance travel within Mozambique was virtually negligible. The Makonde chiefs, therefore, tended to be content with limited independence in their home areas – hence, the accusations of 'tribalism'.

With the victory of the young activists, the war was prosecuted more vigorously. Mondlane was assassinated in 1969, probably as the result of internal dissension within FRELIMO. But in 1970 the Portuguese army switched from defence to a vigorous offensive, *Operation Gordian Knot*, led by General Arriaga, its counter-insurgency expert. It succeeded in destroying most of FRELIMO's advance bases in the north.

Samora Machel became leader of FRELIMO and the internal disputes were not so much resolved as shelved, because of his insistence on the overriding importance of the military struggle. From 1970 FRELIMO's military effectiveness drastically improved when it was allowed to operate from bases in Zambia. At last it had strategic targets to attack in the Trans-Zambesi and Beira railways and the development schemes linked to the Cabora Bassa hydro-electric project. The Cabora Bassa complex, intended to attract a million Portuguese immigrants, the most ambitious development project ever mounted by a colonial government, proved an ideal target for guerrilla harassment.

For all its Marxist discourse, FRELIMO had scant success with the industrial working class, mainly dockers and railwaymen, in Lourenço Marques, Beira and other urban areas, simply because the bulk of Mozambique's working class was Portuguese and, insofar as it was radicalized, gave its allegiance to the Portuguese Communist Party. Like Cabral's PAIGC, therefore, FRELIMO had to find its support among the peasants. It infiltrated areas weakly held by the Portuguese and, again like Cabral, sought to develop them as 'models' for postcolonial Mozambique.[20] They were important in the international propaganda battle between Portugal and the nationalist movements with each side vying with the other for the moral high ground by claiming superior statistics of such aspects of the civilizing mission as literacy classes and medical clinics.

FRELIMO, however, failed to establish an organizational base among the Muslim Makua, the largest ethnic group in Mozambique. In all its African colonies Portugal Africanized its armed forces so that by the end of the wars perhaps 60 per cent of the troops fighting the nationalists were black. Ironically, in view of its proclaimed crusade for Catholicism, many of Portugal's crack troops, such as the Yao, Swahili and Makua in Mozambique and the Fula in Guinea, were Muslims. These peoples, once neglected or harassed because of their resistance to 'Westernization', that is to say Catholic proselytizing, were now courted because their conservative social structures and traditional education made them relatively immune to nationalist propaganda. On the other hand, mission-educated Africans were recruited by the nationalists and sections of the church became openly sympathetic to their cause.

The nationalists in Angola remained split. The MPLA mounted the most consistent military challenge and adopted the most sophisticated revolutionary doctrine. It suffered, however, from internal ideological differences as well as ethnic and personal rivalries. It also faced rivalry from the FNLA, which still enjoyed the support of Zaire, and in 1966 from UNITA (*União Nacional de Independencia Total de Angola*), a movement of the southern Ovimbundu people which drew some support from Zambia.

In 1973–4 the Portuguese regime drifted into crisis. Bad publicity over the Wiryamu massacre, news of which broke when Caetano was making an important state visit to London, damaged Portugal's international prestige and aggravated disputes with the Vatican over African policy. The effects of the world depression following the 1973 Arab–Israeli war worsened industrial disputes. And, above all, there were the cumulative effects of war weariness as the soldiers realized they were fighting a war that they could not win. A total of 7,674 Portuguese military dead during 14 years of war, and only half of those in action, was tolerable. But the nature of the fighting left many more wounded, *mutilados*, blown up by nationalist land mines. The social basis of the *Estado Novo* regime was strongest among the peasants of northern Portugal who, having lost the labour of a conscript son, came to dread his return, crippled, as one more mouth to feed.

In February 1974 General Spinola published *Portugal and the Future*, setting out his ideas on the African wars which he claimed were stunting Portugal's economic development, forcing it into international isolation and 'will finish by leading our country into revolutionary disintegration'; meantime, 'The people in their realism and sometimes naive good sense, simply emigrate, incontestable proof that we must consider certain problems in a new light.'[21] The immediate cause of the coup – the Revolution of the Flowers on 25 April – were grievances over army pay and promotion. Many senior officers, including right-wingers, knew what was in the offing but preferred to secure a place for themselves in the new order rather than preserve the increasingly directionless and demoralized *Estado Novo* regime. The coup was organized by middle-ranking officers of the *Movimento das Forcas Armadas* (Armed Forces Movement or MFA), who invited Spinola to take over the presidency.

The collapse of *Estado Novo* in Portugal, however, was not foreseen by the nationalist insurgents in Africa. Originally, Spinola, far from abandoning Africa, intended to find a political solution involving some degree of devolution culminating, possibly, in a Lusophone federation. But the whole colonial administration collapsed with the Caetano regime. Soldiers returned to barracks. People simply ignored officials and their regulations, pending a new source of authority. There were rumours of a coup by the white settlers but, unlike Rhodesia, they had never controlled the administration and the security forces; they lacked parties and political leaders: hence there could be no UDI.

The nationalists hurried to fill the political vacuum. In Mozambique they penetrated south of the Zambesi for the first time. In Angola all three nationalist movements sought to establish themselves at the capital Luanda. The Portuguese withdrawal was chaotic. All the complex machinery of a modern state was simply abandoned as administrators, managers and settlers left their offices unmanned. On 27 July Spinola announced that negotiations for an early transfer of power, beginning with Guinea, would begin immediately.

Spinola and the increasingly left-wing MFA were more and more at odds with each other. Indeed so much so that there was no coherent representation of Portuguese interests during the decolonization negotiations. Spinola eventually resigned on 30 September.

Before then Portugal had already recognized the independence of Guinea-Bissau as from 10 September. That was relatively easy. There were no important Portuguese – or international – interests involved and no serious competitor to the PAIGC. Indeed, Guinea-Bissau must be categorized as a unique hybrid in the comparative history of decolonization. Being West African it was without settlers and geographically beyond the reach of effective South African destabilization. But because it belonged to the Portuguese it had to fight for its liberation against a regime which regarded the possession of its African Empire in its totality as essential to its continued existence. (And if lusotropicology was taken literally then future Portuguese settlement – however far-fetched that might currently seem – could not be ruled out. Cabral, for one, claimed it was part of Portugal's long-term strategy.) The independence of Guinea-Bissau, therefore, represented both the belated tidying-up of postcolonial West Africa and the first stage in the decomposition of that formidable alliance of Portugal, Southern Rhodesia and South Africa which had so long blocked the further advance of nationalism across the continent.

A further election was held after independence in December 1976. It was conducted more or less on the same lines as the one held in the liberated areas in 1972, with a single slate of PAIGC candidates who piled up huge majorities in eight of the 10 constituencies. (The exceptions being Fula and Mandinka Muslim areas where the electorate followed the lead of their conservative anti-PAIGC chiefs, but even in these cases PAIGC candidates were endorsed by over half the electorate.)

The issues involved in independence for Mozambique and Angola were more complex. In Mozambique FRELIMO, which was the only possible claimant to power, hurried to place its own cadres in power. It rejected a proposal by the Portuguese Foreign Minister, Mario Soares, for an immediate cease-fire followed by elections supervised by the Portuguese army. 'As the Caetano government demonstrated that liberal fascism does not exist, so too it is necessary to make clear that there is no such thing as democratic colonialism', Machel bluntly declared.[22] In other words, with Portuguese military power fast disintegrating, FRELIMO had no intention of disbanding its forces which were, for the time being, the sole disciplined military machine in Mozambique and taking its chances at the ballot box. Quite the reverse. FRELIMO's call to arms, *'Independencia ou Morte! A Luta Continua! Venceremos!'* (Independence or Death! The Struggle goes on! We shall win!) was shortened to *'A Luta Continua!'* after independence. With an attack expected at any time from Southern Rhodesia, and the ever-present threat of South Africa, it warned the party faithful that they could not relax.

But it was also directed against *O Inimigo Interno* (The Internal Enemy) defined as the class enemies of FRELIMO who worked by rumour, economic sabotage and covert force, in clandestine collaboration with the external enemies, to undermine the new regime. Whites, chiefs, and other 'reactionary elements', such as the Catholic Church, were specified at the Third Party Congress in June 1975. In reprisal for Samora Machel's aid to the guerrillas of the Popular Front, the Rhodesians encouraged resistance from sections of the Mozambican population, such as the Makua, who did not accept FRELIMO's legitimacy. This was the origin of RENAMO (Mozambique National Resistance) which, taken over by South Africa after the demise of Rhodesia, was able to put 20,000 warriors in the field. Such a force was sufficient to cripple the economy of the new state, and cause terrible casualties as it swept through large sections of the countryside, but not strong enough to capture the cities and replace the FRELIMO government. Able to inflict terrible wounds, but not to kill, it proved a most effective weapon in the South African armoury of destabilization.[23]

Angola, with no single dominant party comparable to the PAIGC and FRELIMO, was also doomed to suffer a protracted civil war after the Portuguese withdrawal. Here the economic stakes were highest and the existence of three relatively strong nationalist movements offered scope for external intervention. Spinola, concerned to avoid the dominance of the MPLA, sought to establish a coalition government of all three movements. Initally this plan was endorsed by the Organization of African Unity (OAU). It failed partly because of the fall of Spinola and the leftward shift of Portuguese politics which prompted the MPLA to bid for power on its own. The response of the MPLA's external opponents was ill-judged. South Africa, whose indirect methods were to prove so successful in Mozambique, was tempted by the three-way split among Angolan resistance movements into direct intervention. On 23 October 1975 a South African armoured force, variously reckoned at 2,000–6,000 men, invaded southern Angola from Namibia in collaboration with Jonas Savimbi of UNITA and Holden Roberto of FNLA, while Mobutu – backed by the United States and China – supported Roberto in the north.

The MPLA now set in motion an emergency plan, calling on Cuban help. A Cuban force of 13,000 men was rapidly sent to Angola. Joint MPLA and Cuban forces stopped the South African advance then took the offensive against the northern force from Zaire, driving it out of the country in January 1976. South Africa was then faced with the stark choice of reinforcing its troops and facing a prolonged and debilitating war similar to that endured by the Portuguese or retreating with consequent loss of face. It intimated that unless it had direct American support it would withdraw. Henry Kissinger, the United States Secretary of State, facing determined Congressional opposition to his support for the FNLA and UNITA, affirmed that South Africa had invaded Angola on its own initiative. The South Africans hastily retreated across the Namibian border before the end of March and South Africa reverted to the policy it was pursuing so successfully in Mozambique: covert support for groups which rejected the legitimacy of the postcolonial regime.

The collapse of the Portuguese Empire critically affected prospects for decolonization elsewhere. It brought the first break in the chain of buffer states protecting the regional superpower, South Africa. Ironically, though, despite Fanonesque romanticization of the cleansing consequences of violence, the way the change of regime was achieved – by armed struggle – meant that the break was far from clean. The prolonged civil war in Angola severely impeded efforts to negotiate Namibian independence through the auspices of the United Nations. Indeed the Cuban presence, coupled with the onset of a new phase of intense East–West competition – sometimes termed 'the Second Cold War'[24] – produced an international environment in which an aggressive South African foreign policy scored notable successes. At the same time, the victory of FRELIMO, and Samora Machel's firm support for the Popular Front, precipitated the defeat of the UDI regime in Rhodesia. And inside South Africa itself the effects of its withdrawal from Angola when faced by the Cubans were profound. Young blacks in Soweto and elsewhere witnessed the hitherto invincible South African military machine being forced to retreat before the military prowess of a Third World state. '*A luta continua*' became their inspirational battle-cry as they challenged the apartheid state on the streets of Soweto in June 1976.

SOUTHERN RHODESIA: FROM UDI TO ZIMBABWE

The end of the Central African Federation in 1963 left the white-settler regime of Southern Rhodesia – and Britain its nominal overlord – in an anomalous position. It had enjoyed responsible government for 40 years, and a position almost akin to that of a dominion within Commonwealth councils, but now had lesser status than the other members of the Federation, Malawi and Zambia, both within the Commonwealth and, internationally, in the United Nations. If the 1962 election had endorsed Sir Edgar Whitehead's programme of limited reform then the Conservative Macmillan government, with which he had negotiated the constitution, might have seized the opportunity to dump such an embarrassing responsibility whatever the international outcry.

Joshua Nkomo's National Democratic Party considered accepting the White-head package in the hope that further reforms would soon follow. But the party eventually refused to cooperate, expecting that under external pressure Whitehead could be induced to offer more. A majority in the United Nations duly called on Britain to revise the constitution. Demonstrations and riots in 1961, similar to those which propelled African nationalists to power elsewhere, led Whitehead to proscribe the party in December. It was immediately reconstituted as the Zimbabwe African People's Union (ZAPU). Help for ZAPU, including small arms, emanated from the Soviet Union, Egypt and other foreign sympathizers, and it too was proscribed in September 1962. Most of the Africans newly enfranchised by Whitehead boycotted the December 1962 election, contributing to his defeat by Winston Field's Rhodesian Front, a populist white-settler party pledged to securing independence under white minority rule.

When Field baulked at the idea of a unilateral declaration of independence (UDI) he was replaced by Ian Smith, a native-born Rhodesian tobacco farmer. Threats of unilateral Rhodesian action now became common. The new British Labour government, led by Harold Wilson, laid down five principles for independence: first, the franchise had to indicate clearly that majority rule would follow; second, it should be guaranteed that the constitution would not be abrogated after independence; third, there should be an immediate increase in African rights; fourth, there should be an end to discriminatory laws; and, fifth, there must be an assurance that the constitution was acceptable to the majority. The Rhodesian view was that the electoral qualifications introduced in 1961 would eventually lead to majority rule as more Africans acquired the necessary levels of income and education. Rhodesia was not invited to the 1964 Commonwealth Conference, though it had been an observer at all conferences since 1926. (South Africa had quit in 1961 and there was now an Afro-Asian majority.)

The final rupture came on 11 November 1965, when the Rhodesian government declaring itself still loyal to the Crown, proclaimed its own independence, breaking the sequence of Britain's orderly withdrawal from its African Empire. The protestation of loyalty accompanying this Armistice Day UDI deliberately opposed traditionalist sentiments of patriotism and imperialism based on 'kith and kin' to 'wind of change' appeasement of the Afro-Asian Commonwealth. The carefully marketed image of Ian Smith as a plain-spoken ex-Spitfire pilot turned tobacco farmer, functioned to the same effect. Moreover, unlike the Portuguese in Angola and Mozambique, or the *colons* in Algeria, the white Rhodesians controlled the colonial administration with its own security forces, including a modern air force. (Smith had been careful to appoint a sympathetic military commander before UDI.) The Rhodesian Front correctly calculated that the British government would not take the political and military risk of deploying force against it.[25]

London was not alone in being nonplussed by UDI. ZAPU, and its leader, Joshua Nkomo, had done everything which brought nationalist parties to power elsewhere in British Africa, including colonies like Kenya and Northern Rhodesia which contained a substantial settler presence. But the expected scenario of piecemeal decolonization by progressive constitutional changes failed to materialize. Instead Nkomo was faced with a script written in Salisbury rather than London. Whereas other movements, having seized the initiative, were carried forward by the bandwagon momentum of their success, ZAPU faced disappointment and possible defeat. Nationalist discontent focused on Nkomo's leadership. Disagreement over ideology and strategy was compounded by personal and factional rivalry. In August 1963 the Zimbabwe African National Union (ZANU), led by the Reverend Ndabaninghi Sithole was founded in opposition to ZAPU. As so often in Third World politics, divisions over strategy and ideology were transmuted into ethnic or communal rivalry. Most of the ZANU leaders were Shona while Nkomo retained broad support among the Ndebele.

The rift was sustained by some of the most significant supporters of African nationalism as well as its enemies. Successful nationalist leaders of Nkomo's generation, now esconced in power, generally rallied to his support. So, too, did the Soviet Union. The People's Republic of China, though, the only great power with expertise in peasant revolution, supported ZANU as part of its challenge to the Soviet Union's claim to be the authentic voice of international socialism. The Rhodesian Front doubly benefited: it faced an ethnically split African opposition and was handed the propaganda prize of plausibly maintaining that it was opposed by 'tribalism' rather than nationalism.

There was still considerable feeling among the rank and file of the ruling British Labour party that the government must bring the rebellion to an end. The Prime Minister, therefore, while ruling out force, refused to recognize the unilateral declaration of independence. Economic sanctions were implemented and made mandatory by the United Nations. But it quickly became clear that they were being flouted by the Portuguese in Mozambique, South Africa and some important multinational companies. On Commonwealth insistence Britain accepted a new, stiffer formula for recognition of the rebel regime, NIBMAR (No Independence Before Majority Rule). But Smith was far from intimidated. His security forces were effectively containing the nationalist guerrillas and the country was still prosperous enough to attract white immigrants.

The collapse of the Portuguese Empire in 1974 drastically changed the military situation. The Rhodesian military frontier was greatly extended making it increasingly easy for guerrillas to penetrate. At a much later stage than its Portuguese counterpart, the Rhodesian army was 'Africanized' and by the late 1970s about four-fifths of its forces were black, while for the first time Africans were commissioned. At the same time there was an ever-growing need in the Rhodesian economy for skilled and supervisory black labour. White supremacy, the Rhodesian Front's avowed objective, was proving ever more difficult to sustain.

White Rhodesia became increasingly dependent on South Africa while South Africa became less willing to bear the burden of sustaining the Rhodesian regime. In 1976 joint United States and South African pressure finally forced Ian Smith to agree to a phased transfer of power to a moderate black government. At the same time ZANU and ZAPU agreed to join in a Patriotic Front. Robert Mugabe, backed by Samora Machel, rose to the leadership in ZANU through the support of the guerrillas in Mashonaland. In 1979 there was an attempt at an internal settlement which resulted in a government headed by Bishop Abel Muzorewa. He failed to achieve peace with the guerrillas or the international recognition that would end sanctions, and eventually agreed to stand down as Prime Minister in favour of an interim British administration.

Fifteen years after UDI, therefore, Britain was once more constitutionally involved in the transition from Southern Rhodesia to Zimbabwe. New elections held on 29 February 1980 – after the guerrillas had been granted official legitimacy – resulting in a massive victory for Mugabe's ZANU party. (Muzorewa was routed. With 100 seats at stake, Mugabe won 57 of the 61 Shona seats. The Ndebele won 20 seats.) Machel, with his own country's experience of continuous civil war, recommended that Mugabe opt for reconciliation in victory. ZANU had already set the tone of postcolonial politics by contesting the election on an extremely moderate programme given the party's previous commitment to revolutionary Marxist-Leninism. The Soviet Union stubbornly continued to back Nkomo hence it enjoyed much less influence than in postcolonial Angola and Mozambique. The Western powers, on the other hand, provided funds to purchase for redistribution the lands of those white farmers who chose to emigrate, while Mugabe welcomed those who chose to continue farming in Zimbabwe.

In April 1980 Britain transferred the remnants of its constitutional authority to a coalition government led by Mugabe, which emphasized continuity by including two whites in the Cabinet. Whites still served as officers in the armed forces, especially the air force, and a substantial, though rapidly decreasing, number opted to stay on in the civil service. In industry and commerce many remained as managers, entrepreneurs and technical experts. Certainly there was no equivalent to the mass exodus of *colons* from Algeria or Portuguese from Angola and Mozambique.

END-GAME IN SOUTHERN AFRICA

South Africa had played a crucial role in prompting the change of regime in this critical buffer state. Yet its switch from supporting the Rhodesian Front to engineering a pliant black successor regime had hardly gone according to plan. Instead of Bishop Muzorewa, or even Joshua Nkomo, the new Zimbabwe would be ruled by an avowed Marxist, Robert Mugabe. On the other hand, unlike Mozambique in 1975 – yet on the hard-earned advice of Samora Machel himself – Mugabe offered reconciliation to his erstwhile enemies as he turned to the West for governmental aid and private investment in order to reconstruct the crippled Zimbabwean economy.

Two obvious lines of action were open to South Africa. It could continue using its military strength to destabilize the neighbouring black states, forcing them to renounce the internationalist aspirations of African nationalism by preventing the African National Congress (ANC) using them as safe havens from which to launch guerrilla attacks on South Africa. And it could use its economic power to bind its neighbours into dependency as economic satellites in the process developing a comprador neocolonial relationship with the political and bureaucratic bourgeoisie in the new states. Political and economic power would reinforce each other just as they were assumed to have done during the heyday of Pax Britannica or the 'good neighbour' policies of the United States in Latin America. South African business could be expected to expand northwards to compensate for the threat and later the reality of international economic sanctions. But what if the black states of southern Africa suffered such losses from destabilization that the economic benefits derived from dominating the regional economy became threatened? It was the task of South Africa's rulers to prevent the tension between military security through destabilization and economic expansion from becoming destructive.

South African imperialism, though, like British or American, was never monolithic. In the late 1970s the then Prime Minister, John Vorster, and General Heneriek van der Berghe, the head of BOSS, the civil intelligence organization, sought to steer South Africa towards *détente* with black Africa. In 1978 this policy drastically changed when both were forced out of office in the wake of the 'Muldergate' information scandal. Defence Minister P. W. Botha became Prime Minister and General Magnus Malan, a known hawk, replaced him at Defence, while South African military men were placed in other key positions. The military perspective of the 'Total National Strategy' predominated as BOSS, already crippled by scandal, lost power to the Military Intelligence Directorate, (MID). Its main objective was to cut off support to the various domestic groups opposing apartheid. In strategic terms this meant undermining the frontline states by direct raids on any ANC bases sheltered there, economic sabotage and destabilization through support for rebel guerrillas and freelance bandits. Accordingly South Africa took over support for RENAMO from Rhodesia before the end of UDI. Magnus Malan promised his opposite number in the Rhodesian forces, General Peter Walls, that in the event of Zimbabwean independence any unassimilable groups would be incorporated into the South African Defence Forces (SADF) and the MID. The South African Air Force thus participated in the transition to Zimbabwe by an air-shuttle of C130s to evacuate RENAMO fighters, along with such Rhodesian irreconcilables as the crack Selous Scouts, who had often fought alongside them.

South Africa's Western well-wishers, having benefited from its help in dealing with Rhodesia, sought to return the favour by a more active involvement in the region. The unashamedly right-wing governments of Margaret Thatcher, 1979–91, and Ronald Reagan, 1980–8, took the lead in developing policies of 'constructive engagement', a term coined by Dr Chester Crocker, Assistant Secretary of State for Africa and President Reagan's special envoy to the region.[26] This policy encouraged South Africa to embark on reformist domestic policies and a foreign policy of negotiation from strength instead of complete destabilization. Without reform and economic expansion, Crocker feared a rising level of violent confrontation between black and white in South Africa and beyond which would prove disastrous for Western interests. Ironically, the threat of sanctions, and then their limited imposition in the mid-1980s, despite protests from Conservative Western governments, increased the leverage of Reagan and Thatcher. South Africa, already suffering from severe recession with danger-ously high inflation and unemployment, relied on their good offices to induce such bodies as Congress, the Commonwealth, the EEC and the United Nations, to drop or at least mitigate sanctions.

After six years of destabilizing Mozambique, South Africa decided to comply with Crocker's advice. In late 1983 it began talks with FRELIMO which culminated in the signing of the N'komati Accord on Non-Aggression and Good Neighbourliness on 16 March 1984. Both the treaty and the rhetoric of Botha, the white Afrikaner, and Machel, the black Marxist in welcoming its signing are remarkable. The treaty rested on 'the internationally recognized principle of the right of peoples to self-determination and independence and the principle of equal rights of all peoples.' Machel proclaimed that neither Mozambicans or South Africans had any other country, thus putting South Africans in a different category to the Portuguese and other colonialists. And though he still proclaimed the battle cry, '*A luta continua*', now 'the struggle [was] against hunger, disease, ignorance, poverty and underdevelopment' and such like impersonal forces. Botha outdid him in anti-colonial rhetoric, citing his people's seniority in the struggle against European imperialism and the deaths of Afrikaner women and children in British concentration camps 'while their husbands, fathers and brothers fought the might of a great empire.'[27] 'The high contracting parties' undertook not to resort to the threat or use of force against each other and not to harbour each other's enemies – meaning the ANC and RENAMO. The rhetoric maintained the fiction of equality between the 'high contracting parties' but the victory was surely South Africa's. After nearly a decade of destabilization the Mozambican state was close to collapse, unable to suppress its rebellion and desperately short of food. And in the aftermath of N'komati, RENAMO banditry proved much more rooted and difficult to curb than the relatively disciplined cadres of ANC exiles. (There is a special irony in RENAMO's entitling the bulletin in which it denied post-N'komati allegiance to Machel '*A Luta Continua, Orgao Official da Renamo*'.)[28] Hence the posture of Mozambique – in any case desperate for the remittances of its migrant workers from South Africa – was still supplicant.

The other great triumph of 'constructive engagement' was in Namibia. In 1986–7 South African and UNITA forces failed to dislodge a combined Cuban and Angolan government force from Cutio Cuanvale, the southernmost Angolan airbase. Cuba's willingness to increase its presence from 35,000 to 50,000 troops, combined with superior new Soviet weapons (notably Mig-23s and ground-to-air missiles) suggested South Africa might suffer a major defeat if the costly war continued. The army's failure gave weight to the Department of Foreign Affairs recommendation that South Africa revert to diplomacy and economic penetration. Angola, too, with its economy badly damaged by civil war, wanted negotiations. Crocker suggested a way forward by linking Namibian independence to Cuban withdrawal from Angola. The Soviet Union under President Gorbachev had long been signalling that it favoured a more conciliatory policy. Even Cuba, able to claim the credit for successfully defending Angola against South Africa and assisting Namibia to independence, might be willing to rest on its laurels. Crocker's plan thus had the merit of allowing all the protagonists to claim a successful outcome. The government of the new state would be decided by elections conducted under joint supervision of South Africa and the United Nations. All parties, including the almost certain winner, the South West African People's Organization (SWAPO) agreed that, like Mozambique, independent Namibia would deny bases to the ANC. That was the price of South Africa, the *de facto* ruler, agreeing to decolonization.

South African foreign policy had therefore adjusted to the serial collapse of its ring of buffer states by reaching agreements with the new black governments. Yet each victory for African nationalism, from the collapse of the Portuguese Empire to the triumph of SWAPO was perceived throughout the Third World, and inside black South Africa, as a defeat for the apartheid regime. Samora Machel's valediction to the ANC after N'komati forced it to surrender its guerrilla bases was prophetic (and also good Marxism!): the struggle in an industrialized country like South Africa, where even agriculture was highly mechanized, was properly a struggle for citizenship and civil rights. '*A luta continua*' but through mass protest and industrial action.

In February 1990 the South African government responded by releasing Nelson Mandela from over a quarter century's imprisonment. The ANC's struggle for citizenship and national reconciliation culminated in the 'Liberation Election' of May 1994. On 10 May Mandela was inaugurated President.

NOTES

1 P. Anderson, 'Portugal and the end of Ultra-Colonialism', *New Left Review* 15–17 (1962), p. 112.

2 James Duffy, *Portugal in Africa* (Harmondsworth, Penguin, 1962), p. 16.

3 M. Crawford Young, 'Nationalism, Ethnicity and Class', *Cahiers d'Etudes Africaines* XXVI (1986), pp. 423–6.

4 'Lenin, when working out the weighted voting system in the soviets, said that for every one vote that a peasant had, a worker should have four votes.' F. Halliday, 'Revolution in the Third World: 1945 and After' (Ellen Rice, Oxford, Blackwell, 1991).

5 L. Vail and L. White, 'Forms of Resistance: Songs and Perceptions of Power in Colonial Mozambique', in Donald Crummey, ed., *Banditry, Rebellion and Social Protest in Africa* (London, James Currey, 1986), pp. 193–7.

6 David Birmingham and D. Martin, eds., *History of Central Africa* (London, Longman, 1983), II.

7 Eric R. Wolf, *Peasant Wars of the Twentieth Century* (London, Faber, 1971); John Dunn, *Modern Revolutions* (Cambridge, Cambridge University Press, 1972); Ben Turok, ed., *Revolutionary Thought in the 20th Century* (London, Zed Press, 1980) is a useful collection slanted towards Africa.

8 Cited in Kenneth W. Grundy, *The Guerilla Struggle in Africa* (New York, Grossman, 1971), p. 92.

9 Douglas Porch, *The Portuguese Armed Forces and the Revolution* (London, Croom Helm, 1970), p. 32.

10 Antonio de Figueirodo, *Portugal: Fifty Years of Dictatorship* (Harmondsworth, Penguin, 1974) uses this poster for its cover.

11 Portugal finally became a member of the UN in 1955, the Soviet Union having blocked its earlier applications.

12 Gervase Clarence-Smith, *The Third Portuguese Empire, 1825–1975: A Study in Economic Imperialism* (Manchester, Manchester University Press, 1985), p. 193.

13 *Op. cit.*, p. 201.

14 Between 1961 and 1974 an estimated 110,000 conscripts failed to report. Porch, *Portuguese Armed Forces*, p. 32.

15 Cited in R. Blackburn, 'The Test in Portugal', *New Left Review* 86, 87 (1974), p. 6.

16 Tom Gallagher, *Portugal: A Twentieth Century Interpretation* (Manchester, Manchester University Press, 1983), pp. 164–90.

17 Amilcar Cabral, *Revolution in Guinea* (New York, Monthly Review Press, 1969).

18 Porch, *Portuguese Armed Forces*, p. 55.

19 P. Chabal, 'Revolutionary Democracy in Africa: the Case of Guinea-Bissau', in Patrick Chabal, ed., *Political Domination in Africa* (Cambridge, Cambridge University Press, 1986), p. 85; and Malyn Newitt, *Portugal in Africa* (Harlow, Longman, 1981), p. 236, hold somewhat different views on this.

20 Leroy Vail and Landeg White, *Capitalism and Colonialism in Mozambique* (London, Heinemann, 1980) deal with the liberated areas as a 'model' but query whether it could be applied after independence.

21 Porch, *Portuguese Armed Forces*, p. 85.

22 *Op. cit.*, p. 113.
23 Alex Vines, *Renamo: Terrorism in Mozambique* (London, James Currey, 1991).
24 Fred Halliday, *The Making of the Second Cold War* (London, Verso, 1983).
25 The UDI period is covered by David Caute, *Under the Skin: The Death of White Rhodesia* (London, Allen and Unwin, 1983); and David Johnson and Phyllis Martin, *The Struggle for Zimbabwe* (London, Faber, 1981).
26 Chester Crocker, 'South Africa: A Strategy for Change', *Foreign Affairs* (Winter 1980/81), though written before he attained office explains his 'linkage' approach.
27 Dennis Austin, *South Africa, 1984* (London, Routledge and Kegan Paul, 1985), pp. 49–53.
28 Vines, *Renamo*, p. 137, n. 53.

12

Conclusion

The enormous condescension of posterity.
(E. P. Thompson)

Be gentle, as you fold away a cast off creed.
(G. M. Young)

Tracing the history of African decolonization, with the evolution of the study of modern Africa as subtext, illuminates the complex interplay between the two. The proliferation of knowledge, and the rapid supersession of organizing concepts which this involved, struggled to keep abreast of the rapid political change, manifest, first, in accelerated decolonization, and, second, the instability of so many postcolonial regimes. This chapter suggests aspects of the formative experience of that generation of Africans and Europeans caught up in the excitement of independence.

Two pictures leap to mind. For me, they memorialize some truths about decolonization likely to be slighted from the perspective of the 1990s. The first is the frontispiece and sole illustration to R. D. Pearce's fine 1982 book, *The Turning Point in Africa: British Colonial Policy, 1938–48*. The second, again unique, illustrates the 'Conclusion' to Jean-François Bayart's seminal work of the late 1980s, *The State in Africa: The Politics of the Belly*, which even before the publication of its English translation in 1993 – the French edition having appeared in 1989 – had challenged Africanists everywhere to revise their understanding of decolonization and independence.

Pearce publishes a photograph of Arthur Creech Jones – 'Creech' to his friends – dressed as a Yoruba chief, datelined Lagos 1944, without commentary. Creech Jones, a rather shy, bespectacled middle-aged Englishman, is smiling at the camera. He is 53 years old. He was born into the working class in Bristol, an old slave-trading port. As a boy Creech Jones was shocked by the revelations of atrocities in the Congo Free State and acquired an abiding interest in African emancipation. He gained political experience in trade unionism and local government, serving from 1913 to 1922 as Secretary of the Camberwell Trades and Labour Council. His socialism derived from Christianity, rather than Marxism, though certain 'doubts' on points of doctrine technically disqualified him from considering himself a Christian in later life. Nevertheless, firmly held religious principles guided his public career which was interrupted by the First World War when he became a conscientious objector. Although he applied to join the Friends' Ambulance Unit, he was court-martialled in 1916 and imprisoned until 1919. He became National Secretary of the Transport and General Workers' Union, led by that fellow working-class Bristolian, Ernest Bevin, from 1919 to 1929. The two men, very different in temperament but only 10 years apart in age, became close friends as well as colleagues.

Creech Jones served from 1921 to 1928 on the Executive Committee of the London Labour Party. In 1925 he was asked to tutor Clements Kadalie, the founder of the first mass trade union in Africa, on his visit to Britain: 'I eagerly responded. . . . I felt that the struggle of the African workers in South Africa could be helped by an organisation which had contributed so much to the making of British democracy.'[1]

He first tried to enter Parliament in 1929, unsuccessfully contesting the Greater Manchester constituency of Heywood and Radcliffe. He had to wait through the disastrous Labour collapse at the 1931 election before being elected MP for Shipley, on the outskirts of Bradford, in 1935. He was soon dubbed 'the unofficial member of the Kikuyu at Westminster', asking the astounding number of 377 parliamentary questions on colonial affairs during his first four parliamentary sessions. (His closest rival asked 210 during the same period.) Naturally he joined the Labour Party Advisory Committee on Imperial Questions and served as its chairman in 1944–5. In 1940, along with the South African socialist Rita Hinden, he set up the Fabian Colonial Bureau, which increasingly took on the role of Labour Party 'think tank' on colonial issues. He was chairman and Hinden secretary. On top of all this, he served on the executive of the Anti-Slavery Society from 1938 to 1954 and as an active member of several kindred groups.

Serious-minded, patently sincere, and apparently without a trace of humour in his speeches and writings, he reported to Leonard Woolf, just after the outbreak of war, that he was 'an overwhelmingly busy person'.[2] As a good Fabian, Creech Jones decided from the outset that reforms could only be achieved by working through the available bureaucratic structures to have practical effect. In 1936 he joined the Colonial Office advisory committee on education, becoming chairman during the Second World War.

His second war proved very different from the first. When Churchill became Prime Minister in 1940 one of his first acts was to offer the Ministry of Labour to Ernest Bevin as leader of the Transport and General, now the world's biggest trade union, and appoint him to the War Cabinet, though Bevin was not yet an MP. Bevin accepted but on his own terms: the expansion of his ministerial powers and a shift to the left in social policy. Churchill treated Bevin with a respect, bordering on deference, he gave to no other Labour member – and very few Conservative members – of his coalition government. Bevin, in his turn, appointed Creech Jones to be his Parliamentary Private Secretary. In 1943

Creech Jones became a member of the Elliott Commission on Higher Education in West Africa. Hence his appearance in Lagos on his first trip to Africa in 1944.

The picture in Pearce's book shows him seated, wearing a voluminous chief's gown over his suit, his splendidly embroidered chief's cap pushed back on his head. On his right stands the veteran Nigerian nationalist, Herbert Macaulay, a handsome 80-year-old, very much at his elegant ease in well-cut tropical suit, looking not unlike his Hollywood contemporary, C. Aubrey Smith. On his left stands the robust figure of J. O. Balogun of the Nigerian Farmers wearing African dress. In the background various Africans can be discerned, some wearing African gowns, some in European suits. Bunting and flags contribute to the general atmosphere of decorous festivity.

In Bayart's book readers are requested to look at the photograph of Ahmed Sekoum Toure, 'radiant, still young and dressed in a western suit . . . crossing the rope footbridge of N'Zerekore. We know what was waiting for Guinea, on the other side. Nevertheless, how can one be indifferent to the joyous forces which leap out of this snapshot, to the certainty that the film has indeed captured history in the making?'[3] He sees, in the book's last sentence, the rope bridge as an image of the interplay between dominators and dominated in Africa.[4]

If the Lagos picture records the auspicious beginnings of decolonization, Fabian reformers in benevolent cooperation with the long-established tradition of West African nationalism, the snapshot of Sekou Toure advancing towards his prize depicts its brilliant triumph less than two decades later. Like Creech Jones, Sekou Toure had a comparatively humble start in life. With little formal education he worked as a postal clerk and made his way through the trade union movement and left-wing politics. In his case there were strong links with the metropolitan left. In the immediate postwar period he joined a study group organized in Guinea by French Communists, while his trade union was also linked to the metropolitan Communist *Confederation Generale du Travail* (CGT). He became a significant public figure by organizing a successful strike against the new work code for French West Africa in 1953. His political party, *Parti Democratique de Guinée* (PDG), was closely associated with his union; hence when most French West African politicians broke with the Communist Party in 1950, Toure's party maintained its strong bond with metropolitan communism.

The very different structures of European and West African society, however, meant that Toure was able both to rally populist opposition to the chiefs and the French colonial administration by emphasizing the unifying principles of Marxism, Islam and anti-colonialism, and at the same time to appeal to varying regional and ethnic groups by advertising his family ties to traditional leaders of the past. As President he bore the titles 'Supreme head of the Revolution' and 'Supreme Servant of the People'. The picture reminds us that one of Africa's most cruel tyrants, whose close relatives formed a tight-knit and rapacious ruling clique, was once that confident figure on the rope bridge.

Both pictures have a snapshot informality very different from the filmic record of the brilliantly stage-managed rituals of the independence-day ceremonies. They are a reminder of the day-by-day building of networks of goodwill and cooperation by which the political and administrative processes of decolonization and independence advanced. The dark side of this focus on personal relationships was the way a tyrant, such as Sekou Toure later became, insisted on acquiring direct knowledge of every person of potential influence, 'not just students returning to Guinea after studying abroad but also political prisoners released from detention who were obliged to pay him "wholehearted homage" at the risk of appearing to bear a grudge.' The small population of most of the new African states, Bayart observes, helped the postcolonial rulers to exercise benevolent or malevolent surveillance 'in the manner of a village chief'.[5]

By some judgements Creech Jones was a political failure. Attlee had some doubts whether he was 'strong enough for the position' when he was promoted to Colonial Secretary in 1946 and his suspicions were confirmed: 'Creecg [*sic*] Jones despite much hard work & devotion had not appeared to have a real grip of administration in the Colonial office. He was bad in the House and contributed nothing in Cabinet . . .'[6] When he lost his seat in the 1950 election he was not found another. Nor was he given a peerage, although he let it be known he would accept one.

Bevin thought his protégé was 'rather undemonstrative. I sometimes think you hide your light under a bushel . . .',[7] but praised 'the indefatigable way you have applied yourself to your task in this Labour Government.' Attlee was a 'Little Englander', who could not comprehend Creech Jones's interest in the colonies. Bevin was genuinely enthusiastic. He warmly endorsed Creech Jones's achievements:

> Looking back over the history of colonial development I do not think anyone has a greater record – the Constitutional changes you have carried through, the development of education, the promotion of universities, the constant attention you have given to economic development, the way you have applied your mind to the problems of soil erosion and transport. If only it had been done long ago. What a different world it would have been![8]

The temperamental faultline between those decision-makers whose imaginations were captured by African issues, and those – such as Attlee and Hugh Dalton – to whom they were a turn-off, cut across division over policy and differences of generation. However much Creech Jones and Andrew Cohen struck Sir Philip Mitchell as misguided, he was impressed by their goodwill and enthusiasm. Similarly, in the 'unofficial' world of African politicians through which decolonization had to be negotiated, shared concern promoted mutual confidence. Cohen judged the long-awaited 1948 Africa Conference of unofficial Council Members to have been successful, attributing this mainly to the delegates' affection for Creech Jones: 'I have now seen the dry bones of papers transformed so dramatically by personal contacts into something real and human.'[9]

Margery Perham, hoping that the Sudan could be persuaded to join the Commonwealth, suggested that Creech Jones could replicate there the starring role which Mountbatten executed with such panache during the countdown to Indian independence. Whatever he lacked in Mountbatten-style charisma, she believed, was compensated for by his being 'a little less ruthless and tempestuous in his methods'.[10]

All governments have a set of major priorities which determine their approach to lesser issues, sometimes forcing them off the agenda, sometimes focusing on them, but in so doing transforming, even distorting them. Among Labour's political heavyweights only Bevin knew or cared much about colonial issues. For the rest such matters as Britain's survival as a great power, involving coping with the Americans and keeping the Soviets at bay, and the welfare of the metropolitan electorate, entailing concern for the housewife's fat ration, determined their approach to African issues. The Colonial Office was squeezed out of areas that the Labour government considered to be of prime political significance. In some ways Africa was fortunate to have impinged so rarely on the agenda of high politics.

Forty years later the decent sentiments and civilized language of Creech Jones and Margery Perham, appear even more dated than the racist bile released by Hugh Dalton. Most missionaries, Fabians, and the assorted propagandists for the multiracial Commonwealth, the French Union and *Francafrique*, spoke the public language of multiracial reconciliation. Fine words signifying little or so they seemed from the perspective of historians imbued with a *realpolitik* approach to international history.

But late-twentieth-century Francophone political science gives such fine words greater weight. '*Francafrique*' has persisted, Bayart observes, despite failing to find 'institutional and communal expression' in 1958–60, maintaining its own form of organization: 'Its "familial" atmosphere – almost "incestuous" according to one journalist – which gives it its particular tone, and', he slyly comments, 'which irritates Anglo-Saxon observers so much, is due less to the manipulation of the secret services than to the production of an intercontinental cultural sociability.'[11] He observes that Therese Brou, who later married Houphouët-Boigny, was among those first 150 scholars whom he sent to France in 1946. The school she studied at was at Villeneuve-sur-Lot, whose mayor, Raphael-Leygues was later appointed French ambassador to the Ivory Coast, where he remained for 15 years. That Houphouët-Boigny and others of the emergent political élite had enjoyed the camaraderie of Parisian parliamentary politics surely contributed to the persistence of Francophone sociability far beyond decolonization.

Some Anglo-Saxons, once drawn into such Francophone networks of sociability, were astonished rather than censorious at the way they contravened formal hierarchies of class and status, thus the American ambassador to Gabon, 'was surprised one day to meet his own secretary – who had French nationality – in President Leon Mba's waiting-room: she had come to help stop her husband, a butcher – who also had French nationality – from trying to divorce her!'[12]

Bayart lumps the Americans and British together in discussing sociability. Anglophone Africans are more discriminating. Consider the fascinating, highly amusing, autobiography of Phyllis Ntantala, a South African from the landed gentry of the Transkei, whose early life was one of relative privilege.[13] Decolonization, among other things, involved a comedy of manners. Who better to record its subtleties than those élites threatened by the crude polarization between imperialism and nationalism? The Anglo-Irish, the Sierra Leone Krios, and well-born black South Africans like Ntantala, who witnessed British appeasement of Afrikaner nationalism, share similar wry comment on the changing etiquette of ethnic and race relations.

After school at Healdtown and Lovedale, Ntantala at 15 won a scholarship to the University of Fort Hare, where she was one of 30 women among over 200 men. There she met her future husband, A. C. Jordan, a man of prodigious abilities: Xhosa poet and novelist, celebrated cricketer, teacher and pioneering scholar in African languages. (He *chose* to write his novels in Xhosa whereas his scholarly writings had to be in English.)

Against the odds, he prospered as a teacher and scholar at Fort Hare and at the University of Cape Town. She reared their family and made a successful career in teaching. She wrote for the radical journal *Africa South* and worked for teachers' organizations and other voluntary groups opposed to the increasingly powerful thrust of state-sponsored South African racism. But the shift from a segregationist to an apartheid agenda, with the triumph of Afrikaner nationalism in 1948, threatened liberal educational institutions like Fort Hare. In 1959 the South African government passed what it euphemistically named the Extension of University Education Act, correctly described in common parlance as 'University Apartheid'. Four new ethnic universities were created and Fort Hare, hitherto the only university for black South Africans, was henceforth to be confined to Xhosa.

Throughout the Western world universities were suddenly expected to cope with the rapid advance of decolonization by initiating and expanding courses in African Studies. None more so than in the United States, which benefited from the self-exile of much of the liberal and radical South African intelligentsia. A. C. Jordan was awarded a Carnegie Travel Grant in 1961 to tour American universities, with the University of California offering him a visiting professorship for the year after the Carnegie tour. But the South African government refused him a passport, despite the personal intervention of the Vice-Chancellor of the University of Capetown. The American embassy could not issue a visa if

Jordan had no passport. He turned, therefore, to the British authorities and the whole family was granted British citizenship within three days. So, in the very year that South Africa quit the Commonwealth and over 40 years after white South Africa's independence, the sometime British connection still had meaning in international law.[14]

Mrs Jordan had to make a protracted stay in England before joining her husband in the US which allowed a comparison of race relations on either side of the Atlantic. She is scathing about white South Africans who reserved for themselves jobs in such organizations as Defence and Aid and the Anti-Apartheid Movement to the exclusion of black South African exiles. And she found lunch with British academics at the School of Oriental and African Studies (SOAS) unbearably 'stuffy'. She feared what would happen to 'A.C.' – and even more to herself – should he end up working there.[15]

By contrast she found social life at the University of Wisconsin, Madison, where Jordan joined the African Studies Programme, as the only black on the faculty, more congenial in spite of the fact that two homemade bombs were thrown at her home at the height of the tension over open housing in nearby Milwaukee.[16] Here was one of the most significant differences between British and French decolonization: the Anglophone world was much more polycentric than its Francophone equivalent. That English, unlike French, was a multi-national, as well as an international, language was a mixed blessing when the British sought to substitute influence for control. For the Francophone, all routes lead to Paris, whereas a British passport made an American visa feasible, opening up New York, Washington, Madison, Boston, Indiana, the University of California and a host of other glittering study and career possibilities. In addition, the United States, as well as exerting a strong cultural pull on the young of all nations and races through Hollywood and popular music, exercised a special appeal to Africans through the influence of African-Americans within its popular culture.[17]

The 'white' Commonwealth – especially Canada – also beckoned, with higher per capita income, and more generously endowed universities, than Britain. Canada, moreover, has the unique distinction of being both Anglophone and Francophone, an immense advantage in both African diplomacy and Africanist scholarship – as *The Canadian Journal of African Studies*, the most genuinely bilingual of Africanist journals, demonstrates.

The Commonwealth itself became increasingly polycentric. This involved creating fresh machinery for coordination, under a new bureaucratic-cum-diplomatic supremo, the Secretary-General. A Commonwealth Secretariat, separate from the British bureaucracy, was created in 1965, charged with responsibility for organizing the biennial Heads of Government meetings, which were soon no longer automatically held in Britain. The first two Secretary-Generals, Arnold Smith and Sonny Ramphal, ensured that the Commonwealth represented the interests of the majority of its members, which from 1961 were Afro-Asian.

As 'new countries' which had never claimed to be great powers, the more prosperous Commonwealth countries – usually, but not exclusively, drawn from the old 'white' dominions[18] – sustained the drive towards a better international order through decolonization and support for both the United Nations and an increasingly multiracial Commonwealth. And they did so at a time of increasing disillusion with such international institutions and the consequences of decolonization in Britain itself.[19] In Lesotho, for example, Canadian aid and the presence of French Canadian Oblate fathers, drawn mainly from the Maritime provinces, have done something to mitigate the isolating effects of being poor, land-locked and totally surrounded by South Africa.

Knowledge of decolonization has progressed by way of the rapid adoption and no less speedy repudiation of a succession of plausible paradigms. Historical events have shaped, and been shaped by, the dominant patterns of imperialism, nationalism, ethnicity, class and gender in kaleidoscopic succession. G. M. Young's cautionary advice, 'Be gentle, as you fold away a cast off creed' seems especially appropriate to historians charged with explaining such recent, highly controversial, processes as African decolonization. However beguiling the patterns and paradigms currently prescribed by the social sciences, historians must focus on people, their actions and their beliefs. So, by way of postscript, this final chapter has been concerned with individuals' biographies and the institutions and beliefs through which they found expression.

NOTES

1 R. D. Pearce, *The Turning Point in Africa* (London, Cass, 1982), p. 98.
2 *Op. cit.*, p.98.
3 Jean-François Bayart, *The State in Africa: The Politics of the Belly* (London, Longman, 1993), p. 261.
4 *Op. cit.*, p. 272.
5 *Op. cit.*, pp. 232–3.
6 Pearce, *Turning Point*, pp. 91–2.
7 Attlee's failure to register Creech Jones's name correctly persists. Several historians have hyphenated it. *Mea culpa*. Henry S. Wilson, *The Imperial Experience in Sub-Saharan Africa since 1870* (Minneapolis, University of Minnesota Press, 1977), pp. 300, 301, 401.
8 Pearce, *Turning Point*, p. 95.
9 *Op. cit.*, p. 192.
10 W. R. Louis, 'The Coming of Independence in the Sudan', *Journal of Imperial and Commonwealth History* XIX (1991), p. 152. See also her moving tribute at his funeral service; Margery Perham, *Colonial Sequence, 1949 to 1969* (London, Methuen, 1970), pp. 279–82.
11 Bayart, *The State*, p. 197.
12 *Op. cit.*, pp. 197, 232–3.

13 Phyllis Ntantala, *A Life's Mosaic: The Autobiography of Phyllis Ntantala* (Berkeley, University of California Press, 1993), p. 8.

14 *Op. cit.*, pp. 187–8.

15 *Op. cit.*, pp. 191–3.

16 *Op. cit.*, pp. 200–2.

17 See, among so many possible examples, photograph 'Fort Hare Rag, 1935: Phyllis as Harlem girl', Ntantala, *Autobiography*, p. xii.

18 An important exception being Singapore whose leader, Lee Kwan Yew, was a prominent and highly articulate participant in Commonwealth conferences.

19 Donald A. Low, *Eclipse of Empire* (Cambridge, Cambridge University Press, 1991), Chapter 12, 'Little Britain and Large Commonwealth', pp. 326–39.

Select Bibliography

The following bibliography is intended as a guide to further reading. It does not include all the books and periodicals from which material has been drawn. Generally, it concentrates on the most recent studies, the bibliographies of which can in turn provide references to sources and earlier accounts. However, certain early works demand inclusion because of their importance in both reflecting and creating the climate of opinion in which decolonization occurred.

Periodicals are abbreviated thus:

AA   African Affairs
CEA   *Cahiers d'Etudes Africaines*
JICH   Journal of Imperial and Commonwealth History
JMAS   Journal of Modern African Studies

GENERAL WORKS

The most comprehensive survey, not confined to Africa, is Robert F. Holland, *European Decolonization, 1918–1981* (Houndmills, Macmillan, 1985). John D. Hargreaves, *Decolonization in Africa* (London, Longman, 1988) is especially strong on the French side, focusing principally on tropical Africa, though it also deals, more briefly, with the settler colonies of northern and southern Africa. Martin Meredith, *The First Dance of Freedom: Black Africa in the Postwar Era* (London, Hamish Hamilton, 1984) is lively and comprehensive. Volume VIII of *The Cambridge History of Africa: From c.1940 to c.1975* (Cambridge, Cambridge University Press, 1984) covers decolonization through thematic and regional chapters with extensive bibliographical commentaries. The most massive accounts are the proceedings of two international conferences, held in Bellagio and Harare, edited by Prosser Gifford and W. Roger Louis, entitled *The Transfer of Power in Africa: Decolonization* and *Decolonization and African Independence* (New Haven, Yale University Press, 1982 and 1988). Both have indispensable bibliographies. Other useful conference reports are:

Anthony H. M. Kirk-Greene, ed., *The Transfer of Power: The Colonial Administrator in the Age of Decolonisation* (University of Oxford, 1979).

W. H. Morris-Jones and G. Fischer, eds., *Decolonisation and After: The British and French Experience* (London, Cass, 1980).

David K. Fieldhouse, *Black Africa, 1945–1980: Economic Decolonization and Arrested Development* (London, Unwin Hyman, 1986) is indispensable for the economic context of terminal colonialism.

THE COLONIAL PERIOD

The basic reference work is W. M. Hailey, *An African Survey* (Oxford, Oxford University Press, 1938 and the second, largely rewritten, edition, 1957). *The Cambridge History of Africa*, VII, 1905–40, ed. Andrew Roberts (Cambridge, Cambridge University Press, 1986) provides comprehensive coverage and bibliography, as well as penetrating thematic chapters. Raymond L. Buell, *The Native Problem in Africa* (2 vols., New York, Macmillan, 1928) despite the period flavour of its title, epitomizes interwar American criticism of European colonialism. Crawford Young, 'The African Colonial State and its Political Legacy', in David Rothchild and Naomi Chazan, eds., *The Precarious Balance: State and Society in Africa* (Boulder, Co., Westview Press, 1988) pp. 25–66, is sharply focused on the critical issues for students of decolonization. Henry S. Wilson, *The Imperial Experience in Sub-Saharan Africa since 1870* (Minneapolis, University of Minnesota Press, 1977) stresses the role of different educational policies pursued by Britain, France and Belgium in the development of opposition to colonialism. There are many useful chapters and an extensive bibliography (V) in Lewis H. Gann and Peter Duignan, eds., *The History and Politics of Decolonization*, (5 vols., Cambridge, Cambridge University Press, 1969–75). Ralph Austen, *African Economic History: Internal Development and External Dependency* (London, James Currey, 1987) is comprehensive and lucid.

NATIONALISM AND NATION-BUILDING

Three provocative studies appearing in the early 1980s revitalized the general study of nationalism: John Breuilly, *Nationalism and the State* (Manchester, Manchester University Press, 1985); Benedict Anderson, *Imagined Communities* (London, 1983); Ernest Gellner, *Nations and Nationalism* (Oxford, Oxford University Press, 1983). See also Breuilly's review article, 'Reflections on Nationalism', considering Anderson and Gellner, in *Philosophy of the Social Sciences* XV (1985), pp. 65–75. Later important general treatments are Eric Hobsbawm, *Nations and Nationalism since 1870* (Cambridge, Cambridge University Press, 1990); James Mayall, *Nationalism and International Society* (Cambridge, Cambridge University Press, 1990) and James G. Kellas, *The Politics of Nationalism and Ethnicity* (Houndmills, Macmillan, 1991).

Thomas L. Hodgkin's classic, *Nationalism in Colonial Africa* (London, Muller, 1956) appearing in the year of Suez and on the eve of Ghana's independence both reflected and influenced the wave of optimism sustaining decolonization. For a late-twentieth-century revisionist perspective on African politics during decolonization and independence see Jean François-Bayart, *The State in Africa: The Politics of the Belly* (London, Longman, 1993).

For trends in the analysis of African and Arab nationalism see Crawford Young, 'Nationalism, Ethnicity and Class in Africa' in *CEA* XXXVI (1986).

Henry S. Wilson, ed., *Origins of West African Nationalism* (London, Macmillan, 1969) illustrates the history of ideas of nationalism and nation-building, long preceding partition, in that region.

THE INTERNATIONAL CONTEXT

Two definitive studies by Wm. Roger Louis deal with decolonization in an international framework: *Imperialism at Bay, 1941–1945: The United States and the Decolonization of the British Empire* (Oxford, Clarendon Press, 1977) and *The British Empire in the Middle East, 1945–51* (Oxford, Clarendon Press, 1984). John Kent's densely detailed *The Internationalization of Colonialism: Britain, France and Black Africa, 1939–1956* (Oxford, Clarendon Press, 1992) disentangles the complex problems involved in coordinating foreign policy with local colonial and metropolitan policy-making. Herbert G. Nicholas's compact classic *United Nations as a Political Institution* (second edition, London, Oxford University Press, 1962) is a historiographical landmark. Mayall's *Nationalism and International Society* (1990) and the later chapters in Hedley Bull and Adam Watson, eds., *The Expansion of International Society* (Oxford, Clarendon Press, 1985) carry the story forward. For the notion of 'imperial overstretch' and a general introduction to international relations see Paul Kennedy's massive and very influential *The Rise and Fall of the Great Powers* (London, Fontana, 1989). Joseph S. Nye's response, *Bound to Lead: the Changing Nature of American Power* (New York, Basic Books, 1990) encompasses much more than the subtitle implies.

David Killingray and Richard Rathbone, eds., *Africa in the Second World War* (Houndmills, Macmillan, 1986) includes a useful general introduction as well as case studies.

BRITISH DECOLONIZATION

British decolonization has engendered proportionately more historiographical debate than other colonial empires. Three stimulating surveys which examine different approaches are Anthony Kirk-Greene, 'Decolonisation in British Africa', *History Today* XLI (January 1992), pp. 44–50 and Michael Twaddle, 'Decolonization in Africa: A New British Historiographical Debate', in Bogumil Jewsiewicki and David Newbury, eds., *African Historiographies: What History for which Africa?* (Beverly Hills, Sage, 1986) and John Darwin's lucid and compact, *The End of the British Empire* (Oxford, Blackwell, 1991).

W. Keith Hancock, *Survey of British Commonwealth Affairs, 1918–1939* (two volumes in three, London, Oxford University Press, 1937–42) is a classic of contemporary history and a masterly exposition of the political theory of the Commonwealth. W. David McIntyre, *The Commonwealth of Nations: Origins and Impact* (Minneapolis, University of Minnesota Press, 1977) and J. D. B. Miller, *Survey of Commonwealth Affairs: Problems of Expansion and Attrition, 1953–1969* (London, Oxford University Press, 1974) carry the story through decolonization.

Several recent stimulating general studies challenge the traditional whiggish interpretation of British decolonization: Bernard Porter, *The Lion's Share: A Short History of British Imperialism, 1850–1983* (second edition, Burnt Mill, Longman, 1984); John Gallagher's posthumous *The Decline, Revival and Fall of the British Empire* (Cambridge, Cambridge University Press, 1982); John Darwin, *Britain and Decolonisation: The Retreat from Empire in the Post-War World* (Houndmills, Macmillan, 1988); Donald Low, *Eclipse of Empire* (Cambridge, Cambridge University Press, 1991). Brian Lapping, *End of Empire* (London, Paladin, 1985) incorporates valuable interview material.

A. N. Porter and A. J. Stockwell, *British Imperial Policy and Decolonization*, 2 volumes, *1938–51* and *1951–64*, (Houndmills, Macmillan, 1987 and 1989) have judicious introductions as well as essential documents.

R. D. Pearce, *The Turning Point in Africa: British Colonial Policy, 1938–48* (London, Cass, 1982); J. E. Flint, 'The Failure of Planned Decolonisation in Africa', *AA* 1983, pp. 389–411 and Pearce's reply, *AA* 1984, pp. 77–93; J. W. Cell, 'The Colonial Office's Plans for the Transfer of Power in Africa, 1947', *JICH*, 1980, pp. 235–57 are detailed studies of British policy.

FRENCH DECOLONIZATION

Raymond Betts, *France and Decolonisation, 1900–1960* (Houndmills, Macmillan, 1991) provides a brief general survey. John Chipman, *French Power in Africa* (Oxford, Blackwell, 1989) assesses the elements of continuity and change in Franco-African relations through the period of decolonization.

Jacques Marseille, *Empire coloniale et capitalisme français: histoire d'un divorce* (Paris, Albin Michel, 1984) is indispensable for the economic background.

Two pioneering comparative studies of British and French decolonization are Miles Kahler, *Decolonization in Britain and France: the Domestic Consequences of International Relations* (Princeton, Princeton University Press, 1984) and, despite the subtitle, Tony Smith, *The Pattern of Imperialism: the United States, Great Britain and the Late-Industrializing World since 1815* (Cambridge, Cambridge University Press, 1981).

BELGIAN AFRICA

Roger Anstey, *King Leopold's Legacy* (London, Oxford University Press, 1966) is a useful introduction to the terminal colonial period. Pierre de Vos, ed., *La Decolonisation* (Brussels, 1975) reports the public debate. But see the books by Young and Lemarchand listed below under 'Country and Regional Studies' for the best introductions to the political history of the end of Belgian rule in the Congo and Rwanda and Burundi.

PORTUGUESE AFRICA

Some historians were so beguiled by one side or another in the propaganda war between Portugal and the nationalist forces and the protracted civil wars between rival nationalist movements, that they became more or less unwitting court historians. There are two general introductions, though, which maintain an admirable objectivity: Malyn Newitt, *Portugal in Africa* (Harlow, Longman, 1981) and Gervase Clarence-Smith, *The Third Portuguese Empire* (Manchester, Manchester University Press, 1985).

COUNTRY AND REGIONAL STUDIES

John Iliffe, *A Modern History of Tanganyika* (Cambridge, Cambridge University Press, 1979) and Leonard Thompson, *A History of South Africa* (Yale, Yale University Press, 1990) are exemplary single country studies.

James S. Coleman, *Nigeria: Background to Nationalism* (Berkeley, University of California Press, 1958) can be paired with Hodgkin as an early classic which shaped the intellectual climate of decolonization. Crawford Young, *Politics in the Congo: Decolonisation and Independence* (Princeton, Princeton University Press, 1965); Rene Lemarchand, *Political Awakening in the Belgian Congo* (Berkeley, University of California Press) and *Rwanda and Burundi* (London, Pall Mall Press, 1970); Richard Joseph, *Radical Nationalism in Cameroun* (Oxford, Clarendon Press, 1977); Dennis Austin, *Politics in Ghana* (London, Oxford University Press, 1964); Tom Lodge, *Black Politics in South Africa since 1945* (London, Longman, 1983) are among the more illuminating analyses of African politics.

Herbert F. Weiss, *Political Protest in the Congo: The Parti Solidaire Africain During the Independence Struggle* (Princeton, Princeton University Press, 1967) brings out the rural, disaggregated nature of African opposition to the colonial state.

The best regional analysis is I. M. Lewis, ed., *Nationalism and Self-Determination in the Horn of Africa* (London, Ithaca Press, 1983).

Index

Egbe Omo Odudwa 94
Egypt 34, 103, 112, 116, 129–30, 154–76, 190
Eisenhower, President Dwight 155–7, 163, 169
Elections
 Afrique noire, multiplicity 148
 Gold Coast, July 1956 146
 Guinea-Bissau 187
 South Africa (Liberation Election, 1944) 198
 Southern Rhodesian (1980) 192
Electoral colleges 148
Elliot, Walter 56
El-Okbi, Sheikh 44
Emigration
 Algerian 43
 Portuguese 182
Emirates of Northern Nigeria 12
End of Empire (TV series) 166
English language broadcasts, Cairo radio 164; *see also* Anglophone Africa
Equal pay 100
Eritrea 112, 119, 122
Estado novo (New State), Portuguese ix, 24, 73–4, 186
Ethiopia 2, 17, 112, 118–23
Ethnicity 5, 14–16, 17, 19, 92–5
Etoile Nord-Africain 43, 44–5
Euro-Africa 115
Europe, statistics of relative decline 72–3
European Coal and Steel Community 165
European Economic Community (EEC) 7, 127, 152, 182, 194
European Free Trade Association (EFTA) 181–2
Evans-Pritchard, E. E. 123
Evatt, Dr Herbert Vere 80–1, 84, 85
Evening News (Accra) 149
Evloué 6, 57
Ex-servicemen 135
Extension of University Education Act (South Africa) 203

Fabian Colonial Bureau 13, 99
Fabians 56, 134, 142, 145, 200, 202
Facing Mount Kenya (Kenyatta) 93
False consciousness 2
False decolonization 2–3; *see also* Flag decolonization
Fancy franchises 98, 148
Fanon, Frantz 2, 179
Fante Confederacy 22
Farouk, King of Egypt 155
Fascism 3, 16–17, 53, 100
Faure, Edgar 126
Feber, Walter le 167
Federal Grand Council 148

Federation of Elected Muslim Officials (Algeria) 43–5
Female circumcision 93
FIDES (*Fonds d'Investissement pour le développement Economique et Sociale*) 149
Field, Winston 190
Flag decolonization 3, 12, 178
Force de frappe 151
Forced labour, abolished in French territories 147
Force Publique 15, 173–4
Fort Hare 203
Four Power Commission of Investigation 122
France
 army 14, 128
 colonial policies 20, 24, 57–8, 61, 100–1, 148, 174
 Communist Party 43, 146–7, 200
 economy 87, 151–2
 Free French movement 51, 72
 Mouvement Republicain Populaire (MRP) 146–7, 169
 Popular Front 44–7, 62
 Radical Party 44, 127, 146
 Second World War 53, 72
 Socialist Party 146–7
Fraser, Peter 80
Free Officers Movement (Egypt) 34, 130
Freetown 35, 95–6
Free Trade 36
French, Colonel 20–1
Frente de Libertação de Moçambique (FRELIMO) 184, 189, 194
Frente Nacional de Libertação de Angola (FNLA) 182, 186, 188
Freyre, Gilberto x
Front de Libération National (FLN) 127, 128, 161, 169
Fulani language, Cairo broadcasts 164
Fula people 182
Functional agencies 75
Functionalist anthropology ix, 93–4, 102–3
Functional Theory of Politics (Mitrany) ix

Gabon 203; *see also Afrique Equatoriale Française*
Gaitskell, Hugh 164
Gambia 14, 150
Gandhi, Mohandas K. 144
Garvey, Marcus A. 23, 35, 120
Gasperi, Alcide de 120–1
Gaulle, Charles de 54, 56–63, 72, 100, 168–71
Gellner, E. 142
General Agreement on Tariffs and Trade (GATT) 70
General Assembly (UN) 83
Geneva Conference on Vietnamese Independence (1954) 126